WOMEN AND ADJUSTMENT POLICIES IN THE THIRD WORLD

WOMEN'S STUDIES AT YORK/MACMILLAN SERIES
General Editors: Haleh Afshar and Mary Maynard

Haleh Afshar and Carolyne Dennis (*editors*)
WOMEN AND ADJUSTMENT POLICIES IN THE THIRD WORLD

Anna Reading
POLISH WOMEN, SOLIDARITY AND FEMINISM

Rebecca Stott
THE KISS OF DEATH: The Rise of the Late-Nineteenth-
Century *Femme Fatale*

Series Standing Order

If you would like to receive future titles in this series as they are published,
you can make use of our standing order facility. To place a standing order
please contact your bookseller or, in case of difficulty, write to us at the
address below with your name and address and the name of the series. Please
state with which title you wish to begin your standing order. (If you live
outside the United Kingdom we may not have the rights for your area, in
which case we will forward your order to the publisher concerned.)

Customer Services Department, Macmillan Distribution Ltd,
Houndmills, Basingstoke, Hampshire, RG21 2XS, England.

Contents

v

Notes on the Contributors

Haleh Afshar teaches politics and women's studies at the University of York. Born and raised in Iran, where she worked as a civil servant and a journalist, she has been working and living in England since 1974. She is a founder member of the Women and Development Study Group of the Development Studies Association and its joint convenor. She is also a member of the council of the British Association of Middle Eastern Studies, and a member of 'Women Living under Muslim Laws'. The books she has edited include *Iran a Revolution in Turmoil*, *Women Work and Ideology*, *Women State and Ideology*, and, with Bina Agarwal, *Women and Poverty in Asia*.

Georgina Ashworth is Director of CHANGE, writer, editor, publisher and development consultant. She has worked with the European Commission, the Commonwealth Secretariat, UNIDO, many NGOs in Europe and is part of international women's networks in Japan, the Hague, and of Women Living under Muslim Laws'. She is the co-ordinator of the Women in Development/Europe network and an active member of the Development Studies Association's Women and Development Study Group, the Women/Development Advisory Group of the Overseas Development Administration and Gender/Women course organiser of the British Council, among many others. She has edited and produced numerous manuscripts for CHANGE including *Of Violence and Violation: Women and Human Rights* (CHANGE, 1986) and many other publications including *Bridging the Gap: Women Studies and Development* (UN INSTRAW, 1989) with Lucy Bonnerjea, *The Invisible Decade: U.K. Women and the UN Decade for Women* (Gower, 1985) and with Margherita Rendel, *Women, Power and Political Systems* (Croom Helm, 1982).

Carolyne Dennis is a sociologist and a lecturer at the Development and Project Planning Centre at the University of Bradford where she directs the post-experience course in planning rural development projects. She has worked for two years in Cameroon and fifteen years in Nigeria undertaking research on educational administration, rural industrialisation, women's paid and unpaid work, health provision and plantation systems. She has recently worked in Kenya, India and Zimbabwe and has publications in the areas of women's paid and unpaid work and the impact of structural adjustment policies on women in sub-Saharan Africa and is the joint convenor of the Women and Development Study Group of the Development Studies Association.

Diane Elson lectures on development issues in the Department of Economics, University of Manchester. She has written widely on gender and development, and is the editor of *Male Bias in the Development Process* (Manchester University Press, 1991). She has acted as a consultant for the Commonwealth Secretariat, FAO and ILO, and is active in various international women's networks, such as Women Working World-wide.

Maxine Molyneux teaches sociology at the University of Essex. She is completing a book on women and the 'Socialist' states and is working on a research project based at UNRISD on the effects of the transition from 'Socialism' on women in Eastern Europe and the USSR.

Caroline Moser is lecturer in Social Planning in Developing Countries at the London School of Economics. Her research interests include gender planning with special reference to employment, housing and basic services, and the social costs of economic adjustment policy. Caroline Moser is a consultant to UNCHS, UNCRD, UNIDO World Bank; is gender planning trainer for OXFAM, VSO and Christian Aid and in Peru and Egypt. She is the co-editor of *Women, Human Settlement and Housing* and a contributor to *Learning About Women and Urban Services in Latin America and the Caribbean* and *Urbanisation in Contemporary Latin America*. She is currently on leave at the World Bank, Washington DC, where she is undertaking research on the social dimensions of urban adjustment.

Ingrid Palmer is an economist with wide practical experience of gender issues in Africa and South East Asia. She has worked with many international agencies including UNDP, ILO, FAO and the World Bank.

Frances Stewart is a senior research officer at Queen Elizabeth House, a Fellow of Sommerville College Oxford, and the President of the Development Studies Association. She has written widely on economic development. She is the author of *Technology and Under-development* and co-author of *Adjustment with a Human Face*.

Georgina Waylen is currently a lecturer in the Department of Politics and Contemporary History at the University of Salford; she was previously a lecturer in Politics at the School of Development Studies, University of East Anglia. Her research interests include gender and development, feminist theory and the political economy of the state in Latin America and the Caribbean.

Winifred Weekes-Vagliani is a sociologist in the research division of the OECD Development Centre who has worked on women and development and gender issues for a number of years and has numerous publications on the analysis of demographic data and its relation to agricultural development in a number of developing countries.

Acknowledgements

We would like to thank the Development Studies Association for funding and supporting the Women and Development Study Group, and the York Women Studies Centre for hosting the study group's annual meeting where the earlier drafts of the chapters in this book were presented. We should also like to thank each and every contributor for their promptness in delivering the work and the enthusiasm with which they participated in the discussions that have preceded the final draft. In particular we should like to thank those contributors who patiently and with great good humour corrected the misunderstandings and helped to clarify many of the central concepts. Any remaining errors, however, are entirely our responsibility.

We should also like to thank Maurice Dodson and Frank Speed without whose constant support, help and encouragement this book would never have been completed.

HALEH AFSHAR
CAROLYNE DENNIS

Part I
The Framework

1 Women, Recession and Adjustment in the Third World: Some Introductory Remarks
Haleh Afshar and Carolyne Dennis*

The changing political and economic circumstances of the 1980s have resulted in a radical change of policy in many Third World countries. Although the OECD countries and the newly industrialised ones, NICs, have made a recovery from the recession of the early 1980s, the Third World has not. This is in part the result of the debt crisis and deteriorating terms of trade as well as the weakness of state policy and the profligate use of international borrowing in the earlier decade. As a result, many Third World countries have had to move towards a contraction of public sector expenditure and a series of market-orientated development policies. Women in general and the poorest among them in particular have borne to a disproportionate extent, the brunt of the ensuing hardships. This volume will address the general shortcomings of the current gender-blind analytical frameworks of government and international financial organisations. The authors will delineate the specific implications that this has on women's lives and will offer alternative strategies for combating recession and poverty.

As a result of the specific prescriptive policies of the World Bank and the International Monetary Fund (IMF), there has been a marked increase in the dominance of monetarist, market-based economics at the national and international levels: hence the stress on cutting government expenditure, the acceptance of much higher levels of unemployment, devaluation and removal of import controls. These have resulted in a marked contraction in public sector expenditure on welfare, education and social programmes which it is hoped will be provided by the private sector. The intention has been to halt inflation, gain economic efficiency, improve the balance of payments and promote growth by switching resources to production of 'tradeables' and through unhindered operation of the market.

3

Much of the writing on the recession and adjustment has been directed at the shortcomings of the policies in general and the destructive impact of some stabilisation policies in particular. This volume will address these questions, but it will be centred on the experiences of women who both as producers and consumers of wealth, health, education and welfare, have had to shoulder the heaviest burden of poverty and stress resulting from cutbacks in public expenditure.

The changes in levels and composition of public expenditure have also had an adverse impact on women both as consumers of welfare and public sector services and as its providers and employees. Furthermore the adjustment policies tend to reallocate public resources towards repayment of loans, rather than provision of basic needs. In the words of Hans Singer, the attempt to cut back to be lean ('reculler pour mieux sauter'[1]) may backfire, and may result in total collapse. The 'cuts on the back of women' can easily lead to irrevocable failures of health, nutrition and public health. As Caroline Moser's chapter shows, a higher burden of work can result in poorer attendance at school for girls who are sharing the burden with their mothers, lower levels of concentration, more resentment and a breakdown of the family and subsequently of social cohesion. At times, such trends are countered by the emergence of fundamentalist ideologies, backed by the state apparatus. In countries such as Chile, Nigeria and Iran different religions carry the same messages for women: they are to remain in the home and provide salvation for the family, even when economically such an option is not open to them.

Authors in this volume note that countries with such diverse political economies as Iran, which for the decade of 1980 has been less closely integrated into the western capitalist financial markets, and Chile and Côte d'Ivoire who retain close monetary links with the west, have, over the past decade, introduced similar adjustment policies. The common trait for the countries concerned has been the recession of the early 1980s and the heavy burden of debt which followed the heady borrowing days of the 1970s and the need to engage both with its economic and ideological after-effects. For the IMF and the World Bank the question was merely one of providing suitable economic solutions, but for the countries concerned the ensuing problems have been gendered, social and cultural as well as economic. The authors in this volume provide a textured perspective, which analyses and illustrates the multidimensional impact of the recession and economic policies on the daily lives of women in the Third World.

THE MULTIFACETED RELATION OF WOMEN AND THE ECONOMY

The book begins with three introductory chapters by Frances Stewart, Diane Elson, and Ingrid Palmer presenting a gendered theoretical framework for the analysis of these policies and their effect on women. Frances Stewart traces the origins of the crisis and offers a systematic study of the adjustment programmes of the IMF and the World Bank. Stewart notes that the IMF concentrated on a demand restraint approach, which sought to reduce expenditure and curb inflation. This was complemented by devaluation and wage control which was to shift resources away from 'non-tradeable' to 'tradeable' products. The long-term aim has been to move toward a more market-orientated economy. The World Bank has moved in a similar direction but with more emphasis on improving the efficient use of resources through reduction of the role of the public sector and getting prices right. About a quarter of the World Bank loans in the 1980s aimed at structural adjustment. The combined impact of these policies has led to the relaxation of price controls, liberalisation of trade and credit; reform of administrative institutions and parastatals and privatisation.

The advocates and administrators of these measures saw no need for a gender-aware approach and have measured their success and failures in purely monetary terms. But as Frances Stewart points out, women as producers undertake both paid and unpaid labour, making a large but often unrecognised contribution to total output, both marketed and non-marketed. Frances Stewart notes the fourfold roles of women as producers, household managers, mothers, and social organisers. Elson, Moser, and Waylen concentrate on the triple role of women as producers, reproducers and active members of the community. As producers they are predominantly active in subsistence farming or the informal labour market; an area which requires close examination and is discussed in detail by Winifred Weekes Vagliani. Furthermore, Stewart shows that as managers of household consumption, women play a crucial role in negotiating the impact of adjustment policies. Caroline Moser and Georgina Waylen note the further burden of community management which is shouldered by women, who take on this third dimension to their domestic responsibilities.

Stewart delineates the knock-on effects of the demand restraints, which influence the formal and informal labour markets and, by reducing household real incomes, have induced a higher level of participation of women in income generating activities. At the same time credit reforms and higher interest rates mean that credit remains virtually inaccessible to poorer women who both as producers and consumers are also adversely affected by devaluation. Of course women who are producing 'tradables' or have sufficient resources to qualify for credit may well gain from these measures. But for the majority of women these policies, combined with the removal of price controls, result in an increase in the relative price of food which is in turn reflected in an increase in time devoted to shopping and processing food by women. Thus women as producers, consumers and household managers have to allocate increasing amounts of time to stretch their limited resources. The case studies in this volume support Stewart's conclusion that women as producers and household managers have been adversely affected by structural adjustment policies, and that as social organisers they have taken over some of the functions previously shouldered by the state and have to spend ever-increasing amounts of time to produce strategies to deal with these problems.

Caroline Moser's study has a different methodological approach in defining the many roles that women have. Moser delineates management by women as that which relates to community work and the political part they play in that context. Moser shows that these demands, combined with increased prices and falling incomes, result in women spending more time on domestic and community duties. As a result the provision of food and overall levels of nutrition have deteriorated markedly for households as a whole.

GENDER BIAS AND ECONOMICS OF EFFICIENCY

The misleading concepts of economics of adjustment, imbued with gender bias, have proved extremely costly for many women. Diane Elson notes that apparent gender neutrality hides a gender bias which stems from the omission from the models of adjustment of the process of production and maintenance of human resources. This conceptual bias, notes Elson, means that the 'economic' sphere has been defined (primarily) in terms of marketed goods and services. But the unpaid reproductive labour of women has been excluded from the analysis. This is partly because economists have implicitly assumed that the reproduction and management of human resources is likely to be carried out by women regardless of the way in which marketed resources are reallocated. Women's unpaid labour is assumed to be unproblematically available and infinitely elastic, capable of stretching to cover shortfalls in other resources needed for survival during adjustment. But although most women do their best to absorb the shock of structural adjustment, it is not without cost to their health. Moreover not all women can cope, as illustrated by Caroline Moser in her study of women in Guayaquil.

Transfers of costs of education, health care and welfare provisions from the public purse to that of poor urban households, highlights the problem of defining costs and efficiency, an issue which is addressed by Elson, Stewart, and Palmer. Diane Elson notes that the drive for efficiency as conventionally defined may mean shifting these costs from the public and paid to the private and unpaid economy.

Ingrid Palmer notes that given the imperfection of the market economy, governments intervene to improve short- and long-term inefficiencies by countering market distortions to achieve short-term and long-term efficiencies of resource utilisation. Similarly the World Bank and IMF adjustment policies seek to reduce the 'distortions' that have prevented the efficient operation of the market economy. But they have not noted the two main sources of gendered-based distortions: unequal terms of participation of men and women in the labour market, and the reproduction tax on women. These result in a failure on the part of the economists to recognise the value of women's labour. The ensuing profligate use of this resource distorts the subsequent economic analysis. Ingrid Palmer demonstrates that without an integrated and gendered analysis of efficiency, policy-makers will remain entangled in a highly inefficient market and unable to allocate resources according to their best price and competitive value.

GENDER IMPACT ON ADJUSTMENT

Ingrid Palmer addresses the need for a gendered approach by distinguishing between the impact of adjustment on women and the impact of gender on adjustment. To achieve real efficiency, which is the stated objective of adjustment policies, Palmer argues that it is necessary to overcome the barriers that hamper participation of women in the labour market and the conversion of unpaid labour or reproduction to paid labour and thus prevent the efficient allocation of resources through perfect competition in the market place. Market efficiency is anchored in the effective operation of the price mechanism as a means of allocating resources to obtain maximum value from each and every unit of input. Inputs and factors of production and production and consumption processes all seek the highest possible return. To succeed, this process demands unhampered access to all factors of production and freedom of movement of labour.

But the subordination of women within the family and society has resulted in a major distortion. Confined to unpaid family labour, women cannot move freely between employers, nor are they able to produce the best return for the highest pay. Women's labour is wasted and, Palmer notes, this static inefficiency permeates through society and hinders the dynamics of efficiency.

Gender-based distortions have resulted in the inability of women to participate in the market on equal terms. This is exacerbated by what Palmer calls the reproduction tax placed on women. Women's participation in the labour market is hampered by their reproductive responsibilities. Since resources in reproduction are domestic and provided free of charge, then clearly they are not properly costed. Thus the labour of women is effectively taxed at the domestic level. This has a knock-on effect in distorting the factor market. Thus gender influences lead to inefficiencies which should be countered by governments through selective measures to overcome domestic handicaps and allocative structured gender discrimination. To do so it must be recognised that women's labour is not cost-free and resources in reproduction need to be properly priced and used. Such pricing would eliminate allocative inefficiencies at the basic level which are reflected throughout the economy. Thus what Palmer calls the gender impact on adjustment would rid the market of the basic inefficiencies which prevent the successful operation of adjustment policies.

ADJUSTMENT AND WOMEN

The authors in the early chapters note that adjustment policies affect women as consumers, producers, and participants in community politics. Their income is affected through changes in wages, levels of employment, the price of consumer goods and demand for the products of the self-employed. The rise in the relative price of food combined with the fall in real income, tightening of credit and shortage of cash have resulted in the necessity for women to buy ever smaller quantities of food and ever cheaper varieties. This in turn has meant both a greater input of time for repeated trips to markets, longer time spent on processing food and fewer and fewer meals for the family – that is a rise in the burden of work for women and a fall in the levels of nutrition for the entire household (Elson, Stewart, Palmer and Moser).

Elson notes the complexities of the relationship of women to the market and state and the difficulties of disaggregating the different dimensions of their impact on women of various classes. Hence Elson argues for the use of specific parameters to analyse the impact of adjustment in terms of changes in incomes, prices, levels and composition of public expenditure and changes in working conditions for both paid and unpaid work.

There is considerable difference in the experiences of women of different classes and between rural and urban women. In theory the rise in official prices should benefit rural women by raising farm-gate prices. But it is necessary to distinguish between well-off farmers who have easy access to credit and the urban markets to enable them to produce and sell food, and the poorer farmers. Poor women in rural areas fare no better than their urban counterparts. As Stewart points out, they are unable to gain access to the formal credit mechanism and the restrictions on loans would have severely adverse effects on their prospects. Furthermore, poorer rural families need to resort to buying food at the end of the agricultural cycle, since they do not produce enough to feed the family and sell to the market. Thus they suffer from the increased prices and cuts in public sector food support policies.

GENDER BIAS IN PRACTICE

The case studies of countries currently implementing the mainstream adjustment policies, link theory and practice. Caroline Moser analyses the differing socio-economic roles of low-income women and households in Guayaquil, Ecuador. Winifred Weekes-Vagliani addresses the need to adopt adjustment with growth and equity. Weekes-Vagliani, based on her work in the context of the multidisciplinary research team at the OECD Development Centre on 'Adjustment and Equitable growth in Côte d'Ivoire', advocates a threefold effort to improve the gathering of gender-differentiated data and its inclusion in macro-planning. Such analysis would enable planners to see that women-orientated policies could increase the efficient use of resources and would form part of the solution to development problems such as population, lagging food production and improvement of family nutrition, as well as questions concerned with the future of the rural and urban informal sectors.

The contradictory impact of ideology and economics is addressed by the three chapters that follow. Georgina Waylen discusses the case of Chilean women. Carolyne Dennis looks at the religious impact of these measures in Nigeria, and Haleh Afshar notes the combined effect of religion and economic shortfall on the lives of working women in Iran.

The case studies highlight the experiences of women as they cope with the policies that have been formulated. In the very different countries of Latin America, Africa and Asia, with differing governments, ideologies and political approaches, there is a marked similarity in the experiences of women. The subordination of women and their shared familial responsibilities know no national or ideological barriers. As a result, despite specific variation in the articulation of economy, society and ideology, and the relative success of enclaves of development, poorer women the world over have had to cope with the intensification of the exploitation of their paid and unpaid labour. In this respect there has often been, as shown by the case studies of Chile and Iran in this volume, a contradiction between the stated aims of government in terms of women's role in society and the participation of women in the formal and informal labour markets. Both Chilean and Iranian governments have had a stated policy of confining women to the domestic sphere or to specifically feminine occupations. In both cases they have had to accommodate the necessity for women to work – in Iran to meet the demands of the government for a segregated labour market, and in Chile to meet the demands of the restructured economy for the cheapest source of labour. In both cases, as in Ecuador, the women have become far more politically active as a response to the intensification of their triple burdens. The politicisation of women has not been necessarily reflected in the level of representation at the formal state and governmental hierarchies. But they have been exercising more influence across the board, using local community-gathering, work-place groups or the media.

Not all efforts have been directed towards formal political activities: there has also been an ideological dimension in the participation patterns of women. In Iran as in Nigeria and to a lesser extent elsewhere, religion has emerged as a means of negotiating the intensified demands on women. But whereas in Iran religious observance has become an important form of demonstration of political solidarity, in Nigeria it is a form of 'coping' mechanism. So, unlike the Latin American experience, in Nigeria religion has provided an individualistic and privatised response to adjustment, rather than a forum for political resistance. But religion, like the economy, is the domain of men, and its hidden agenda carries the same marked gender bias that has been noted in the formulation of economic policies.

As the case studies in this volume show, women in some countries have been marginalised in the formal sectors. Even in Iran where official policies have led to an increase in the employment of women in the civil service in departments such as health, education and welfare, the cutbacks in public sector expenditure have led to an overall fall in the numbers of women working for a wage. But, as Winifred Weekes-Vagliani notes, it is essential to construct a methodology for recognising and evaluating women's work in the informal sector. As Moser, Weekes-Vagliani, Waylen, Dennis and Afshar show, the shortcomings noted in the introductory chapters are reflected in the practices of policy-makers in different countries. Women's unpaid labour is not recognised, or, as in the case of Nigeria, it is accepted and reinforced. But the absence of formal recognition does not make the burden any less real. Feminists need to adopt different and more effective means of observing women's work such as those offered by Stewart, Elson, Palmer, Moser, and Weekes-Vagliani. These would enable us to understand that such indicators as lower availability of domestic labour, as in Chile for example, may denote a shift in patterns of informal labour employment.

They would also facilitate the removal of gender bias which applies at all levels, from the collection of basic data to implementation of policies. In Iran there is evidence that the formal segregation of the labour market has resulted in the census-takers being urban men asking questions from rural men. Not surprisingly, there has been a marked under-reporting of women's participation in agricultural production.

As the case studies indicate, the gender bias in practice has proved not only detrimental to women, but also to governments and nations. It has created misinformation as well as inefficiencies. There is an undeniable need for targeted specific policies to remove the inefficiencies that have occurred as the unintended result of the slowing-down of growth and adjustment policies.

GENDERED POLICIES

Not surprisingly the authors argue for alternative policies. They demand a gendered and disaggregated approach which seeks to modify the process of adjustment with a greater degree of selectivity, seeking to benefit poorer women and giving higher priority to health and education, than to prestigious larger-scale urban projects. As the contributors to this volume point out, such a disaggregated approach would prevent the deterioration of health and nutrition among poorer households by provision of specific help to those who are in greatest need. By securing a minimum standard of health, education and welfare it would be possible to achieve adjustment through growth.

The book concludes with clear evidence that women academics and activists have struggled to obtain both an awareness of the problems at the international level, and stated and practical means of overcoming these shortcomings and obtaining a gendered development perspective for adjustment policies. The difficulty of this task is demonstrated by Georgina Ashworth's account of the participation of activists at governmental and non-governmental levels. The 'final declaration', reported by Maxine Molyneux, demonstrates that women can and do successfully collaborate to provide a clear strategy for development and delineate the way forward.

In the final section of the book Gwyneth Morgan offers a selective bibliography to enable readers to come to terms with the existing academic material in the field and facilitate further research which it is hoped will be provided by readers of this volume.

Notes

* We are most grateful to Diane Elson, Caroline Moser and Winifred Weekes-Vagliani for their helpful comments on an earlier draft of this introduction. Any mistake or misrepresentation, however, is entirely our responsibility.

1. Hans Singer and Rene Prendergast (eds), *Adjustment and Development* (London: Macmillan, forthcoming).

2 Can Adjustment Programmes Incorporate the Interests of Women?
Frances Stewart[1]

INTRODUCTION

The 1980s were a decade of economic crisis for many developing countries, especially in Africa and Latin America. They were also years of continuous adjustments, as governments with the support, and often following the dictates, of the International Monetary Fund (IMF) and World Bank (WB), tried to push their economies onto a more satisfactory path. Change, of course, is part of the normal process of development. Growing economies need to adjust ceaselessly to both exogenous and endogenous developments. But the acute problems faced by many countries in the 1980s – especially shortage of foreign exchange and often accelerating inflation – led to a special focus on the need for structural adjustment (SA). This chapter reviews how the policies aimed to bring about structural adjustment and the subsequent adjustments impinged on women in developing countries.[2]

To assess the impact of SA policies on women, it is necessary to trace the effects of the policies adopted – which are mainly macro – and see how these impinge, at a micro level, on women. The impact then depends not only on the nature of the policies but also, critically, on the role women perform in the economy and society. This chapter attempts to trace the interaction in five stages. First, there is a brief analysis of the origin of the economic crisis; second, we describe the major features of the policies followed; third, the chapter analyses relevant features of women's role in society. The fourth stage is to bring together the earlier analyses, in order to examine the main ways in which SA has affected women in Third World economies. The concluding section considers alternative policies which might be less harsh in their impact and make more use of the productive and social potential of women.

13

I   ORIGIN OF THE CRISIS OF THE 1980s

In the late 1970s and early 1980s very large imbalances developed in many countries' balance of payments on current account (see Table 2.1). In 1980, non-oil developing countries as a whole faced a deficit of $86 billion. The large deficits differed from earlier ones because bank lending was not forthcoming to finance them, as it had been in the 1970s, and because the crisis was so widely shared – with at least two-thirds of the countries of Latin America and sub-Saharan Africa, and a number of Asian countries finding themselves simultaneously in a similar acute situation.

The crisis had its main origin in exogenous occurrences – in developments in the world economy, outside the control of developing countries. Policy decisions of Third World governments in the 1970s, however, allowed these developments to have such a devastating effect. One basic problem was that in the 1980s there was a sharp worsening in both the trade and capital accounts *simultaneously*, whereas previously a worsening in the trade account had often been offset by an improvement in the capital account.

At the end of the 1970s, a series of adverse developments in the world economy worsened the trade prospects for LDCs. The oil-price rise of 1978–9 not only affected the terms of trade of non-oil developing countries negatively, but also precipitated a slow-down in world economic growth. There was a major recession among the industrialised countries in the early 1980s; although economic recovery followed and has been sustained, on average world growth in the 1980s was about three-quarters of the 1970s rate. Commodity prices were sharply affected by the recession and when growth resumed did not rise as expected. Commodity prices, which had fallen by 1.1 per cent p.a. 1970–9, fell by a further 1.2 per cent p.a. 1980–9. Another problem was the rising protectionism among industrialised countries in the 1980s. One review concluded: 'By the early 1980s, protection was unambiguously growing with only minor offsets. . . . This was most pronounced in industrialised countries' trade with developing countries' (Page, 1987, p. 49).

Developing countries' trade thus suffered from the combined effects of a slower growth in world trade, deteriorating terms of trade and increasing restrictions on market access. However, it was the deterioration on the capital account which precipitated and prolonged the crisis.

During the 1970s many countries had financed big trade deficits,

Table 2.1   Balances on current a/c of balance of payments ($b.)

	1978	1980	1982	1984	1986	1988	1990 (est.)
Industrial countries	+14.5	−61.8	−25.3	−53.6	−25.1	−52.4	−95.8
Developing countries:							
Africa	−12.8	−1.6	−21.6	−7.7	−10.3	−10.3	−9.1
Asia	−6.8	−19.3	−16.0	−3.8	+4.2	+8.8	−2.3
Europe	−7.1	−12.3	−3.3	−0.7	−0.7	+6.7	+2.9
Middle East	+11.2	+90.7	+4.8	−13.6	−17.2	−8.4	+13.7
Western Hemisphere	−19.0	−29.5	−40.3	−0.8	−16.7	−10.8	−10.1
All non-fuel exporters	−28.4	−67.1	−62.0	−26.1	−10.0	+6.7	−16.7

Source: IMF, *World Economic Outlook*, April 1986; October 1990.

largely caused by the oil price rise of 1973–4, by heavy borrowing from the commercial sector, at low interest rates. But interest rates rose sharply at the end of the decade, as governments of industrialised countries espoused monetarist policies. The high interest rates imposed a very heavy burden on those countries which had borrowed a lot. Some countries could no longer meet their debt servicing obligations. Mexico's near default in August 1982 frightened bankers and led to the collapse of voluntary bank lending to developing countries. Although aid flows held up, they did not expand to fill the gap. The result was a turnaround in the capital account of enormous proportions. Net external lending by developing countries from the commercial banks was only $8.8 b. in 1987 compared with $91.5 b. in 1980. The net transfer to developing countries (net external borrowing less the outflow for interest) fell from $44 b. in 1980 to minus $63 b. in 1989. There was a particularly large negative transfer from Latin America (see Table 2.2).

The crisis of the 1980s was concentrated on two groups of (to some extent overlapping) countries – the heavy borrowers of the 1970s, and countries highly dependent on primary commodities for exports. The worst affected countries were in Latin America, which contained most of the major borrowers of the 1970s as well as some primary commodity dependent countries, and Africa, where most countries are dependent on a few primary commodities, the prices of which moved particularly unfavourably, and where production trends were generally poor over this period. However, some countries in Asia were also badly affected, for example the Philippines, while most others suffered losses as a result of the adverse movement in commodity prices.

Table 2.2   Net transfer to developing countries ($b)

	1980	1982	1984	1986	1988	1989
All developing countries						
Net external borrowing	+101.0	+98.4	+49.5	+43.6	+15.8	+37.2
Interest payments	− 57.5	−83.4	−88.0	−84.9	−92.2	−100.1
Net Transfer	+ 43.5	+15.0	−39.5	−41.6	−76.4	−62.9
Africa						
Net external borrowing	+10.9	+17.6	+8.1	+8.0	+6.9	+9.2
Interest payments	−7.4	−8.6	−10.7	−12.1	−13.7	−14.2
Net Transfer	+3.5	+9.0	−2.6	−4.1	−5.8	−5.0
Western hemisphere						
Net external borrowing	+38.5	+40.6	+14.0	+7.5	−0.7	+10.0
Interest payments	−26.4	−45.2	−44.1	−36.3	−37.6	−41.7
Net Transfer	+12.1	−4.6	−30.1	−28.8	−36.9	−31.7

Source: IMF, *World Economic Outlook*, April 1988, October 1989.

Faced with unfinanceable deficits on current account, countries were forced to make some adjustments. The question at issue was not and is not whether to adjust but how to adjust. The number of countries approaching the International Monetary Fund (IMF) for financial support in the 1980s was almost double the number of the 1970s. This finance was conditional upon agreement to IMF policy packages, and IMF finance was withdrawn if the required conditions were violated in what was considered a significant way. The Fund programmes were primarily directed at short term stabilisation. But as the 1980s progressed, and the crisis continued, it became evident that medium-term structural adjustment policies were also needed.

The World Bank initiated structural adjustment policy-based lending in response to the evident need for more growth-oriented adjustment. These loans included Structural Adjustment Loans (SALs) which involve macro-economic policy packages, and Sectoral Adjustment Loans (SECALs) which consist of sectoral policy packages and sectoral loans. WB lending for structural adjustment supplemented IMF stabilisation programmes, as almost all WB adjustment lending occurred where an IMF facility was in place. New IMF facilities were also introduced combining IMF and WB policy-conditionality and financing – the Structural Adjustment Facility (SAF) in 1986 and the Enhanced Structural Adjustment Facility (ESAF) in 1988.

Adjustment efforts were not confined to countries with Fund or

Bank programmes. Some countries introduced adjustment policies on their own. Nonetheless, the Fund and Bank have dominated adjustment policy-making, and it is their programmes that we focus on below.

II THE NATURE OF ADJUSTMENT PROGRAMMES

IMF Stabilisation Packages

Fund programmes covered the majority of countries in Latin America and sub-Saharan Africa in the 1980s. Over 40 countries had Fund programmes in each year in the 1980s (compared with around 20 in the 1970s). The Fund's influence has been particularly pervasive because most countries have had a succession of agreements, so that policy-making was dominated by Fund agreements for most of the decade. Despite the large number of programmes, the Fund's financial contribution was not very big, and in recent years has become negative, as shown in Table 2.3.

Although the policy packages are not identical, there has been considerable homogeneity in Fund-supported programmes in different countries. Three categories of policy have formed part of almost every programme: *demand* restraint, *switching* policies and policies related to *long-term supply* or *efficiency*.

The *demand restraint* element consists in policies aimed at reducing demand in the economy, with the objective of reducing expenditure on imports, and releasing resources for exports. Demand restraint, and particularly control over the money supply, is also thought to be essential for the control of inflation. Policy instruments include reductions in government expenditure (or in its rate of increase), and in the budget deficit; controls over the money supply and credit creation; and policies to hold down (or cut) real wages. Particular emphasis has been placed on reducing subsidies, partly as an instrument of demand restraint, partly because this is regarded as necessary for the promotion of efficiency.

Switching policies are aimed at shifting resources from non-tradeables to tradeables, by changing incentives. Devaluation is the main policy instrument. Policies towards wage control have a switching element.

Long-term supply policies are reforms believed to raise the long-term efficiency of the economy. The policies are designed to secure a

Table 2.3   Finance from Fund and Bank ($b)

	1981	1982	1983	1984	1985	1986	1987	1988
Net credit from IMF	6.6	6.9	11.0	4.7	–	–2.7	–5.9	–5.0
No. of countries with Fund programmes	49*	45*	54*	45*	42*	25**	20**	n.c.
Net transfer from World Bank	3.20	4.34	4.55	5.34	4.68	2.90	2.50	–0.5
of which IBRD	1.45	2.45	2.16	3.05	2.60	0.05	–0.2	–3.5
IDA	1.75	1.92	2.40	2.29	2.21	2.81	2.7	2.9
No. of countries with Bank SAL/SECAL programmes	11	8	16	16	16	25	29	25

* With a Fund programme for at least one month during the year.
** Signed an Agreement in the year.

Sources: Commonwealth secretariat, PMM (88)5; IMF, World Economic Outlook, April 1988, October 1989; Cornia et al. (1987).

more market-oriented economy, subject to less restrictions and segmentation. Reforms include trade liberalisation, financial reforms to raise interest rates in the formal sector and to unify credit markets, and price reforms.

Analysis of the composition of Fund programmes from 1980 to 1984 shows that demand restraint policies were implemented in almost every case. Limits on credit expansion were applied in 99 per cent of the cases, restraint on central government expenditure in 91 per cent, reduction in the budget deficit as a percentage of GDP in 83 per cent and wage restraint in 60 per cent. Switching policies – as indicated by exchange rate changes – were adopted in 54 per cent of the cases, and price reforms in 40 per cent of the cases. Interest rate reform occurred in 27 per cent of the cases and development or restructuring a sector in 65 per cent. Consequently, demand restraint policies dominated over more supply-oriented policies (Cornia et al., 1987, ch. 2).

Fund programmes have usually been of quite short duration – one year to eighteen months being typical, although the SAF and ESAF are on a three-year basis. The programmes consist almost entirely of macro policy instruments; and have not been concerned with the distributional effects on different groups within the country. Monitoring variables reflect the concern with macro-values, normally consisting in such items as total money supply, or total credit creation; they do not include elements relating to the real performance of the economy (e.g. incomes or growth), nor real welfare of people.

The Fund programmes are invariably negotiated through a country's Ministry of Finance and Central Bank. Economic planning ministries and those concerned with the social sectors are never directly involved.

World Bank Structural Adjustment Loans

The proportion of resources going to structural adjustment lending rose over the 1980s, accounting for one-quarter of all Bank lending by 1987, and extending to 29 countries. Consequently, the SALs and SECALs had an increasing influence on developing-country policy-making. However, as with the Fund programmes, not very large financial flows are involved, as shown in Table 2.3. The net transfer of finance from the Bank peaked at $5.3 billion in 1984 and has since fallen sharply, and is becoming negative in 1988. The flow of finance is important because availability of finance conditions what type of adjustment programme a country can have.

Analysis of SALs shows that the philosophical basis and values were the same as Fund programmes, being strongly market-oriented. 'Like the IMF it stresses monetary and fiscal orthodoxy, appropriate real exchange rates, positive real interest rates, and liberal approaches on external account (Helleiner, 1988).

Categorisation of the major SAL policy instruments (see Mosley, 1987; and Table 2.4) suggests four major elements:

1. Mobilisation of domestic resources through fiscal, monetary and credit policies, and improved financial performance of public enterprises.
2. Improving the efficiency of resource use throughout the economy: in the public sector, measures include reform and privatisation; in the private sector, price decontrol, reduced subsidies, competition from imports and credit reform.
3. Trade policies: liberalisation, with import quotas removed and reduced and rationalised tariffs; improved export incentives and some institutional reforms to support exports.
4. Institutional reforms: strengthening the capacity of the public sector generally and increasing the efficiency of public enterprises; improved institutions to support the productive sectors.

The major difference between Fund and Bank programmes is the Fund emphasis on demand restraint, while the Bank supports more

Table 2.4   Types of policy measure requested in return for SAL finance, 1980 to October 1986

Measure	Percentage of SALs subject to conditions in this area
Trade policy:	
Remove import quotas	57
Cut tariffs	24
Improve export incentives and institutional support	76
Resource mobilisation:	
Reform budget or taxes	70
Reform interest-rate policy	49
Strengthen management of external borrowing	49
Improve financial performance by public enterprise	73
Efficient use of resources:	
Revise priorities of public investment programme	59
Revise agricultural prices	73
Dissolve or reduce powers of state marketing boards	14
Reduce or eliminate some agricultural input subsidies	27
Revise energy prices	49
Introduce energy-conservation measures	35
Develop indigenous energy sources	24
Revise industry incentive system	68
Institutional reforms:	
Strengthen capacity to formulate and implement public investment programme	86
Increase efficiency of public enterprises	57
Improve support for agriculture (marketing, etc.)	57
Improve support for industry and subsectors (including price controls)	49

Source: Paul Mosley, 'Conditionality as Bargaining Process: Structural-Adjustment Lending, 1980–86', *Essays in International Finance, Princeton University*, no. 168 (October 1987) p. 5.

specific instruments than the Fund. However, since almost all countries that get SALs have to have an agreed Fund programme first, this difference reflects the differing specialties of the two agencies, rather than differences in view. The SALs are of longer duration – being from three to five years. In the past, Bank SALs notably omitted the social sectors, and neglected the distributional impact of the programmes. But recently some sector loans have been directed at the social sectors and the Bank began to consider the 'social dimensions of adjustment'. No changes have been made in the broad design of programmes to take these considerations into account, but special initiatives have been taken in a few countries, to compensate those adversely affected.

The Bank talks to a wider range of representatives in the country with which it is working, including the planning ministry, and sector ministries, such as the Ministry of Agriculture. However, unless there is a sector loan to them, the social sectors are not involved in formulation of the programme, although they may be consulted in the design of a compensatory programme.

In summary, the stabilisation policies of the Fund and the structural adjustment policies of the Bank have six major elements, which we shall focus on in the analysis below. These are:

1. Demand restraint
2. Price decontrol
3. Reform of trade regimes
4. Credit reform
5. Parastatal reform and privatisation
6. Administrative reforms.

III WOMEN'S MULTIFACETED ROLE

The ways in which SA policies affect women depends on women's role in society. While both women and men perform a number of functions, women are different in having so many demands on their time and capacities in most societies. From our present perspective, it is useful to highlight four main roles: women as producers, as managers of household consumption, as mothers and carers, and as active in the community.

Women as Producers

This consists in women's contribution to the national economy through productive activities – which extends both to employment in the formal sector and informal sector activity. In many countries much of women's productive activity takes place within the household, and much of the output is consumed within the household. Measurement of such activities is usually incomplete and large segments of women's productive activity are omitted. In the Philippines estimates of 'full income', including the value of work done inside the household, suggested that this was twice as high as marketed income; women's share of the household's marketed income was 20 per cent, but they contributed almost 40 per cent of full income (King and Evenson, 1983). Altogether it is estimated that unpaid household work would add on a third to estimates of world production (Sivard, 1985).

Women's role as producer fulfils two functions: it contributes to the national product and national welfare (whether measured or not); and it generates income for the household. Income generation by women is particularly important for poor households.

The nature of women's contribution to production and income generation varies across societies, according to culture and history, stage of development and government policy. Moreover, the precise contribution in any society is unknown because of the weak statistics on aspects of women's productive activities, especially in the informal sector and within the household. Nonetheless, below we present some 'stylised facts' to help in the analysis of the impact of SA on women:

- In most developing countries women's activities outside the household – as indicated by participation rates – are lower than those of men, but have been rising over the past thirty years in many areas. As a result women have formed an increasing proportion of the total labour force. In Asia, women have formed a rising proportion of the total labour force – from 29 per cent in 1950 to 33.8 per cent in 1985; in Latin America from 18 per cent to 24.2 per cent; in Africa they have remained roughly constant at around 32 per cent. (But the statistical problems, and especially failure fully to incorporate informal sector activities, must be noted.)
- Within the formal sector, women are paid significantly less than men in every country for which there is data. Data for earnings in manufacturing for eighteen developing countries show that women's earnings vary from 45 per cent of men's (S. Korea) to 89 per cent (Burma). This differential arises from women being proportionately more concentrated in industries which pay low wages, in less skilled occupations within each industry, and also in being paid less than men when doing the same job.
- Women's education and skill levels are significantly below those of men. In general the lower the level of education in the society, the greater the disparity.

- Women are proportionately most significant in the agricultural labour force, taking developing countries as a whole, and of lesser importance in industry and services. (However, the data on services is particularly suspect where much female activity is omitted.) Women account for over 36 per cent of the agricultural labour force, in developing countries as a whole. However, in Africa, women are the majority of the farmers, producing 90 per cent of the food, but they are of lesser importance in export crops.
- Women's role is especially large in the informal sector, where they often form the largest part of the workforce. In urban Tanzania, for example, about 80 per cent of the female workforce is self-employed, and 53 per cent of all informal-sector workers are women (Shields, 1980). In Peru, 40 per cent of the labour force in the informal sector are women, compared with 18 per cent of the formal-sector labour force (Mazumdar, 1976). Women entrepreneurs are to be found almost exclusively in this sector. Informal-sector earnings are, on average, substantially less than formal-sector earnings. For example, in Brazil informal-sector earnings for men are 53 per cent of formal-sector earnings and for women, 47 per cent.
- Women spend much more time on work within the household for subsistence, which has no exchange value, than men. This includes food production, processing and preparation, health care and education.
- On average, women's income per hour worked is very significantly below that of men. This the combined effect of lower wages in formal-sector employment, disproportionate importance in agriculture and the urban informal sector, where incomes tend to be lower than in the rest of the economy, and the great significance of unpaid subsistence activities.
- In many countries, the number of female-headed households has been growing. In Kenya, 40 per cent of rural households are headed by women; in Ghana, almost one-half; in Zambia, one-third. It is estimated that women are the sole breadwinners in one-quarter to one-third of the world's households (Sivard, 1985).
- Female-headed households account for a disproportionately large proportion of the very poor. For example, in Costa Rica in 1982, 37 per cent of destitute households were headed by women, compared with only 13.8 per cent of non-poor households (Pollack, 1988).
- Women's contribution to national production is seriously under-

stated because so much of it is unmeasured, and because women's pay (which is taken as the measure of their contribution to national product) is below that of men, even for the same job. Women's contribution to national *welfare* is even more seriously understated because their unpaid activities are particularly high in low-income households, where any addition to output has a large effect on welfare, and because of the focus of these activities on basic needs.

• Women's contribution to income generation is particularly important for the survival of low-income households.

Women as Managers of the Household Consumption

Women normally organise household consumption – especially in the area of basic needs. As they are responsible for securing the basic needs of the household, they, therefore, are particularly affected by changes in the conditions of consumption. It is their obligation to try to ensure adequate consumption for basic needs when circumstances change.

Women as Mothers and Carers

In pregnancy and after, women are responsible for the welfare of children and thus of future generations. It is estimated that three-quarters of all health care takes place at the family or individual level (Cocytax, 1984), and probably as large a proportion of education is household-based. Women have prime responsibility for most informal health care and education as well as feeding; they are also primarily responsible for ensuring that children have access to formal education and health care.

Women in the Community

Women's role extends beyond the household to a network of social/community relationships. In this role women contribute to the nature, viability and cohesiveness of the community. The community can play a vital role in contributing to household survival at times of hardship, as well as in raising social welfare in more normal times.

The multifaceted role of women is subject to one major constraint – the time constraint. Each of the four functions takes time. Adding together time spent on work outside the household and household activities – without even making allowance for social activities – shows that women's activities very often take most of their waking hours, even in normal times. A study of Buenos Aires, for example, showed that women who worked outside the household spent 55.9 hours on household work and 35.4 hours in paid work, a daily rate of 13 hours. Studies across the world have shown that women consistently work longer hours than men, with daily work hours ranging from 6 to 16.

IV STRUCTURAL ADJUSTMENT: THE IMPACT ON WOMEN

The impact of structural adjustment on women depends both on the role of women in society when the adjustment takes place, which determines how they are initially affected by the SA package, and on women's response to the changing situation. There are important differences between societies in both respects, so that simple generalisations are likely to be wrong. But there is sufficient in common in women's role across societies to make it possible to come to some important and widely applicable conclusions.

In this section we take the six major elements of an SA package, identified above, and consider how each affects women, in the light of the earlier analysis of women's functions in society. Since the adjustments of the 1980s occurred because of deteriorating economic circumstances, it is sometimes very difficult to separate accurately the effects of the adjustment policies from the effects of this general economic deterioration. In the discussion below, no attempt is made to delineate responsibility for the changing circumstances of women, where it is difficult to do so.

1. Demand Restraint

Demand restraint has an aggregate economic impact. In addition, the particular measures adopted to achieve this restraint have specific impacts. Both affect women.

The aggregate impact of demand restraint is to reduce real incomes, either absolutely or compared with what they would have been. In effect, in the short term, demand restraint produces – or accentuates – recession. Demand restraint is achieved by cuts in government expenditure, credit restraints and reductions in real wages. The impact of these measures is to reduce formal sector employment, and reduce the real wages of those employed.

In the first half of the 1980s, most countries experiencing stabilisation packages also experienced declining real per capita incomes, although not all this decline can be attributed to the stabilisation package. For example, in the Philippines real GDP per head fell sharply from 1982 to 1985; real wages fell for every category of worker over this period, with average wage and salaries in 1985 being 30 per cent below the 1982 level. The UNICEF study found that GDP per capita fell in six out of the ten countries they examined; and in each of the six real wages fell and unemployment rose (Cornia *et al.*, 1987).

The immediate employment impact is on the formal sector; however, the informal sector suffers knock-on effects as more people seek work there, while opportunities decline with the general decline in the economy.

The decline in formal-sector employment reduced employment opportunities for women. Where cuts in employment were focused on the public sector – as they typically are in adjustment packages – women suffered especially because in general there are relatively more women, employed on better terms, than in the private (formal) sector. There is some evidence that women's employment opportunities have suffered more than proportionately, as labour markets tighten. For example, in Sri Lanka and Taiwan, when employment of both men and women fell during recession, that of women fell more than proportionately. Women's unemployment rates are usually higher than those of men. There is some evidence that this disparity increased over the 1980s. For example, in Jamaica female unemployment reached 36.5 per cent in 1984, as compared to 15.8 per cent for men (Boyd, 1987). In Barbados, in 1981 the unemployment rate was 15.1 per cent for women and 7.4 per cent for men; this increased to 24.1 per cent for women and 13 per cent for men in 1985 (Massiah, 1988).

Falling real wages affect both men and women, but again there is some evidence to suggest that women were worst affected, and there was a further deterioration in their relative wage. In Peru, for example, women's real wages fell by 15 per cent during the period from 1976 to 1984, while men's wages fell by 11.4 per cent (Francke, 1988).

Participation rates among women have tended to rise in most countries during recession/stabilisation, as women try to sustain household incomes. This was the typical response in Europe in the 1974–5 recession (Rubery, 1988). There is similar evidence of rising female participation rates – with stable and sometimes falling rates among men – in developing countries during the recent crisis. In the Philippines the female participation rate rose from 60 to 64 per cent between 1982 and 1984. Rising female participation rates were also noted in Jamaica, in Costa Rica, in Chile and Uruguay in the late 1970s and early 1980s (Berger, 1988). The need for incomes has forced women into the labour force to protect their families' survival. The effect is particularly strong among low-income families. For example, the greatest increase in participation rates occurred among the lowest income group, and there was a fall among upper income women in Chile 1974–5.

Additional female participation was concentrated in the informal sector, which grew as a proportion of total employment, while average earnings fell. For example, in twelve Latin American countries, workers employed in the informal sector increased by more than 18 per cent between 1981 and 1983, while average earnings in the sector decreased by 21 per cent (PREALC, 1985).

Cuts in government expenditure on the social services formed an important element in the package. Although the social sectors were not, on average, cut back more than proportionately, there were significant falls in real expenditure per head in these sectors in about two-thirds of the countries of sub-Saharan Africa and Latin America in the early 1980s. In some countries there were very substantial falls. In Jamaica, for example, real expenditure on education per head fell by over 30 per cent, 1980–5, and on health by 20 per cent (Boyd, 1987). In Zambia real expenditure on health fell by 22 per cent from 1982 to 1985, or over one-third in per capita terms. Table 2.5 gives some figures of cuts in the social sectors. The cuts were particularly heavily concentrated on non-wage recurrent expenditure and on capital expenditure (Cornia *et al.*, 1987, ch. 3).

Cuts in government expenditure on health and education caused a deterioration in facilities both for women and their families. In many countries, some health centres closed down; in those that remained open, there was an acute shortage of drugs. In Zambia the real value of the drugs budget in 1986 was only a quarter of the 1983 level, while only 10 per cent of this budget was actually released because of shortage of funds (Oxfam, 1988). A survey of rural health centres showed that most critical drugs had been out of stock for long periods. For example, oral rehydration salts had been out of stock for

Table 2.5   Countries with the most severe cuts in per capita GDP and health and education expenditures (annual percentage change)

	Health	Education	GDP
Africa	1979–83	1979–83	1980–85
Ghana	−15.8[a]	−9.5[a]	−4.4
Malawi	−9.8[a]	+7.0[a]	−1.0
Sudan	−9.5	−16.8[a]	−2.6
Togo	−7.5	+3.3	−3.7
Liberia	−6.9	−0.6	−7.1
Mauritius	−6.6	−7.7	
Tunisia	−6.4[a]	−16.6[a]	+1.4
Latin America	1980–84[b]	1979–83[c]	1980–84[b]
Bolivia	−77.7[d]	−14.1	−27.5
Guatemala	−58.3	n.a.	−14.8
Dominican Republic	−46.5	−4.1	+1.8
Surinam	−44.2[e]	n.a.	n.a.
El Salvador	−32.4	−8.1	−25.6
Chile	−23.8	+0.7[a]	−6.7
Barbados	−21.3	n.a.	−5.0
Jamaica	−18.5	−24.1[f]	−5.6
Costa Rica	−16.5	−16.5[a]	−12.3
Honduras	−15.2	n.a.	−11.5
Argentina	−13.9	−8.9[a]	−13.9
Uruguay	−13.4	−6.1[a]	−12.0
South and East Asia	1979–83	1979–83	1980–83
Sri Lanka	−12.9[a]	+1.6[a]	+2.5
Philippines	−1.3[a]	+0.8[a]	−2.7
Middle East			
Israel	−3.8[a]	−0.4[a]	−0.1
Jordan	−3.1[a]	+2.3[a]	+1.3

Note: The list extends only to countries for which data are available. Full data are only available for 15 countries in Africa (out of a possible 38). [a]1979–82 [b]Cumulative. [c]Per annum. [d]To 1982. [e]To 1983. [f]Cumulative 1980–85.

Source: As Table 2.4.

17 weeks over the previous year, and in some areas for 31 weeks; chloroquine had been out of stock for 4 weeks, on average, and in the worst area for 10 weeks. Schools were similarly affected as teachers were often unpaid, and there was no money for books.

The cuts in government expenditure on these services had significant negative effects on women's own welfare – with worsening health care, especially during pregnancy. It also affected women in their role as mothers, as the facilities available deteriorated. The incidence of recorded diseases rose significantly. In some countries – e.g. Zambia – immunisation programmes broke down because of lack of funds for drugs and for transport. In Chile, typhoid fever and hepatitis increased. In Peru, increasing deaths were recorded due to tuberculosis. In many countries a trend improvement in infant and child mortality rates came to a halt; in some – e.g. Brazil, Ghana, Zambia, Uruguay – infant mortality rates rose in some years in the 1980s, in part due to the worsening health facilities, in part to worsening nutrition.

The deteriorating educational facilities – together with the other adverse changes experienced by low-income families – was reflected in lowered educational performance. Drop-out rates rose and school completion rates fell – for example, in Sri Lanka, Ghana, Peru, the Philippines and Brazil; rising illiteracy rates and deteriorating educational attainment were recorded in Sri Lanka, the Philippines, Jamaica, Zambia, Nigeria and Peru. In many countries, the number of children living on the streets increased significantly.

All these changes severely and adversely affected women in their role as mothers. The quality of family care women could provide worsened and new demands were imposed on them to try to provide some domestic substitutes for the deteriorating public facilities in health and education.

2. Price Decontrol

The structural adjustment package affected prices in five ways: through the reduction/abolition of subsidies, especially on food; through price decontrol; through raising producer prices for farmers; through the impact of devaluation on domestic prices; and through the imposition of charges for various publicly provided services.

The net effect was to increase relative food prices. In most countries for which there is evidence, food price indices rose significantly faster than the overall consumer price index during the adjustment period (Cornia *et al.*, 1987, ch. 1). Removal of the maize subsidy in Zambia together with devaluation led to a doubling of the price of maize meal. Rising food prices combined with declining earnings meant a sharp fall in real household incomes. This affected women in their role as household managers. Women had to spend more time on organising consumption – for example, shopping more frequently and buying less at a time (see Raczynski and Serrano, 1985), buying less convenience foods and spending more time on food preparation.

In some poor urban areas, where real incomes had fallen almost below survival levels, women got together to organise collective shopping and cooking. This occurred for example in *comedores populares* in Peru. This increased the time women devoted to social organisations, while reducing some household tasks.

Price reform has also involved the introduction of charges for some health and education services: for example, school fees for primary schools were introduced in Bendel State in Nigeria leading to a reduction of one-third in the enrolment rate. In Ghana, the introduction of health charges was associated with reduced attendance at clinics. Such charges reduced the ability of women to meet the basic needs of the family.

These changes in prices led to reductions in real incomes for many poor households, often to below the minimum subsistence level, which worsened nutritional standards. There is evidence of rising malnutrition among children in at least 23 countries in the 1980s. Some of this was due to drought, but much was associated with falling real incomes among poor households. While there is little direct evidence on female nutrition, there is evidence of an increase in the proportion of low-birthweight babies in a number of countries where this data has been collected: in north-east Brazil the proportion of low-birthweight babies rose from 10.2 per cent in 1982 to 15.3 per cent in 1984 (Dias *et al.*, 1986); increases were also recorded in Barbados and Jamaica from 1979 to 1982 (UNICEF). This data indicates rising female malnutrition. It is likely that rising malnutrition among women – especially pregnant and lactating women – has been extensive, including most of the countries where rising child malnutrition was recorded.

3. Trade Regimes

Various changes are typically involved: devaluation, foreign exchange auctions and import liberalisation.

Devaluation – together with domestic price changes – increases the price of tradeables relative to non-tradeables. Women are particularly affected by developments in the agricultural sector, because of their heavy activity in this sector. SA packages have aimed to raise agricultural prices, with the highest rises for export crops. However, women may not benefit as much as the sector as a whole, or even at all, for three reasons. First, the subsistence crops in which women specialise experienced a significantly lower price rise than export crops. Second, women farmers frequently lack access to essential inputs, such as fertilisers, and to technological advice through extension officers, so that it is very difficult for them to take advantage of the improved prices in terms of greater production. Third, the greater increase in the price of export crops may increase the amount of (unpaid) time women are required to put in on these crops, and reduce land available for the subsistence crops (Joekes, 1988). In Zambia, an ILO report found that the cash income per economically active member of the subsistence farming sector (who are mainly women) fell by 13 per cent from 1976 to 1985. The report concluded that 'this sector has borne the brunt of the recession in all aspects'.

The terms of trade of the service sector tend to deteriorate, as a consequence of devaluation and price decontrol. This therefore, further reduces the real incomes of women as producers in this sector. This adverse effect was particularly felt in the urban economy.

The effects on the industrial sector depend on the nature of the sector, and also of the measures taken. Trade liberalisation, together with devaluation, is intended to increase the efficiency of the sector, orienting it more towards exports, and reducing some inefficient import-substitution. Where there is already a viable export sector, these effects may indeed occur, and expansion of labour-intensive exports ensue. Since women are relatively heavily employed in the production of labour-intensive exports, this will increase their employment opportunities, albeit at low wages. It has been estimated that women account for 75–80 per cent of the labour force in labour-intensive manufactured exports (Joekes, 1987). The adjustment process may increase employment in these activities, but wages are not likely to rise.

In economies which have a smaller industrial base and little experience in exporting, it appears that liberalisation frequently leads to reduced industrial output and employment, and in these circumstances does not have these beneficial effects, but rather adds to the recessionary effects, with reduced employment opprtunities and further downward pressure on wages.

Foreign exchange auctions have been introduced in countries with heavy restrictions to permit market allocation of the limited foreign exchange, and to bring about a market determined exchange rate. The policy is intended to produce a more efficient allocation of imports than reliance on administrative controls. However, in Zambia the auction was dominated by large-scale and foreign-owned companies. Small-scale firms and the agricultural sector received very little foreign exchange.

Allocation of foreign exchange by unstructured auction was certainly not helpful to women as producers or consumers. The small-scale, informal and agricultural sector were all squeezed. These sectors do not, however, generally benefit from administrative controls (see Ncube, 1987), although on balance it seems they did even worse under the auction. The structured auction that followed in Zambia did somewhat better for these sectors – and for women as producers. It also ensured that some foreign exchange was reserved for medical supplies, in contrast to the unstructured auction.

4. Credit Reform

Credit reform is intended to raise interest rates for large-scale borrowers who are often subsidised, and to lower rates and increase credit to the small-scale sector, which usually has very limited access to the subsidised loans, and has to pay enormously high interest rates to borrow on the informal money markets. The informal sector sometimes pays rates as high as 100 per cent p.a., five to ten times the rates paid in the formal sector. Credit reform is intended to bring the two markets closer together. Women are unlikely to be much affected by these changes. For the most part they had almost no access to the subsidised rates, and borrowed on the informal sector market, if at all. But the credit reforms do not help them much for two reasons. First, the major problem about borrowing for low-income borrowers is lack of collateral. Without new rules about collateral, reforms do not benefit low-income borrowers significantly. Second, women are disadvantaged in approaching most formal-sector institutions in developing countries, and this applies as much to the reformed credit institutions as to the old ones, unless their procedures are changed.

Credit reform in Sri Lanka provides an example. The benefits of the reforms went almost entirely to the large-scale producers. Bank requirements for small-scale producers, including higher margins, and higher equity requirements, made credit virtually inaccessible to small firms (Joekes, 1988).

5. Parastatal Reform/Privatisation

This is aimed at increasing the efficiency and profitability of parastatals. Such changes do not affect women significantly, since they generally do not form an important part of the bureaucracy which runs the parastatals, nor of the private sector owners/managers which replace parastatals. Women may be indirectly affected, however, by any cuts in employment and increase in prices. In the longer run, they would gain if these changes brought about increased efficiency and thereby contributed to higher economic growth. The precise effects depend on the context. For example, some of the marketing parastatals in West Africa may compete directly with women who market produce. Reform might help these women, but this depends on the nature of the reform. In most countries, the public sector has not been successful in extending their services to women – e.g. credit, extension. But most reforms envisaged do not make any explicit attempt to improve access for women. Reform which permits greater influence of market forces, without any special attempts to incorporate women into the market, is unlikely to help women significantly, but equally they probably do not lose significantly either.

6. Administration

This class of reforms tends to be rather imprecise, calling for 'improvement' on administrative capacity, training, etc. Whether such measures help women depends on whether women are explicitly brought in as a major target for training. If they are not – and there is not explicit mention of women in most of the documents – the schemes are likely to have very little positive effect on women's administrative capacity, although they would gain, as citizens, from any general improvement in male capacity.

Summary of Effects of SA on Women

As *producers*, women have been adversely affected by recession and demand restraint. The limited evidence suggests that reduced employment and real wages in the formal sector has usually been worse for women than men; there have been reduced real earnings in the informal sector; increased female participation in the work force has moderated the loss in household income but has increased female work hours.

Restructuring of the economy, towards tradeables, has probably improved women's position a little as agricultural producers, but less than men who specialise in export crops; it has worsened women's position in the service sector, where they are heavily concentrated;

and has increased employment opportunities for women in labour-intensive exports in those economies where these are significant.

Other changes to the economy – including credit reform, parastatal reform, administrative reform – have had little effect on women, who were not beneficiaries of the unreformed system, but are not beneficiaries of the reformed system either.

Women as *household managers* have been badly affected by demand restraint and recession which has severely reduced family income in many economies, often to below subsistence, and consequently imposed increasing demands on women's time, as consumers, as they shop more often and spend more time trying to stretch their income to meet the subsistence needs of the family. These effects have been made worse by price decontrol, devaluation, reduced food subsidies, and increased charges.

With respect to the conditions of women as *mothers*, the adjustment package has worsened the health and educational facilities available, and increased the time women need to spend on the health, education and feeding of their families, as a result of the cuts in these services, increased charges and higher food prices.

The role of women as *social organisers* has been increased, as local social organisations have taken over some of the functions previously fulfilled by the state, and as women have acted collectively to contribute to their mutual survival.

The income women control has fallen in countries undergoing adjustment. Women's health, nutrition and education has fallen along with that of the rest of society, especially in the worst affected countries. No data has been collected on whether women have suffered more than proportionately in these respects. The hours of work necessary for women to fulfil their four functions have increased with respect to every function.

Overall, there has been a marked deterioration in the conditions women face with respect to each of their major functions in most countries undergoing stabilisation and structural adjustment. The deterioration is largely associated with the stabilisation aspect of the package; the effects of the longer-term reforms are more ambiguous, offering some increase in employment and earnings in some sectors, with decreases elsewhere. But much of the long-term packages, as at present designed, are irrelevant to women, as they are not involved in the most important reforms. The marketisation of the economies, which form a central aspect of the longer-term reforms, will not benefit women unless institutions are changed so that women can participate on equal terms in the market, and unless social support and services are improved so that women can afford the extra time that successful participation in the market would require.

V ALTERNATIVE ADJUSTMENT STRATEGIES

If the negative effects of SA on women are to be avoided, the present SA policies will need to be radically altered. The aim should not merely be to eliminate the negative effects, but to generate positive effects so that women's productive potential can be fully realised, and their welfare enhanced during the process of adjustment. Alternatives are especially urgent because of the prolonged nature of the crisis and therefore the extended influence of SA policies.

Alternatives to current SA policies are also needed to avoid harmful effects of SA on the poor in general, and specially on children (see Cornia *et al.*, 1987). While this chapter focuses on women, the need to protect the poor is equally urgent (and in fact overlaps, as the poorest groups are often female-headed households). Many of the proposals outlined above would also contribute to a programme which protects the most vulnerable.

An alternative approach to structural adjustment, fully incorporating the interests and concerns of women, would contain three elements:

1. the adoption of more expansionary macro-policies, reducing the recessionary elements in SA;
2. the redesign of the adjustment package so that women's interests are built into it, and do not rely, as at present, on some unlikely 'trickle-down' effects; and
3. the introduction of special measures to support women in their efforts to maintain standards for themselves and their families during adjustment.

We discuss these three elements below and the fourth element of the necessity of monitoring the impact of adjustment policies.

1. Macro-Policies

Much of the cost of the adjustment policies has arisen from the sharply deflationary element. This deflationary element was mainly due to the need for very rapid improvement in the balance of payments, which itself reflected a deficiency of medium-term finance. For most economies, any significant improvement in the trade balance in such a short time-period could only come from deflation, which would lead to a cut in imports. While a major turnaround on the current account balance was achieved in the 1980s in both the Western Hemisphere and Africa, it was due to a fall in the volume of imports. Exports made no contribution to the adjustment: in both regions they fell in value terms over this period, partly because of the adverse movement in the terms of trade. There were severe cuts in investment in both regions, reducing growth prospects and also the potential for export expansion. In Africa gross capital formation as a proportion of Gross Domestic Product fell from 28 per cent in 1981 to 19 per cent in 1987, in the Western Hemisphere from 23 per cent to 17.5 per cent.

It is essential that adjustment policies should avoid this deflationary posture, and *achieve adjustment through growth*, rather than contraction, if women's incomes and employment are to be protected. A number of major changes are needed in the world economic and financial system to make adjustment with growth a real possibility. The changes include: (i) a longer time perspective in terms of finance and conditions, on the part of the IMF; (ii) much *more* net finance for adjusting countries. (At present as noted above, the net financial flows are negative.) Potential sources include multilateral institutions, bilateral aid donors, commercial banks and multinational companies. The additional finance could be given in the form of new flows of money, or it could take the form of reduced reverse flows, to be achieved by lower interest rates, and generous rescheduling/write-offs of existing debt. While the Brady plan appears to be moving in the right direction, the actual sums involved are far too small. (iii) In the absence of large additional medium-term financial flows, developing countries should be permitted to make use of import controls as a way of reducing imports with a smaller negative impact on output and employment levels. (iv) The world economic system should support expansionary adjustment among developing countries. This involves growth in the advanced countries, and a liberal trading environment towards imports from developing countries, and the support of mechanisms to uphold commodity prices.

All adjusting countries would prefer expansionary adjustment. The domestic policies necessary to achieve it are not complicated: they include less tight budgetary and credit restrictions, and support for investment, especially in priority areas including the export sector; and probably selective import controls, to make sure that priorities are met, and that unnecessary deflation is avoided.

The Need for Gradual Changes

The macro-policy reforms are usually introduced very abruptly with large changes in a very short period. As a result there are very large losses in incomes in some occupations, almost overnight; as it takes time for new jobs to be created in alternative occupations, in the interim people may suffer very acute hardship, leading to malnutrition and even deaths, and also to political unrest which may bring the programme to a halt. Changes which affect people's lives in this way should be more gradual. Those who advocate rapid change argue that this is the only way to secure change at all: the evidence for this view has not been produced. Moreover, the sudden changes have been so devastating in effects that they have frequently been reversed after a short time (see e.g. Zambia, Nigeria, and many other examples of abandoned IMF programmes).

2. Redesign of Adjustment Policies to Incorporate Women

Neither the macro-policy instruments, which form the core of IMF programmes, nor the structural reforms embodied in World Bank programmes, have any explicit concern with the distributional impact of their programmes, yet each have important distributional effects. These effects need to be considered when policies are formulated, so that the objectives of protecting the poor and fully incorporating women into the adjustment affect the design of policies.

Meso Policies

Meso policies concern the distributional impact of macro-policies, determining which income group, sector and gender bears the brunt of the changes.

Any given macro-policy target may have a range of distributional effects, according to the meso policies adopted. For example, a given public expenditure cut may fall more or less heavily on different sectors (e.g. defence or health), and within sectors on different groups (e.g. on curative or preventative health, on health activities directed at men, women or children). Meso policies can design expenditure cuts to protect certain services and certain groups in society. In some countries vulnerable groups were protected during the 1980s, through well-designed meso policies (e.g. in Costa Rica or Chile), while in others (e.g. Bolivia) the social sectors were cut more than proportionately with total expenditure, and vulnerable groups suffered greatly.

Other macro-policies, e.g. credit targets, tax or tariff changes, also have distributional implications. With appropriate use of meso policies, vulnerable groups may be protected. Changes in the tax and subsidy system, for example, can be designed to fall heavily on some groups, and protect others. Credit allocation can similarly be biased towards or against the small-scale sector or women borrowers.

The Structured Market
One important form of meso policy is the adoption of structured markets. Most of the policy reforms involve an increasing role for the market in the allocation of resources. But without any guidance, the market is a clumsy instrument, especially when there is considerable disequilibrium. Resource allocation then takes place according to existing purchasing power and creditworthiness, which may not accord with a society's priorities. Women and low-income groups typically suffer in an unguided market. What is needed is a *structured market* in the allocation of resources, in which a certain proportion of resources (of foreign exchange, or of credit, for example) is reserved for particular groups, including the small-scale sector and women entrepreneurs. The use of such a structured market has been successful in getting resources to the Self-Employed Women's Association in India, for example. Similarly, Indonesia has introduced measures to reserve credit for the small-scale sector.

The use of structured markets to ensure that women and low-income groups get adequate resources is an essential aspect of an alternative package.

Sectoral Policies
Much can be achieved by reallocating resources within each sector. Thus by shifting expenditures towards preventative health care and primary health care and away from curative and hospital health care, considerable improvement can be secured in the average health of women and children. In some cases, cost-effective substitutes can reduce costs and improve standards – e.g. the use of oral rehydration therapy as a substitute for intravenous cures for diarrhoea. In the health sector, UNICEF has recommended some core interventions, which are low cost and can improve child health, and appear particu-

larly appropriate for use as a means of protecting child and female health during economic adjustment. However, some of these interventions impose an additional time burden on women, which may mean that they are not adopted, or that they reduce other female activities which are also of importance to the health of the family (see Leslie *et al.*, 1986). Consequently, restructuring must take into account this time dimension, as well as the need to increase cost-effectiveness and improve the conditions of health.

The principles behind meso- and sectoral policies designed to protect women during adjustment should be the following:

1. Basic needs provision for poor households should not be adversely affected, and efforts should be made to improve resource allocation in these areas. This requirement applies to public expenditure policies, aid policies, taxation and charges. A similar requirement holds for aspects of resource allocation affecting the earnings of low-income households: namely that credit restraints should not apply to informal sector activities, to small farmers or for the most part to labour-intensive activities.
2. With respect to those macro-policies that affect other households (middle-income, upper-income), efforts should be made to ensure that women are not disproportionately adversely affected.
3. Careful and regular monitoring is needed.

Institutional Change
The reforms contain significant institutional change. But while they may enhance efficiency, they do not improve access of women. Additional institutional reforms are needed. (i) Female access to resources must be improved. Women suffer from centuries of legal discrimination against them in most societies, and from a disproportionate lack of assets. To offset this may require land reform and new credit institutions, such as the Grameen Bank in Bangladesh, where women form 70 per cent of the membership and receive 56 per cent of the disbursements. The repayment rate of the Bank has been over 99 per cent. (ii) Reforms of government institutions must ensure that women are included in management and operations, and that the institutions provide adequate access to women. Extension services, for example, are often male-dominated and rarely make special efforts to reach female farmers, which reduces the efficiency of the programmes as well as their equity. (iii) Reform is needed in female education, which lags behind male in most economies at most stages

Table 2.6   Education, female and male, 1986

	Primary enrolment[a] %		Secondary enrolment %	
	F	M	F	M
China	120	137	35	48
India	76	107	24	45
Other low income	68	83	20	29
of which				
Bhutan[b]	17	29	9	14
Sri Lanka[c]	102	104	70	63
Lower				
mid-income	100	108	50	57
of which				
Yemen Ar. Rep.[b]	79	125	3	26
Chile[c]	109	110	73	67
Upper				
mid-income	101	107	67	71
of which				
Oman[b]	86	101	25	45
Korea, Rep.[c]	94	94	93	98

Notes: [a] % may exceed 100, if repetitions mean that more than the total age group is at school.
[b] Country with lowest female secondary school enrolment in group.
[c] Country with highest female secondary enrolment in group.

Source: World Bank, World Development Report, 1989 (Washington D.C.).

of education (see Table 2.6). Educational (and training) inequalities are one of the basic explanations for women's lower incomes and worse employment opportunities than those of men. Inequalities in incomes and employment will be perpetuated unless this basic inequality is put right. Building up female education will not only help ensure equitable development, but will also increase the economic efficiency of the labour force, improve household and especially child health, and reduce fertility. Therefore, the promotion of female education at every stage should be a central element in structural reform.

3. Support Policies

Some hardship is inevitable for some groups during stabilisation and adjustment. The hardship would be less if the changes suggested above were introduced, but even so some people may suffer drastic loss of incomes during the interim, and this is likely to be borne especially by women in low-income households, in terms of additional work (paid and unpaid) and lowered consumption. Consequently, support policies are essential to help women during this period, and to prevent the worst suffering. Support policies include:

(a) Employment Schemes
Effective and extensive employment schemes have been launched in a number of countries – e.g. Morocco, Chile, Maharashtra in India, Botswana – to provide basic employment and incomes to people adversely affected by economic or climatic disaster. In Chile at one time 13 per cent of the workforce were employed on such schemes. In Botswana nearly one-third of the income lost through drought was replaced by public works schemes. The schemes are also often effective in improving infrastructure and have been shown to be economically efficient (see Cornia *et al.*, 1987). Women have been active participants: 75 per cent of those involved in the Peruvian Temporary Employment Scheme from 1985 to 1987 were women, and since it was stopped women have formed a pressure group for its reinstatement (Francke, 1988). Women outnumbered men in the Chilean scheme (Pollack, 1988). In Botswana most of the beneficiaries of the labour-based relief programme were women. However, while these schemes are valuable in maintaining incomes, they also impose new time demands on women. This poses particular problems for rural-based schemes, where the time demands can conflict with agricultural as well as domestic tasks. In the urban areas, the time demands can conflict with child caring, and additional facilities may be needed.

(b) Food and Nutrition
A prime objective of any government – at all times and especially during crisis and at normal times – must be to ensure that everyone has access to adequate food. This objective is not being met in many countries during adjustment. Subsidies should be maintained for basic staples during adjustment. It may also be necessary to provide free food for very needy groups, especially young children and pregnant and lactating women. Such food can be delivered through health clinics or schools, for example.

(c) Support for Communal Activities
During economic crisis, the community can play a major role in

supporting poor households by providing communal shopping, cooking, and child caring facilities, and also supporting local health and educational facilities with labour, materials and sometimes money. The state can do a lot to support these sorts of activities through active encouragement, the removal of legal obstacles and small amounts of money.

Monitoring

It is essential that the effects of structural adjustment on women and on low-income households be monitored regularly and rapidly during adjustment. To date, most monitoring activities have concerned major economic variables, like money supply, credit creation and trade, and no attention has been paid to social variables or to the position of women. This is one reason why it is only now – almost a decade after the crisis started – that the position of low-income groups and of women is being recorded, and even now the data is very scarce. Monitoring is essential to draw political attention to developments, to permit good design of policies and secure appropriate action.

Summary of Alternative Strategy

The discussion above has reviewed major elements in an adjustment strategy that would incorporate women into the adjustment process in an equitable way, paying special attention to women in low-income households. The main proposals covered were:

- More expansionary adjustment policies, with substantial additional medium-term financial flows to adjusting countries; and more gradual adjustments.
- Meso and sectoral policies to protect the needs of women, especially in low-income households, in the allocation of public expenditure, aid, taxes and subsidies, credit and foreign trade regime; this would involve the use of structured markets, especially in foreign exchange and credit allocation.
- Policies towards institutional reform to be reformulated so as to incorporate the interests of women, and small-scale producers, with redistribution of access to assets and promotion of female education at all levels. Policies to improve administrative capacity need explicitly to include women.

- Support policies during crisis include public works, feeding schemes, and support for communal initiatives.
- Monitoring of the participation and welfare of women on a regular and speedy basis is essential.

The alternatives proposed here would not only avoid unnecessary hardship and be more equitable, but they would also increase the efficiency of the programmes in both economic and social terms, because women have very large underused potential for increasing the productivity of the economy.

Notes

1. This chapter relies heavily on work done for the Commonwealth Secretariat. I am grateful for their permission to use it. Much of the analysis – and more material than could be included here – has appeared in Commonwealth Group of Experts, 1989, *Engenderimg Adjustment for the 1990s* (London: Commonwealth Secretariat). The ideas in this paper were stimulated and influenced by discussions among the Group of Experts, and by background papers prepared by Susan Joekes, all of whom I would like to thank.
2. There are of course structural adjustments in developed countries too, which often have important effects on women. These are not discussed here because of space.

References

Berger, M. (1988) 'Women's Response to Recession in Latin America and the Caribbean: A Focus on Urban Labour Markets', paper presented to the Workshop on 'Economic Crisis, Household Survival Strategies and Women's Work', Ithaca, New York, Sept.

Boyd, D. (1987) 'The Impact of Adjustment Policies on Vulnerable Groups: The Case of Jamaica, 1973–1984', in Cornia *et al.* (1987).

Cocytax, X. F. (1984) *The Role of the Family in Health: Appropriate Research Methods* (Geneva, WHO)

Cornia, G. A., R. Jolly and F. Stewart (1987) *Adjustment with a Human Face* (Oxford: Oxford University Press).

Dias, L., R. Camarano and A. Lechtig (1986) 'Drought, Recession and Prevalence of Low Birth Weight Babies in Poor Urban Populations of the North East of Brazil', letter to editor of *Journal of Tropical Pediatrics*.

Elson, D. (1987) 'The Impact of Structural Adjustment on Women: Concepts and Issues', paper prepared for Commonwealth Secretariat.

Francke, M. (1988) 'Weathering Economic Crisis: Women's Response to the Recession in Lima, Peru', paper presented at 'Weathering the Economic Crisis: Women's Response to the Recession in Latin America and the Caribbean', Racine, Wisconsin, June.

Helleiner, G. K. (1988) 'Growth-Oriented Adjustment Lending: A Critical Assessment of IMF/World Bank Approaches', paper prepared for the South Commission, Geneva.

ILO (1987) 'Employment and Incomes in Zambia in the Context of Structural Adjustment', ILO/SATEP, Lusaka.

Joekes, S. (1987) 'Evaluation of Research and Policies on Female Employment in Developing Countries', paper prepared for OECD Development Centre, Conference on Evaluation of Urban Employment Research and Policies in Developing Countries, Paris, November.

Joekes, S. (1988) 'Gender and Macroeconomic Policy', paper prepared for AWID Colloquium on Gender and Development Cooperation, Washington, D.C., April.

King, E. and R. Evenson (1983) 'Time Allocation and Home Production in Philippine Rural Households', in M. Buvinic, M. A. Lycette and W. P. McGreevey (eds), *Women and Poverty in the Third World* (Baltimore: Johns Hopkins Press).

Leslie, J., M. Lycette and M. Buvinic (1986) 'Weathering Economic Crisis: The Crucial Role of Women in Health', paper presented at the Second Takemi Symposium on International Health, Harvard, May.

Massiah, J. (1988) 'Weathering Economic Crisis: Women's Response to the Recession in Commonwealth Caribbean', paper presented at 'Weathering the Economic Crisis: Women's Response to the Recession in Latin America and the Caribbean', Racine, Wisconsin, June.

Mazumdar, D. (1976) 'The Urban Informal Sector', *World Development*, 4, pp. 655–79.

Mosley, P. (1987) 'Conditionality as Bargaining Process: Structural Adjustment Lending 1980–86', *Essays in International Finance*, Princeton University, no. 168.

Ncube P. D. (1987) 'The International Money Fund and the Zambian Economy' in Hevenik, *The IMF and the World Bank in Africa* (Uppsala: Scandinavian Institute of African Studies).

OXFAM (1988) 'Debt and Poverty: A Case Study of Zambia', by J. Clark with D. Keen, Oxford.

Page, S. (1987) 'The Rise in Protection Since 1974', *Oxford Review of Economic Policy*, 3, 1, pp. 37–51.

Pinstrup-Andersen, P. (ed.) (1987) *Consumer-Oriented Food Subsidies: Cost, Benefits and Policy Options for Developing Countries* (Baltimore: Johns Hopkins).

Pollack, M. (1988) 'Women's Poverty in Latin America: A Three Country Study of Short and Long-Term Trends', paper presented at 'Weathering the Economic Crisis: Women's Response to the Recession in Latin America and the Caribbean', Racine, Wisconsin, June.

PREALC (1985) *Mas Alla de la Crisis* (Santiago, Chile: ILO).

Raczynski, D. and C. Serrano (1985) 'Vivir la porbeza: testimonio de mujeres', Santiago: Corporaciom Investigacciones Economica Latino America.

Rubery, J. (1988) 'Women and Recession: Some Problems of Comparative Analysis', paper presented at 'Weathering the Economic Crisis: Women's Response to the Recession in Latin America and the Caribbean', Racine, Wisconsin, June.

Shields, N. (1980) *Women in the Urban Labour Market of Africa: The Case of Tanzania*, World Bank Staff Working Paper, 380, Washington D.C.

Sivard, L. (1985) *Women . . . a World Survey* (Washington, D.C.: World Priorities).

3 Male Bias in Structural Adjustment

Diane Elson

INTRODUCTION

The last decade has been marked by a contrast between rising awareness of the importance of women's contribution to the economy and continued deterioration of the world economy. Encouraged by the UN Decade for Women, many governments have set up Women's Bureaux, or Departments for Women's Affairs. Women's groups across the world have campaigned for proper recognition of women's work both as producers of goods and services, and as reproducers of human resources; and for access to the resources women require to improve the productivity of their efforts. There have been some successes in opening up new activities to women through special training programmes; and in enhancing women's income earning opportunities through projects with women's components, or specifically directed to women. Much of the energy of Women's Bureaux in developing countries has been directed towards women's projects, often in partnership with aid agency officials who have special responsibility for women and development. In market economy developed countries, much of the emphasis has been on introducing new equal opportunities legislation and enabling women to fight their cases through the courts.

But more important to the economic well-being of women than either projects or legislation is the general condition of the economy. Low rates of growth of output and exports and employment undermine the efforts put into projects and legislation. The 1980s saw not just *low* rates of growth, but *absolute declines* in many of the key indicators of economic well-being in Latin America and Africa. The period 1980–2 was one of deep *recession* in the international economy and subsequently recovery was very hesitant. Despite rapid growth in the second half of the decade in the developed countries and in parts of Asia, the world economy remains in an uneasy and unsettled state. In many developing countries the problems have been compounded by falling export prices, protectionist barriers to their exports, and

46

the mounting burden of debt. Real *per capita* incomes declined in both Latin America and sub-Saharan Africa between 1980 and 1988: in some countries in Latin America real *per capita* GNP by the end of the 1980s was less than at the end of the 1970s; in some African countries it was less than at the end of the 1960s (World Bank, 1989, p. 6).

There are no signs of a decisive improvement in the international environment facing such countries: primary commodity prices are at their lowest level since the 1930s; protectionist pressures are growing in the developed market economies; interest rates remain at an historically high level; the difficulties of debtor nations are intensifying. Major imbalances within the industrialised world, in particular the large US fiscal and balances of payments current account deficits, are likely to perpetuate volatility in the international financial system.

It is thus of the utmost importance that those concerned with the well-being of women should develop the capacity to analyse the implications of global economic deterioration for women and to make an input into the formulation of strategies to cope with that deterioration. It is no less important that those concerned with the design and implementation of policies to cope with the adverse international economic environment should develop an awareness of the significance of gender for economic processes.[1]

Here it will be argued that the analysis on which structural adjustment programmes are based, the choice of policy instruments, and the evaluation of the impact of structural adjustment programmes on living standards, are all susceptible to male bias. The term 'male bias' indicates as orientation that tends to work to the benefit of men more than to the benefit of women (Elson, 1991a). There is no implication that all men are necessarily male-biased; nor that all men are better off than all women. An analogy can be drawn with the term 'urban bias', indicating an orientation that tends to work to the benefit of urban people more than rural people. Male bias stems from a failure to take into account the asymmetry of gender relations; the fact that women as a gender are socially subordinated to men as a gender through both social structures and individual practices.[2] In this chapter, some steps that could be taken to diminish male bias in structural adjustment programmes are considered; and it is argued that they would both improve the position of women and improve the chances of creating new social political and economic structures that would facilitate more appropriate forms of adjustment than those currently being undertaken.

CONCEPTUAL TOOLS: MALE BIAS IN ADJUSTMENT ANALYSIS

Economic trends and economic policies are usually presented in a language which appears to be *gender neutral*. No specific mention is made of gender or of the sexual division of labour. The focus of attention is on the gross national product; on imports and exports and the balance of payments; on efficiency and productivity. Macro-economic policies, such as structural adjustment programmes, are supposed to reallocate resources so as to restore balance of payments equilibrium, increase exports and restore growth rates. Questions of gender have been considered irrelevant to those objectives.

However, this apparent gender-neutrality masks a deeper *male bias*. Three important kinds of male bias are implicit in the conceptual framework underlying structural adjustment programmes: male bias concerning the sexual division of labour; male bias concerning the unpaid domestic work necessary for producing and maintaining human resources; and male bias concerning the household, which is taken to be the basic unit from which the macro-economy is made up (Elson, 1991b).

The first kind of male bias consists in ignoring the fact that some kinds of work are socially constituted as 'women's work', while other kinds of work are socially constituted as 'men's work'. Changing the relative monetary rewards of different kinds of work will not result in a smooth reallocation of labour from one to the other in the face of gender barriers. Taking no account of gender leads to the belief, expressed by the Chief of the Trade and Adjustment Policy Division in the World Bank, that 'it is relatively easy to retain and transfer labour originally working in, say, construction or commerce for employment in the export . . . of, say, radios or garments' (Selowsky, 1987). But all the available evidence about the sexual division of labour suggests it would be far from easy to transfer male labour from construction to the production of radios and garments, where the preference of employers is universally for female labour (Elson, 1991b). If a structural adjustment policy has the aim of reducing employment in the construction sector and increasing employment in activities such as radio and garment assembly, as in the case in many countries undergoing structural adjustment, then a more likely outcome than a smooth transfer of labour is unemployment for men; and for women, factory work in addition to the unpaid work they do as daughters, wives and mothers. A key question to ask is: does the adjustment work by adding new kinds of paid work to the paid and unpaid work that women are already doing?

The second kind of male bias consists in ignoring the unpaid work required for the process of reproduction and maintenance of human resources. This process is not explicitly included in macro-economic thinking. The economy is defined principally in terms of marketed goods and services, with some allowance made for subsistence crop production in developing countries. The work of caring for children, of gathering fuel and water, processing food, preparing meals, keeping the house clean, nursing the sick, managing the household, is excluded from the economy. It is, of course, work which largely falls on the shoulders of women, even in the most developed countries. By excluding explicit consideration of this work, and of the resources it requires, structural adjustment analysis and policy has a built-in conceptual bias against women.

This conceptual bias has important practical consequences. When macro-economic policies are formulated to reallocate resources, the lack of explicit consideration of the process of reproduction and maintenance of human resources tells against women. For the implicit assumption of macro-economic policy is that the process of reproduction and maintenance of human resources which is carried out unpaid by women will continue regardless of the way in which resources are reallocated. Women's unpaid labour is implicitly regarded as elastic – able to stretch so as to make up any shortfall in other resources available for reproduction and maintenance of human resources.

Now it is perfectly true that the process of reproduction and maintenance of human resources is different from the production of any other kind of resource. It does not respond to economic signals in the same way: if the price of a crop falls far enough, it may be uprooted or left to rot; if there is insufficient demand for a manufactured good, the factory is closed and the machinery mothballed, sold off second hand, or scrapped. But if the demand for labour falls, if unemployment rises, and wages fall, mothers do not 'scrap' their children or leave them to rot untended. Human resources have an intrinsic, not merely instrumental value.

However, women's unpaid labour is not infinitely elastic – breaking point may be reached, and women's capacity to reproduce and maintain human resources may collapse. Even if breaking point is not reached, the success of the macro-economic policy in achieving its goals may be won at the cost of a longer and harder working day for many women. This cost will be *invisible* to the macro-economic policy-makers because it is *unpaid* time. But the cost will be revealed in statistics on the health and nutritional status of such women.

Terms like 'cost' and 'productivity' and 'efficiency', which play a large role in discussions of economic policy, are in fact ambiguous. What is regarded by economists as 'increased efficiency' may instead be a shifting of costs from the *paid economy* to the *unpaid economy*. For instance, a reduction in the time patients spend in hospital may seem to economists to be an increase in the efficiency of the hospital, but may in fact result in a transfer of the costs of care for the sick from the paid economy to the unpaid economy. The money costs of the hospital per patient fall but the unpaid work of women in the household rises. This is not a genuine increase in efficiency; it is simply a transfer of costs from the hospital to the home.

In considering structural adjustment programmes, we need to be able to make the link between 'the economy' and 'human resources' by way of women's unpaid labour. A key question to ask is: does the adjustment work by increasing the amount of unpaid labour women have to do?

The third kind of male bias consists in the assumption that the economy is built up from households, which can be treated as units whose internal functioning does not require any analysis. The design and implementation of structural adjustment programmes is now recognised as requiring some consideration of the allocation and enjoyment of resources between households. But there is still a tendency to assume that households are pooling and sharing institutions capable of absorbing the shocks of adjustment, and that there is no need to analyse the allocation and enjoyment of resources within them.[3]

However, there is now available a wealth of theorising (Sen, 1983; Folbre, 1986a; Folbre, 1986b) and evidence (Beneria and Roldan, 1987; Blumberg, 1988; Dwyer and Bruce, 1988) which undermines this complacency. The household is a site of conflict as well as of co-operation; of inequality as well as of mutuality; and conflict and inequality are structured along gender lines. This does not mean that women are passive victims within the household and play no decision-making role. Rather, it means that women do not enjoy the same decision-making power as men; their bargaining power is weaker, and they do not enjoy the same control over resources. A key question to ask is: does the adjustment add to women's responsibilities within the household without adding to the resources women require to discharge those responsibilities? Is it *women* who are the shock absorbers of the adjustment process?

POLICY INSTRUMENTS: MALE BIAS IN METHODS OF STRUCTURAL ADJUSTMENT

A sustainable strategy for coping with the deteriorating international environment facing many LDCs requires some form of structural change. The important question is what form this change should take and how to organise this change. The World Bank and IMF have placed great faith in the efficacy of market forces as the best way to organise structural change.

The World Bank holds the view that a major reason for poor economic performance in LDCs, and for inability to cope with the deteriorating international economic environment, is *distortions* in resource allocation; distortions caused, it is argued, by government policy, in particular, by over-extension of the public sector and by the use of direct controls and subsidies, and regulations like minimum wage legislation. These policies, it is argued, distort prices and hamper the efficient allocation of resources. A major element of World Bank structural adjustment programmes is the removal of controls and regulations; a reduction in the role of the public sector; and more incentives for the private sector.

The thinking that underlies World Bank adjustment programmes is shared by governments of some important donor countries. Former US President Reagan spoke of the 'magic of the market' and US Secretary of State, George Schultz, instructed USAID officials that policy dialogue should be 'used to encourage LDCs to follow free market principles and to move away from government intervention in the economy' (Killick, 1986).

How far is this emphasis on market forces imbued with male bias? The relation between women, the market and the state is complex. State agencies do *not* always operate *in* the interests of women, and markets do *not* always operate *against* the interests of women.

The state frequently plays a major role in perpetuating social, economic and ideological processes that subordinate women (Agarwal, 1988). Women are frequently treated as dependents of men in legal and administrative procedures, rather than as persons in their own right. The state frequently upholds patriarchal family forms in which women do not have the same access to resources as men. Examples of public sector projects and programmes which ignore the needs of women as producers and direct resources towards men abound.

The market appears to treat women as individuals in their own right. If women can sell their labour or their products and get a cash income of their own, this lessens their economic dependence upon men, increases their economic value, and tends to increase their bargaining power within the household. Access to an income of their own tends to be highly valued by women, not only for what it buys, but also for the greater dignity it brings.

However, so long as women carry the double burden of unpaid work in the reproduction and maintenance of human resources, as well as paid work producing goods and services, then women are unable to compete with men in the market on equal terms. Equal pay and opportunities legislation, and diminution of 'traditional' barriers to women working outside the home, cannot by themselves free women from domestic burdens and expectations. Access to markets has benefits for women, but those benefits are always limited, even if markets are entirely free from gender discrimination. They are limited because the reproduction and maintenance of human resources is structured by unequal gender relations, and because the reproduction and maintenance of human resources *cannot* be directly and immediately responsive to market signals, so long as human resources have intrinsic as well as instrumental value.

Women with high incomes can reduce their disadvantage in the market relative to men by buying substitutes for their own unpaid work – employing cleaners, maids, nannies and cooks. But even this does not obliterate their disadvantage, as they still have responsibility for household management. Women who are not in the highest income groups do not have this option.

If most women are to gain from access to markets, they also need access to public sector services, such as water supplies, electricity, waste disposal facilities, public transport, health care and education, which will lighten the burden of their *unpaid* work and enable them to acquire the skills they need to enter the market. For all but well-off women, there is a *complementarity* between state provision of services required for human resource development, and the ability to make gains from participation in the market. For most women, the choice is not between dependence on the state and independence, but between dependence on the state and dependence on a man.

This suggests that most women have an interest not so much in reducing the role of the state and increasing the role of the market, as in *restructuring* both *the public sector* and *the private sector* to make them both more responsive to women's needs and contributions as both producers and reproducers.

It is necessary to disaggregate the public sector and the private sector. In the public sector, we need to distinguish different categories of expenditure and agency (social services; transport and energy; police, legal system and armed forces; state-owned factories, farms and marketing and distribution facilities – often called parastatals). Within each category we need to examine exactly what is being supplied (primary health care or open heart surgery, for example) and to identify who is benefiting from these activities. We need to examine the relation between producers and users of public sector goods and services. How responsive are producers to the needs of users? What mechanisms are there for users to influence the allocation of resources in the public sector? The structural adjustment required in the public sector may not simply be a reduction in expenditure and costs, but a change in its priorities and in its relation to users of services. The mobilisation and organisation of women who use public sector services may be a way to achieve this.

The private sector needs disaggregating into the formal sector and the informal sector; foreign-owned and locally-owned enterprises; large and small enterprises; those which employ wage labour and those which employ family labour; joint-stock companies and co-operatives; farmers, traders, manufacturers; activities directed by women and activities directed by men. If greater reliance is to be placed on private enterprise, we need to ask *whose enterprise?*: the enterprise of the women farming or trading on her own account or the enterprise of agribusiness and merchants with monopoly power; the enterprise of a women's co-operative or the enterprise of a multinational corporation? The mobilisation of women's enterprise in activities that provide a decent income and a basis for sustained economic growth requires support from state agencies, particularly in the provision of credit and training, and in services that free women's time from domestic duties. A one-sided emphasis on market forces as the principal instrument for structural adjustment amounts to male bias.

EMPIRICAL INVESTIGATIONS: MALE BIAS IN THE
ASSESSMENT OF IMPACT

The process of adjustment affects households in the following ways:

• changes in *incomes* and *employment*, through changes in wages
  and job opportunities for employees, and through changes in
  product prices and product demand for self-employed;
• changes in *prices* of important purchases, especially food;
• changes in *levels* and *composition* of public expenditure, particularly those in the social sector, including possible introduction or
  increase of *user charges* for services;
• changes in *working conditions*, through changes in hours of work,
  intensity of work, job security, fringe benefits and legal status; this
  applies to *unpaid* work as well as paid work.

These changes will not affect all households in the same way: some
will lose and some will gain. Nor will these changes affect all members of households in the same way. The *intra*-household distribution
of resources has to be taken into account as well as the *inter*-
household distribution of resources. This is a crucial point for the
avoidance of male bias in empirical investigations of the impact of
structural adjustment on living standards. It is of some use to chart
the impact of structural adjustment on the poorest 20 per cent or the
richest 20 per cent of households; it is even more useful to chart the
impact on particular social classes, such as the urban poor, or public
sector employees, or own-account small farmers. But within all these
groupings there is a strong likelihood of a gender-differentiated
impact.

One important form of gender differentiation is between male-
headed and female-headed households. But to disaggregate households on this basis is only a first step to avoiding male bias. It must be
complemented by an investigation of gender-differentiated impact
within households which are male-headed.[4] When households have
to reduce food consumption because of rising prices and falling
incomes, available evidence suggests it is quite likely that the consumption of women and girls will be reduced by more than that of
men and boys. If charges are introduced or increased for education
and health services, there is a strong possibility that the access of girls
will be reduced. When attempts are made to compensate for reductions in purchased resources by increases in unpaid labour (e.g.

buying cheaper food that requires more preparation time), it is likely to be women who bear the main burden.

Neither joint decision-making nor equal sharing of resources within households is at all common (Dwyer and Bruce, 1988). It is quite possible for the standard of living of wives to be lower than that of husbands; and for the standard of living of girls to be lower than that of boys. Nevertheless, it is generally women who have the responsibility of 'household management', of seeing that members of the household are fed, clothed and cared for. Women are generally closely associated with the 'collective' aspects of household consumption, and their obligation to meet children's needs is generally regarded as stronger than men's (Blumberg, 1988). Men's obligation is limited to providing some of the cash or productive assets required by women to carry out their household management tasks. Women, then, must meet their families' needs by 'stretching' the husband's cash contribution with 'good housekeeping', or earning an income themselves, or producing food or clothing themselves, or engaging in barter and petty trade. It is women who must cope and devise survival strategies when household incomes fall and prices rise.

CHANGES IN INCOMES AND EMPLOYMENT

To avoid male bias in assessing the implications of changes in income and employment, it is necessary to compare the implications for women and for men, and the way they are mediated by the household. Many adjustment programmes include limitations or complete freezes on wage and salary rises in the public sector; and may also include reduction of the degree of price indexation of wages and reductions in the coverage of minimum wage legislation. Employment in the public sector may also be frozen or reduced. Public sector employees are thus likely to face adverse changes in their incomes; and there will be a knock-on effect in that part of the informal sector which supplies goods and services to public sector employees. Wage freezes for teachers, nurses, doctors, clerical workers and administrators, means less demand or lower wages for domestic servants, for instance.

It may be argued that this affects men more than women since more public sector employees are men than are women.[5] But it is worth emphasising that jobs in the public sector have hitherto provided some of the better urban jobs for women; many of them skilled, professional jobs with a high degree of security. Wage differentials between men and women are smaller in the public sector (Standing, 1989). In most cases, far more professional and managerial jobs for women are provided by the public sector than by the private sector. The best career opportunities for educated women have in many countries been in the public sector. In some countries this is no longer the case. In Jamaica, nurses and teachers are leaving the public sector because of the low levels of pay. Professional women remaining in the public service have been driven to doing extra jobs at night in the informal sector, such as running snack shops.

Moreover, even when it is male rather than female public sector employees who suffer loss of income and employment, there is a spillover effect on women, because as wives they must manage the adjustment of the household budget to the loss of income. The measured rate of female participation in paid work may well rise as more women are propelled into the market. But if job opportunities are not expanding at the same time, the result is likely to be a fall in the rate of remuneration. Great care must be taken in evaluating the significance of rising rates of female participation in paid work. This is not always a sign of progress for women. For poor women coping with the loss of male income to the household, participation in the market may represent 'distress sales'. It may represent not an enlargement of choice and an enhancement of bargaining power, but an additional burden and restriction. For such participation is unlikely to be matched by a compensating reduction in domestic responsibilities. It is women's free time that will be sacrificed.

One category of employment that has expanded for women in some countries is work in export-oriented labour-intensive manufacturing. For example, as part of their adjustment strategy, Sri Lanka and Jamaica have set up Export Processing Zones (Free Trade Zones) which employ women in garment production. Wages for women in EPZs do tend to be higher than the average for comparable work outside the zones, and employers in the zones have no difficulty in recruiting women to work for them (ILO, 1988). But workers in EPZs tend to enjoy fewer rights than workers in private formal sector factories outside the zones; and they have proved vulnerable to the ups and downs of the world market, and to the changing investment strategies of multinational corporations (Heyzer, 1989).

In the rural areas, some groups are likely to enjoy increases in incomes as a result of higher prices for producers of marketed crops. For instance, Ghana increased cocoa prices by more than seven times between 1982/3 and 1986/7 as part of a major World Bank supported programme to rehabilitate the cocoa industry. In most sub-Saharan countries, nominal producer prices for food crops have risen substantially since 1980, mainly as a result of dismantling price controls. For instance, Zambia increased the official (or nominal) price of maize by 142 per cent between 1980 and 1985 (ODI, 1986). However, the impact of high prices for the things farmers sell has been eroded by higher prices for the things farmers buy. Many of the things farmers buy, both consumer goods and production inputs, are imported; and devaluation raises their prices. The real prices that farmers face depend not only on the nominal crop prices in local currency, but also on the prices of what they buy. Calculations by the US Department of Agriculture show that the real price rise for farmers is much less than the nominal price rise. Though the nominal price of maize rose in Zambia by 142 per cent, the real price rise for farmers, taking into account the rising prices of what they buy, was only about 6 per cent (ODI, 1986). So the incentive effect is much less than the change in nominal producer prices would suggest. In any case, the gender impact of such price increases depends crucially on the intra-household resource allocation process. We need to know if extra cash income accrues to men or to women; and if it accrues to men, how they dispose of it. How much goes to increase men's personal consumption, and how much is made available to wives to increase family consumption?

The benefit from higher crop prices also depends on producers' capacity to respond by increasing output. While there is evidence that rural producers do switch from one crop to another in response to changing relative prices, it is far less clear that they will be able to increase output of a wide range of crops in response to a general increase in crop prices (Chibber, 1988). For this depends on their ability to mobilise more of the inputs required – in particular, fertilisers, credit, and labour. Women's double burden of crop production and human resource production and maintenance leaves little spare time. There are ample time budget studies showing the long working day of women farmers. Moreover, other elements of structural adjustment programmes may also make increasing demands on women's time; cutbacks in the public provision of rural health, education and water supplies, for instance. There is a limit to the extent to which women can switch time from human resource production and maintenance to crop production. As has already been argued, children will not be left untended because another crop becomes more profitable. Thus, the provision of public services, which reduces the time women must spend in domestic duties, is *complementary* to their ability to respond to higher crop prices with higher output.

Even if they do have some 'spare capacity', women may be reluctant to increase their agricultural work load because they are not confident of enjoying the proceeds of extra work. This has happened in the past in cases where production is under the management of men, who then control the resulting proceeds. There have been instances of women refusing to spend extra time weeding and harvesting in their husbands' fields, preferring to work on activities which generate an income that they directly control (Elson, 1991b).

CHANGES IN PRICES OF CONSUMER GOODS

Increased food prices for consumers are major features of adjustment programmes. Where food imports are high, devaluation, which increases the price of imports, will have a substantial impact on food prices. Removal of food subsidies is also a major feature of adjustment programmes. It is advocated as a major contribution to reducing public expenditure. In Sri Lanka, following the removal of food subsidies, prices rose by 158 per cent for rice, 386 per cent for wheat flour, 331 per cent for bread and 345 per cent for milk powder in the period 1977–84. In Zambia, the price of maize meal, the main consumer staple, was raised in one step by 50 per cent in 1985, as the first stage in removing the subsidy (ODI, 1986). If wages are frozen while food prices (and prices of other essential items, like kerosene) are rising, then *real* income will fall. Urban wage earners in Tanzania faced a 50 per cent fall in real incomes between 1980 and 1984, while in Ghana over the same period, they fell by 40 per cent (ODI, 1986).

In such circumstances, it is important to look at the distribution of food within households. UNICEF studies reveal a widespread deterioration in the nutritional status of children and pregnant and lactating mothers in both rural and urban areas in countries with IMF stabilisation and World Bank structural adjustment programmes (Cornia, Jolly and Stewart, 1987). Mothers are unable to buy enough food of the right type to feed the whole family; priority in feeding may be given to adult males, though this appears to be more likely to happen in South Asia than in sub-Saharan Africa.

The intra-household resource allocation system constrains the extent to which total household expenditure can be reallocated in response to rises in food prices and must be taken into account to avoid male bias in the evaluation of the impact of food price rises. A recent study of one hundred households in low-income areas of Lusaka, capital of Zambia, found that in only a tiny minority of cases was money management a joint responsibility of husband and wife (Munachonga, 1986). In the majority of cases, wives were given fixed housekeeping allowances by their husbands, who were generally reluctant to tell wives how much they earned. These women have the traditional responsibility of ensuring that meals are prepared each day for their families, but they do not have a say in the total allocation of household expenditure. They can only determine how their housekeeping allowance is spent. When prices rise, this requires a high degree of ingenuity in making ends meet, involving extra stress and time. Increases in the housekeeping allowance and reductions in husband's personal expenditure requires conjugal negotiations which are often fraught with tension (Dwyer and Bruce, 1988). Female-headed households do not face this kind of constraint in expenditure reallocation – but they are generally worse off in terms of total income because of the poor earning power of most women.

CHANGES IN PUBLIC EXPENDITURE

It is well known that structural adjustment policies have involved cutbacks in public expenditure on health and education services, leading to reduction in provision and in take-up where user charges have been introduced (Cornia, Jolly and Stewart, 1987). For instance, ODI Briefing Paper, 1986, reports that in Jamaica social services expenditure fell by 44 per cent in real terms between 1981–2 and 1985–6. Some schools have been closed and services offered by some hospitals and health centres downgraded. Charges have been introduced for health services, even for the low paid and unemployed. In Nigeria, state governments have imposed fees on both primary and secondary education, and the enrolment rate among poor children has fallen drastically.

Expenditure cuts have often hit recurrent expenditure harder than capital expenditure, leaving schools short of books, paper and pens, and hospitals short of bandages and drugs, even while new hospital and school building has gone ahead. The process of project funding in which aid is available for capital expenditure but not recurrent expenditure may be a factor here. Expenditure cuts have also often hit rural services harder than urban services.

In Sri Lanka, a serious deterioration in the delivery of health care has been noted. Large investments in new and more sophisticated hospitals and equipment have gone ahead while rural services and preventive medicine have remained short of resources. Private practice by doctors employed in the Health Service has been introduced, and studies have found that private patients get preferential access to health service facilities. Privatisation of social services has probably gone furthest in Chile. For example, educational coupons have replaced state-sponsored education. But at a time of recession, poorer households have endeavoured to survive by cashing in their coupons, rather than spending them on schooling. Literacy levels have fallen.

Such deterioration in public provision of health and education is likely to hit women harder than men, since it is women who are likely to have to spend time making up the shortfall, and it is women (and girls) who are more likely to be deprived of health and education services when these are in short supply. Recent work on Zambia by Evans and Young (1988) indicates some of the possible effects. In Zambia, real per capita expenditure on health fell by 16 per cent between 1983 and 1985. For the majority of Zambian people, the only alternative to health services provided by the state are those that have been traditionally available in the community and household. The result of health expenditure cutbacks has been to shift more of the burden of health care to the community and household – which in practice means women. In the rural areas, the decline in rural health provision has had a direct effect on services which are particularly important to women and children, such as immunisation and mother and child health clinics. People now have to travel further to get treatment and drugs; and wait longer in queues. Women interviewed for the study said they themselves could not afford to be ill because of the time it would take away from their work. They reported having to spend more time caring for other household members when they are sick. If husbands or children have to attend hospitals for treatment, shortages of equipment and personnel mean that women are expected to go with them to provide meals and care for the duration of the treatment. One woman reported missing the entire planting season for this reason (Evans and Young, 1988), a perfect example of the interdependence between public provision and ability to respond to market opportunities.

The transference of costs from the public sector to women in the household and community has been explicitly advocated under the banner of promotion of self-help practices by some exponents of 'Adjustment with a Human Face': 'there is scope for decentralising many activities in health, nutrition, child care, sanitation, etc., to the family (or community) level . . . while such an approach may increase time costs for women, it will place extremely modest monetary costs on the household; and will lead to substantial savings in the public sector' (Cornia, Jolly and Stewart, 1987, p. 174). The implication that increased time costs for women do not matter, a result perhaps of a belief that women have lots of spare time, has been criticised by Antrobus (1988), who points to the enormous pressure on the time of poor women. Avoidance of male bias in the assessment of public expenditure cuts requires close attention to the implications for women's time use.

CHANGES IN HOURS OF WORK AND WORKING CONDITIONS

Here again we need to compare the situations of women and men. It is very likely that adjustment programmes have a gender-differentiated impact on the total length of the working day. For many women they mean longer hours of work, both of paid work and unpaid work. Maintaining a household on reduced resources takes more time – hunting for bargains, setting up informal exchange networks with neighbours and kin, making and mending at home rather than buying, etc. Increasing agricultural output takes more time. Making a living in the informal sector in conditions of falling demand takes more time. Women are resourceful in devising survival strategies for their families. However, there is a difference between mere survival strategies and activities that can form the basis for sustained growth and development on both a personal and a national level. There is likely to be growing differentiation between profitable informal sector activities that provide a basis for accumulation and 'dead-end' activities that are undertaken out of sheer necessity and in which most women are concentrated. Dennis (1991) points to such differentiation in informal-sector trading in Nigeria; while Scott

(1991) shows that in Lima, Peru, women tend to be concentrated in precisely those informal sector activities that do not provide a basis for accumulation.

The concentration of women into 'dead-end' informal-sector activities is part of a tendency towards the casualisation of work which also extends as far as male skilled workers in the formal sector (Standing, 1989). Labour market deregulation and privatisation of public sector activities are tending to erode distinctions between the 'formal sector' and the 'informal sector', as many jobs in the 'formal sector' are being made more 'flexible' – which frequently means loss of job security, loss of rights to sick pay, pensions, redundancy compensation, and maternity leave, and increasing intensity of work as job boundaries and the technical division of labour are altered. There is evidence that structural adjustment programmes are tending to undermine compliance with ILO labour standards (Standing and Tokman, 1990). Of course, women's employment, even in the formal sector, has always tended to be characterised by inferior working conditions to those enjoyed by men: 'women wage workers are more often than men classified in that peculiar category, "permanent casuals", and thereby unable to acquire legal entitlement to benefits or statutory forms of protection' (Standing, 1989, p. 1093). Ironically, the one area in which structural adjustment programmes may be reducing the bias in favour of men is through a levelling down of the working conditions of many male workers to those of women.

DIMINISHING MALE BIAS IN STRUCTURAL ADJUSTMENT

Can male bias in structural adjustment be diminished? Let us first clarify our objective. It is not to diminish male bias by worsening in absolute terms the position of men; but to diminish male bias by improving in absolute terms the position of women. In other words, the objective argued for here is one of levelling up rather than levelling down. For this to be possible, changes are required in the international economic environment so that developing countries do not have to bear all the burden of adjustment. Some of the necessary changes are discussed by Stewart in Chapter 2 of the present volume. Levelling up still means a reduction in male privilege, but there are likely to be some long-term benefits to men in a reduction of male privilege, since such privilege in many cases acts as a barrier to the achievement of sustainable development. For instance, there is evidence that African women farmers are just as good as men in farm management, but in the past they have had lower productivity because they have been denied investment. Channelling more investment to them would raise the overall productivity of investment (Herz, 1988). It would also improve satisfaction of basic needs since women tend to use a higher proportion of income under their control for the satisfaction of basic needs than do men (Blumberg, 1988).

Overcoming male bias is a long and complex process which has nowhere been completed.[6] Here we briefly indicate three steps which need to be taken in order to diminish male bias in structural adjustment.

The first step in diminishing male bias in structural adjustment is to win recognition of the significance of gender divisions in work and consumption for the process of resource reallocation and determination of living standards. This means dialogue with economic policy-makers in government and in international institutions; with women's units in government and in international institutions; and with non-governmental women's organisations. The last kind of dialogue is particularly important, because without a push from women's organisations, gender divisions are unlikely to have much salience on official agendas.

The second step is to win recognition of the complementarity between public sector provision of services and productive inputs to women, and their ability to reallocate their time and effort in ways that contribute to a sustainable and more appropriate structural adjustment. A one-sided emphasis on market forces will be biased against women, even though an enhancement of women's market opportunities is important for reducing male bias in the household. Reduction of male bias requires a restructuring of the public sector to make it more accountable to women and a restructuring of the functioning of markets to make them responsive to women's needs rather than to narrow criteria of profit.[7] Such restructuring is not just a matter of improvements in the management of public sector organisations, or of more sensible ways of guiding markets – for instance, through reserving a certain proportion of credit for women – though these can help. It requires a change in the balance of power in the relation between women as users of public sector services and those who provide them; and a change in the balance of power between women as buyers and sellers and the merchants, and employers with whom they deal.

The third step is to reconsider the form of structural adjustment.

The kind of structural adjustment promoted by the World Bank is a very partial and limited process of change. It accepts as parameters most existing structures of social power in developing countries. It judges the desirability of outcomes by valuing output produced by paid labour at world market prices (so-called 'efficiency prices'). This fails to allow for the riskiness of markets in general, and international markets in particular; and fails to value at all the output of women's unpaid labour in human resource production and maintenance. Much thinking about alternatives concentrates on ameliorating the destructive side of current structural adjustment measures – for example, the UNICEF proposals for adjustment with a human face. More recently, the UN Economic Commission for Africa has gone beyond this and emphasised the need to transform some of the structures that World Bank thinking tends to take as given. It has argued, for instance, for the need to get more popular participation in the design of structural adjustment programmes, and to reshape demand in LDCs so as to get a better match between what people buy and what the economy can produce (UNECA, 1989).

There is a need to go beyond these alternatives to consider more explicitly the issue of control over investment in the adjustment process. Any programme for structural adjustment will put control over accumulation in some hands rather than in other hands. There is certainly a need to put control over accumulation in hands that will use investment productively rather than waste it; and that will use it in ways that will make best use of scarce foreign exchange rather than intensify the demand for foreign exchange. The rhetoric surrounding many World Bank structural adjustment programmes suggests that they will achieve this by diminishing the control enjoyed by urban bureaucratic elites, and relocate accumulation in the hands of a largely rural popular class of farmers and artisans and small traders. But critics argue that in reality control is being concentrated into the hands of large-scale merchants, agribusiness and manufacturers, often with strong links to multinational companies, or with strong links to the urban bureaucratic elites (Mbilinyi, 1988). In the process, the control of people over even their own labour power is diminished (Standing, 1989). Standing (1989) and Mbilinyi (1988) suggest that the loss of control over their labour is particularly serious for women. Fears have also been voiced about women farmers losing control of land and crops to husbands, as farming becomes more profitable. There is little doubt that large-scale farming, trading and manufacturing is mainly in the hands of men, and that women have little voice in determining the process of accumulation within such activities.

A design for structural adjustment that diminishes male bias has to begin from the standpoint of redressing women's lack of control over resources and locating more accumulation in the hands of women, particularly poor women, so that a reduction in male privilege does not lead to an increase in the privilege of the wealthy. Some of this relocation of accumulation to women may be effectively accomplished on an individual basis, through the redirection of credit and technical assistance to individual women farmers, traders and artisans (as is suggested by other authors in this volume). But emphasis should be placed on relocation of accumulation to organisations of women[8] – co-operatives, community associations, savings associations, trade unions, research and action groups – as this is much more likely to ensure that women do not lose control to male relatives; that the accumulation process is not hampered by too small a scale of operations; and that women employees are able to exercise some modifying influence over the decisions of their employers.

This requires a much wider definition of the kind of institutional reform that is required. So far, the emphasis in structural adjustment programmes has been on privatisation, administrative reform and self-help groups. Institutional reform must be defined much more widely to include the fostering of groups with the capacity for advocacy and effective intervention in the political process on behalf of those who have been excluded. A link between adjustment and democratisation has been made in recent contributions from both the UN Economic Commission for Africa and the World Bank. But genuine democratisation requires the growth of precisely the kind of autonomous campaigning groups that are regarded as creating 'distortions' from the economic viewpoint underlying World Bank programmes, which privileges an exceedingly narrow view of efficiency. A more appropriate approach to adjustment would start from the question: efficiency for whom? And to pose this effectively requires the fostering of groups which seek to empower those whom present power structures are biased against.

Groups concerned with the empowerment of women would be particularly well placed to improve the linking of production decisions with the effective satisfaction of basic needs, the foundation of long-run sustainable development. Available evidence suggests that women, through their experience in trying to meet the daily needs of other household members, tend to have both a better appreciation of the scale and intensity of basic needs, and to give greater priority to the satisfaction of such needs, than do the men who have dominated resource allocation in both the market and the state, both before and during the current phase of structural adjustment.

Notes

1. For earlier attempts to promote these twin objectives, see Elson (1989a and 1989b).
2. The concept of male bias is explained at greater length in Elson (1991a).
3. This assumption appears to characterise much of the work being undertaken under the World Bank/UNDP programme on the Social Dimensions of Adjustment in Africa.
4. This point does not yet seem to be fully understood by many of the researchers contributing to the programme on the Social Dimensions of Adjustment.
5. Figures for the female share of public service employment for 27 LDCs are provided in Standing (1989, table 7). The country with the highest share is Jamaica (50 per cent in 1980). Figures for Africa ranged from 11 per cent to 41 per cent, and for Latin America and the rest of the Caribbean from 23 per cent to 47 per cent.
6. For a fuller discussion of the complexities of trying to overcome male bias in development, see Elson (1991c).
7. There is no space here to explore this argument more fully. It is discussed at greater length in Elson (forthcoming). For an interesting discussion of attempts to make part of the public sector in the UK more accountable to women (and men), see Mackintosh and Wainwright (1987).
8. Mention of this point is also made by the Report of the Commonwealth Expert Group on Women and Structural Adjustment (Commonwealth Secretariat, 1989).

References

Agarwal, B. (ed.) (1988) *Structures of Patriarchy* (Kali for Women, New Delhi).

Antrobus. P. (1988) 'Consequences and Responses to Social and Economic Deterioration: The Experience of the English-Speaking Caribbean', Workshop on Economic Crisis, Household Strategies and Women's Work, Cornell University.

Beneria, L. and M. Roldan (1987) *The Crossroads of Class and Gender* (Chicago: University of Chicago Press).

Blumberg, R. (1988) 'Income Under Female Versus Male Control', *Journal of Family Issues*, vol. 9, no. 1.

Chibber, A. (1988) 'Raising Agricultural Output: Price and Non-Price Factors', *Finance and Development*, vol. 25, no. 2.

Commonwealth Secretariat (1989) *Engendering Adjustment for the 1990s* (London).

Cornia, G., R. Jolly and F. Stewart (1987) *Adjustment with a Human Face* (Oxford: Clarendon Press).

Dennis, C. (1991) 'The Limits to Women's Independent Careers: Gender in the Formal and Informal Sectors in Nigeria', in Elson (ed.), *Male Bias in The Development Process* (Manchester University Press).

Dwyer, D. and J. Bruce (eds) (1988) *A Home Divided: Women and Income in the Third World* (Stanford: Stanford University Press).

Elson, D. (1989a) 'The Impact of Structural Adjustment on Women: Concepts and Issues', in B. Onimode (ed.), *The IMF, the World Bank and the African Debt, Vol. II, The Social and Political Impact* (London: Zed Books).

Elson, D. (1989b) 'How is Structural Adjustment Affecting Women?', *Development*, no. 1.

Elson, D. (1991a) 'Male Bias in Development: An Overview', in D. Elson (ed.), *Male Bias in the Development Process* (Manchester University Press).

Elson, D. (1991b) 'Male Bias in Macroeconomics: The Case of Structural Adjustment', in Elson (ed.), *Male Bias*.

Elson, D. (1991c) 'Overcoming Male Bias', in Elson (ed.) *Male Bias*.

Elson, D. (forthcoming) 'From Survival Strategies to Transformation Strategies: Women's Needs and Structural Adjustment', in L. Beneria and S. Feldman (eds), *Economic Crises, Household Strategies and Women's Work*. (Westview Press).

Evans, A. and K. Young (1988) 'Gender Issues in Household Labour Allocation: The Case of Northern Province, Zambia', ODA/ESCOR Research Report.

Folbre, N. (1986a) 'Hearts and Spades: Paradigms and Household Economics', *World Development*, vol. 14, no. 2.

Folbre, N. (1986b) 'Cleaning House: New Perspectives on Households and Economic Development', *Journal of Development Economics*, vol. 22.

Herz, B. (1988) 'Briefing on Women and Development', World Bank/IMF Annual Meeting, Berlin.

Heyzer, N. (1989) 'Asian Women Wage-Earners: Their Situation and Possibilities for Donor Intervention', *World Development*, vol. 17, no. 7.

ILO (1988) *Economic and Social Effects of Multinational Enterprises in Export Processing Zones* (Geneva).

Killick, T. (1986) 'Twenty-five Years of Development: The Rise and Impending Decline of Market Solutions', *Development Policy Review*, vol. 4.

Mackintosh, M. and H. Wainwright (1987) *A Taste of Power: The Politics of Local Economics* (London: Verso).

Mbilinyi, M. (1988) 'Agribusiness and Women Peasants in Tanzania', *Development and Change*, vol. 19.

Munachonga, M. (1986) 'Impact of Economic Adjustments on Women in Zambia', University of Zambia, Lusaka.

ODI Briefing Paper (1986) *Adjusting to Recession: Will the Poor Recover?*.

Scott, A. M. (1991) 'Informal Sector or Female Sector? Gender Bias in Urban Labour Market Models', in Elson (ed.), *Male Bias*.

Selowsky, M. (1987) 'Adjustment in the 1980s: An Overview of Issues', *Finance and Development*, vol. 24, no. 2.

Sen, A. K. (1983) *Resources, Values and Development*, ch. 16, 'Economics and the Family' (Oxford: Blackwell).

Standing, G. (1989) 'Global Feminisation Through Flexible Labor', *World Development*, vol. 17, no. 7.

Standing, G. and Tokman, V. 1990 *Labour Policy Issues in Structural Adjustment* (Geneva: ILO).

UN Economic Commission for Africa (1989) *Adjustment with Transformation*, (Addis Ababa).

World Bank (1989) *World Development Report* (New York: OUP).

4 Gender Equity and Economic Efficiency in Adjustment Programmes
Ingrid Palmer

INTRODUCTION

Most writing on gender and adjustment points out the disproportionate negative impact on women of the new policies. There are good reasons why UNICEF sounded the alarm bells on the welfare of women and children in its 'Adjustment with a Human Face'. Evidence was gathered about precipitous falls in maternal and child health and the parlous state of social services alongside sharp declines in real income. The economic cost of all this was depicted in terms of disinvestment in human resources. In addition there were chapters in the two volumes of the UNICEF study which described how women's economic capabilities were especially debilitated by adjustment measures. Even before this publication there was a warning about the uncertain net outcome for women of new incentives and extra burdens in *Development, Crisis and Alternative Visions: Third World Women's Perspectives* (Sen, 1985) written for the United Nations Conference in Nairobi. More recently the Commonwealth Secretariat's *Engendering Adjustment for the 1990s* (1989) has put the issues, raised elsewhere, in the logical order of describing women's roles, the impact adjustment has had on them and what attempts have been made to help women. The bulk of the report tends to focus on the non-economic roles of women and on their welfare and well-being. However there are some succinct pages on women's difficulties in responding to new economic opportunities and on some desirable interventions in infrastructure and markets to release women's production potential. Concern over the social dimensions of adjustment has led the World Bank and UNDP to assist 20 African countries with detailed surveys on the economic position of households and to identify projects and programmes which not only aid particularly vulnerable groups but go beyond firebrigade action to enable the poor to respond positively to adjustment opportunities. In

Tanzania, for instance, UNDP's Social Dimensions of Adjustment is concentrating on four groups in the population, one of which is described as those always so poor that their position could scarcely have been worsened by structural adjustment policies but who can be helped to a position from which they can benefit from the results of adjustment when they finally come through.

While crucial arguments about the adjustment process are raised by these publications, as well as by other chapters in this present volume, they are raised from the point of view of women as an interest group. The focus therefore is on what is happening to women, or the *impact of adjustment on women*. This is not the only way gender issues can be included in an approach to today's policy-makers who are in the business of allocating scarce resources as never before. Adjustment strategies mean that demands for resources must now be supported by persuasion that there will be an economic dividend.

Yet it is this very stricture which could offer the Women in Development (WID) lobby its best chance of making gender issues an integral concern of planning rather than an afterthought in the form of special projects or amendments to programmes. That is to say, if it can be argued that *gender issues impact on adjustment* at every turn then it might be easier to persuade policy-makers to review gender issues at the earliest stage of planning, before options on overall adjustment strategies are closed off and certainly before policy packages are detailed. The literature on gender and adjustment is nudging in this direction but always with a backward look at the WID lobby. The effect is that there is constant swinging between regarding women as producers and as consumers.

Another reason for distinguishing the impact of adjustment on women from the gender impact on adjustment is to distinguish between practical and strategic gender needs. The concept of these gender needs was developed by Moser (1989) who defined practical gender needs as a response to an immediate perceived necessity which does not challenge prevailing forms of women's subordination, and strategic gender needs as measures to overcome women's domestic handicaps and structured gender discrimination. Practical gender needs do not, for instance, change the terms of women's access to and control over resources (including income). A strategic gender need, on the other hand, makes a change to women's economic status in this way.

This chapter is intended to help policy-makers to think systematically about gender issues purely in terms of their own economic brief. There are grounds for believing that the time is propitious for a new initiative. Second thoughts about the earlier oversimplified adjustment packages have produced a new policy environment in which periods of stabilisation and adjustment (and even the longer-term transformation) are seen to mingle and to need more time, in which it is considered that adjustment loans are more appropriately disaggregated by sector, in which experience has led to more sensitive sequencing and packaging of policies, and in which institutional reforms and infrastructural improvements are seen as preconditions for the success of market liberalisation. This provides scope for imagination, sensitivity and flexibility. And in this there is a unique opportunity to permeate gender issues throughout the planning process.

But what is the economic brief of policy-makers that has to be taken into consideration? It should be remembered that structural adjustment is about improving the efficiency of resource allocation in the present economy through freeing markets from restraints, while long-term adjustment (or economic transformation) is about developing new comparative advantages through an economically efficient distribution of investments in higher factor productivities.

THE MEANING OF ECONOMIC EFFICIENCY

It would be useful when examining the meaning of economic efficiency to bear in mind women's particular problems of access to resources and income, and of free deployment of their labour.

At the centre of the idea of an efficient allocation of resources is the proposition that the economy is working most efficiently when there is no rearrangement of resources that would produce greater total output. For this to occur in a free market economy every input and output must be priced at the level which reflects its true economic value (or opportunity cost) to the whole economy. That is to say it should be priced just high enough to bid it away from the next most profitable or gainful use. If it were priced less than this then it could be successfully bid for by less profitable enterprises or by consumers who do not prize it most. If priced higher then the user is paying more than required to bid it away from other uses.

So what determines the price a producer is prepared to pay for a resource to bid it away from another user? Economic efficiency would decree that this price is equal to the market value of the output of the last unit of the resource applied. If the value of this marginal output is greater than the cost of the unit of the resource utilised to produce it then it would profit the enterpreneur to use more of the resource; if less then it would profit her to cut back on production.

This optimal position for the individual producer is totally different from the situation when the producer applies units of a resource up to the point where its marginal product falls to zero. In the literature on economic development this latter situation is often ascribed to family labour use. In practice it occurs when the resource, for one reason or another, cannot be deployed elsewhere: hence its economic opportunity cost is zero. While it can still yield something it might as well be used because it is 'costless'. This reveals the first assumption of the efficiency model: that resources are free to move between different uses and between different employers.

Another assumption of this description of economic efficiency is that every producer is faced with the same set of prices which are determined by competitive market forces. In reality there are distorting influences from both government and private sources.

The distortion of markets that comes from government intervention is well known. Taxes and subsidies divert resources from their optimal economic use – taxes by penalising the use of resources or demand for products, and subsidies by encouraging the use of resources and consumption of products beyond what is intrinsically economic. Subsidies effectively bid (demand) resources away from their proper economic usage, while taxes impose a premium on the use of a resource. Resources are further misallocated through quotas in both factor and product markets. Unravelling these distortions is what structural adjustment is all about.

Ideally for markets to operate efficiently there should be perfect competition among a host of buyers on one side and among a host of sellers on the other. Perfect knowledge on the part of all participants is assumed as is completely free entry and exit. And all this in every factor and product market. No individual or group should be able to influence prices. Otherwise monopolistic selling practices will raise resource prices and lower resource utilisation artificially and monopsonistic buying practices will lower resource prices and raise resource utilisation artificially. In practice the criteria for full competition are always lacking, sometimes seriously. Restrictive practices of various kinds are present. Among the restrictive practices are those caused by gender influences.

The assumption of competition has to hold in all markets. For demand and supply in one commodity market to represent 'true value to the whole economy' there must be allocative efficiency in all markets. If there is imperfect competition in just one market, whether a factor or product market, this has a knock-on effect in others because distortion in one market leaves a derived influence on supply and demand in others. In reverse order the removal of just one distortion will send ripples through other markets.

But if there are different sources of market imperfection, how are some affected by the removal (or intensification) of others? For instance, if the government withdraws its intervention and thereby 'liberalises' markets, are other sources left unaffected? Or could they move into some kind of vacuum? Does the end of government monopoly procurement leave the field for private monopoly procurement? And if the 'urban bias' is ended by free market costing of foreign exchange does another bias acquire a stronger lease of life? On the other hand, could another distortion be weakened by the removal of government intervention? For instance, does the end of a fertiliser subsidy reduce the cost advantage of large farmers because they were able to appropriate most of the subsidised fertiliser? As Elson shows, the termination of subsidies does not always have a negative effect on the poor.

So far only the issue of short-term, or static, efficiency has been referred to. But governments are concerned with going beyond structural adjustment to structural transformation which would allow sustainable growth in the direction of new comparative advantages. Dynamic efficiency can therefore be defined as the most economically efficient distribution of investment in the means of higher productivity. But where should this investment lie? Short-term supply and demand would lead to different prices from a longer-term view of supply and demand. Therefore static allocative efficiency need not resemble long-term allocative efficiency. Moreover, even if there were perfect markets in technology and capital there might also be long-term societal goals which would influence choice of technology and factor productivities to invest in. There are different opinions on the relation between adjustment and transformation. The minimalist approach to the outcome of structural adjustment is that the underlying economy should operate with less economic waste, but that nothing much else changes. The maximalist approach is that the process of unimpeded allocative efficiency itself leads to growth because prices which are allowed to reflect true scarcity show where productivity increases are most needed and entrepreneurs follow up on this. But in reality the path of equilibrating marginal returns and marginal costs between enterprises and industries is not nearly so smooth.

In a highly imperfect world strategic government intervention to counter other distortions can improve the short- and long-term efficiencies of resource utilisation. The instruments chosen for this intervention must depend on the degree of static efficiency and the development objectives of government. However, if dynamic efficiency is pursued before static efficiency has been achieved, then certain distortions will be carried through to the long-term structure of the economy. On the other hand, waiting for the elimination of short-term inefficiencies could mean waiting for a long time, during which opportunities to start growth and transformation are passed up.

Because private market forces fail to equate marginal returns and marginal costs a strategy of moving towards static efficiency gives government a role in developing counterbalancing distortions. But government intervention can do the same for longer-term dynamic efficiency because private investors' horizons do not stretch into the very long term. The case of investing in environmental restoration is now obvious. But the same applies to investing long term in overcoming social and cultural disadvantages of a target group.

The debate here accepts the desirability of proper costing of all resources and of convergence on open competitive markets to guarantee that prices reflect true scarcities, which is the best guarantee of efficient investments in higher factor productivities. Deviation from this should only be for stated political or social objectives or for taxing the present to invest in the future. It should not be because of ignorance or indifference. A return to theories of the market offers the opportunity to raise gender issues in the framework of economic accounting. But the verity of this approach depends on an accurate and adequate description of the gender context. So far that has been lacking in economic tracts.

THE GENDER CONTEXT

There are two main sources of gender-based distortions in markets:

1. unequal terms of women's and men's participation in markets;
2. the reproduction tax on women.

Unequal Terms of Market Participation

The causes of discrimination against women in markets are legendary. They have social and cultural origins. Some specifically arise from women's immobility due to domestic responsibilities, although this in itself is related to social and cultural factors. Gender discrimination occurs in human resource development and in access to fixed and variable factors of production as well as to credit. Discrimination starts in primary education and health care. The effect of gender differentiation in these markets is all too apparent by the age of 14 years. But it is worsened by what happens later in training and in terms of access to resources. A picture emerges of the infraction of gender equality in 'primary markets' of early life being compounded by discrimination in other markets later on. In the final market, say that of credit, we see not just the innate inequality of the credit market due to cultural hostility to female borrowers but a greatly distorted gender profile of people approaching the credit market. The access points of credit services are more elusive to women than men for reasons associated with gender discrimination in other markets, such as women's higher rate of illiteracy or lower asset status. All these sources of sequential discrimination would lead to great inefficiency in the deployment of credit.

The labour market suffers several sources of gender bias. There is the derived effect of discrimination in human resources development. There are cultural attitudes to what are appropriate jobs for women and men, respectively, and to the value of women's jobs relative to men's. Gender-typing of employment can make nonsense of 'equal pay for equal work'. And there is protective employment legislation which can work to restrict women's employment opportunities.

But there are also markets within the household economy. Even where there is only one joint household enterprise family labour is often deployed in a way that does not resemble the distribution of the returns to labour. Whenever culture bonds women's (and children's) labour to the household production unit, this labour is not free to move to more efficient uses outside the household economy and it is invariably used beyond the point which marks its most efficient deployment in the wider economy. The head of household is effectively the only buyer in that micro labour market. Ironically this resource misallocation is often heralded as efficient enterprise in the literature on development. Standard economic analyses of agricultural development frequently point to small family farms being more efficient than large farms. What is meant by this is that they have higher land yields, and sometimes that they absorb less capital. When a correct gender context is applied, we see that this enterprise is far from efficient and offers long-term hostages in the form of unnecessarily high population growth. In the great majority of cases the reason why land yields are higher for small farms is because of the more intensive application of female family labour. But this labour, not land, is the scarcest of all factors of production. Its lavish use makes no economic sense. The scarcest factor of production should be used sparingly and if there is not enough of it to combine with all the other factors of production in some optimal way, resources should be targeted on raising its productivity before all others.

In the case of small family farms so much female labour is applied that its product per unit of labour is very low. Yet it is noticeable that the labour technology for female typed agricultural tasks is much more traditional than that for male typed tasks. The cause of this gross misallocation of resources is women's lesser control over resources and their general low status. In strict economic terms family labour operates in its own spatially monopsonistic market with only one 'buyer' of labour. The wider effect of this is that the excessive use of female labour sends ripples of subsidies throughout the economy starting with the price of the output of the household.

But in some countries, noticeably African ones, the household economy is not a single enterprise internalising some rate of return over all household resources. Separate economic accounting units exist within the household, each having its own rate of return. Labour is exchanged between the units according to the gender division of labour. Credit may be supplied to family partners with interest attached, and produce exchanged or used to pay for the labour of other household members. This situation can pertain to informal sector activities as well as to agriculture. It is nearly always accompanied by the managers of the separate economic units participating in some factor or product market above the household level. This encourages a measure of allocative efficiency of household resources, especially labour, by giving bargaining power to each manager. Approximate opportunity costs are implicit in the way members of the household mobilise variable resources for their own accounting units. But competition in the household is far from perfect. Men enjoy favoured access to resources, leaving women with fewer or inferior resources. Women tend to labour more for men than men for women, and the deficit is rarely covered fully by a gift of produce or cash. One can speak therefore of an asymmetry of access to resources (and income) between women and men: in other words, gender-based imperfection in markets for resources. Another way of putting it is that the terms of trade are loaded against women's economic activities: women have to work harder for one unit of personal disposal income than men. The single household enterprise which subordinates all household resources to itself is merely an extreme form of asymmetry when women have no separate bargaining power whatever. There is nothing to temper allocative inefficiency. In that the returns have to go to support the family because there are no other sources of income for this, female family labour is not left unpaid; although there are likely to be fewer leakages of the income on its way to family maintenance if women controlled it. However, the fundamental point to be made here is that this gender asymmetry of access to household resources and incomes leads to allocative inefficiency.

Much of the gender bias in early human resource development arises from intra-household markets. Boys are usually favoured by parents' expenditure on education, nutrition and medicine, perpetuating the disadvantages of women. The long-term scarcity of quality female labour that intra-household markets generate is impervious to wider market influences. Intervention of a distinct nature is required to counterbalance this hidden waste.

Gender influences act as restrictive practices. That is to say, conditions of market participation are different for women and men, and men are advantaged. There does not exist a free flow of resources to their best economic use. Monetisation, commoditisation and technological modernisation have acted to worsen this asymmetry and therefore the misallocation of resources. The market place is most easily exploited by the stronger and better equipped. Those who start at a handicap rarely overcome it without some compensating government intervention. This is basically the case for intervention in the cause of allocative efficiency.

There are four basic ways in which structural adjustment programmes worsen gender-based misallocations. First, it makes the informal sector more overcrowded and with fewer starting assets women will experience a greater fall in income than men from this. Second, cutbacks in social sector expenditure mean a greater work burden for women and aggravated misallocation or superexploitation of their labour. Third, the introduction of user charges for education and health will exacerbate discrimination against investment in female human resources. Fourth, devaluation and higher agricultural prices will increase the asymmetry of access to resources in the farm household by giving greater incentives to the crop portfolios of men who have the power to swing increments of land, working capital and family labour in their favour.

In the climate of government trying to save on expenditure it might be supposed that innovations have to be postponed. And yet some of the more effective innovations to improve women's access require only legal and institutional reforms. Allocative intervention is an additional measure that can be used as a countervailing distortion to the one that exists. For instance, training and/or credit resources can be set aside for women while aggregate expenditures remain constant. These would be examples of the meso policies of UNICEF's 'Adjustment with a Human Face'. They act to introduce compensatory lower barriers to access by women. The purpose is to encourage the emergence of individual merit.

For agriculture there is a need to monitor the effects of changes in relative crops prices and profitabilities. This might lead to considering the desirability of meeting certain preconditions before changing prices.

There are many implications in all this for the revision of adjustment packages. The agenda for marshalling them in some order might be outlined by a few simple questions that policy makers ought to be asking:

- what are the major gender biases in markets and how damaging are they to short- and long-term adjustment?
- which biases are amenable to some corrective action in the short term?
- for which biases is corrective action contingent upon some basic precondition being met?
- what counterbalancing distortions are justified on the grounds of cost effectiveness?
- what institutional and legal reforms to counterbalance gender biases would be both feasible and effective in the short, medium and long term?
- what are the reasons why long-term adjustment might be jeopardised by postponing the rendezvous with different kinds of gender biases?

• how should the present prioritisation of correction of gender biases in markets be influenced by long-term adjustment considerations?

The Reproduction Tax on Women

Frances Stewart has described the multiple roles of women, so there is no need to repeat them here. What has to be pointed out is that these extra unremunerated tasks act as a labour tax on women. Corvee labour if you like. Like all taxes it influences the allocation of resources, in this case in the form of penalising women's labour time in other activities which are both more remunerative and more open to productivity increases. Resources in reproduction are not properly costed (and therefore not properly used).

We can see at once that women's reproduction activities distort the 'productive' labour market. How does this inefficiency operate? Any labour market entrant who is tied for periods of her/his working life to other responsibilities is unable to compete equally and for an equal length of time on the basis of intrinsic merit. Skilled and capable women will be underemployed in a qualitative sense working under men of lesser competence. But what happens in one market has a derived influence on other markets. A distortion in a primary determining market, such as the labour market, has a knock-on effect in other factor markets; and distortions in factor markets create distortions in product markets. In this way the reproduction tax on women sends ripples of inefficiencies throughout the economy.

When government ameliorates conditions in the domestic sector through social sector expenditure it enables women to cope better. Meeting this practical gender need is often motivated by the fear that women's domestic work threatens 'economic' output. However, while it meets an immediate need of women it may support an underlying misallocation of labour resources which distorts all other markets. It may even worsen that misallocation. The only guarantee that resources in the domestic sector are absorbed and used efficiently is when these activities are exposed to free market forces. This can only be done by meeting Moser's strategic gender needs.

The very fact that women's reproduction work leads to immediate use values of goods and services means that it is productive to the household economy. At the least it displaces expenditure or saves cash income. Therefore it might be supposed that it is not strictly a tax of corvee labour from which women would gain nothing. But it is a tax in the sense that in this sector labour productivity is unnecessarily low because it has been so long and so thoroughly neglected, and that if resources used are viewed as part of the wider economy, the allocation of resources to and in this work is hopelessly inefficient. More importantly it is a tax in the sense that women thereby supply a resource, free of charge, to the wider community: namely, a replacement for the present labour force. When capital equipment has to be replaced employers draw on their depreciation accounts which are clearly seen to lower profits and company tax. Biology and culture oblige mothers to bear almost the entire cost of a depreciation account for the labour force. Therefore when women return use values to their families with their domestic work it is because society has imposed upon them the responsibility for this particular (labour force) depreciation account. There is no intention here to comment on societal values and the worth of family life. The purpose is solely to help policy-makers to think systematically about the economic cost of these reproductive arrangements.

What is the impact of structural adjustment programmes on this labour tax on women? Cuts in social sector expenditure increase it, and therefore worsen the misallocation of resources. And this occurs at a time when women in agriculture will be expected to work longer hours in the fields and when urban women seek and carry out any gainful employment in increasingly time-consuming ways.

Any agenda for revisions of adjustment packages to limit the distortions caused by the reproduction tax on women would include two basic questions:

• what are the identifiable economic costs, in terms of markets' inefficiencies, of this reproduction tax to the wider community?
• how does the increase in the reproduction tax caused by structural adjustment programmes thwart the objectives of those programmes?

Means to Reduce the Reproduction Tax

Women's labour participation in the formal sector is inhibited by child care responsibilities. Therefore labour is not absorbed by the formal sector most efficiently. Solutions to inefficiency in the formal labour market include investment in labour productivity in domestic/reproduction work and full (health-giving) maternal leave and child care facilities. This has a cost. We can immediately dispense with the idea of imposing the cost on particular employers of women (as is widespread now with maternity leave and creches). This merely sets up a new distorting effect. Women will not be employed. But if governments are able to raise company taxes and mainstream provident funds, then a levy on *all* wage employers for a communal maternity leave fund can just as easily be arranged. In effect this would amount to using fiscal measures to award transfer payments to a group which starts in market exchange with a handicap.

This scheme will carry its own distorting effect, such as weighing on the formal sector, and more heavily on labour-intensive production because of inflation of the wages bill. But these are minor compared with the continued drain on resources from role conflicts of women. This might be seen as helping women to cope better. But it is more than this if women's greater activities in market exchange bring them direct increments of produce or cash income. It will significantly deflate the reproductive labour tax on women and thereby improve the efficiency of their labour deployment. Therefore the shift of the tax from women to employers should improve the allocation of labour resources.

Applying the same principle to child-minding facilities will lead to a further improvement. Child-minding facilities could also be made available for women working in the informal sector and even in agriculture. The point at which a fiscal levy is made may differ, but what is at issue is compelling the wider economy to end the huge subsidy that women give it at present.

The total reproduction tax on women is affected by the number of children born to them. There are several well-known reasons, sound in the micro economic world of women, for women to desire above normal replacement fertility. But if those reasons were displaced by new goals the reproduction tax can be reduced without infringing on women's right to choose how many children they have.

As presently packaged, adjustment policies offer the demographic legacy of continued high fertility. Women's labour use is intensified. The demand for children's assistance will increase. Breastfeeding is further jeopardised. Infant morbidity and mortality are likely to rise. As income declines, girls' schooling will be further disadvantaged.

There is another reason for long-term planners to include reproduction on their agenda. In an era of long-term environmental concern we cannot leave population issues to demographers' fiddling with extrapolations. Does population planning (as so far practised in Population Planning Units attached to government machineries) have to be exclusively about predicting human numbers and planning housing, jobs, education and health services? Is it not possible to design economic growth in a way which actively influences population growth?

An agenda to revise adjustment policies to encourage lower fertility would include the following points:

- secure continued investment in health and education services;
- make the support services of the social sector budget that are most relevant to women more effective, whether or not this entails more financial input;
- encourage the free movement of women's labour by all means possible (including maternity leave and child-minding facilities).

Creating Revenues to Fund the Capitalisation of Women's Unmarketed Work

Hopefully governments will realise that their budgets can only benefit from the growth induced by reducing gender biases in the market and improving the efficiency of resource allocation. But there is a final point to make.

The policy environment has changed to allow other possible scenarios. Budget reforms, extra resources and further meso policies in 'social dimensions of adjustment' packages can be pressed into service to counter the impact for some women. But these are ameliorations of crisis conditions. They do not answer the question 'what is to be done to reduce this huge labour tax on women in the long run?' Tap water and electrification of homes would bring about the greatest reductions. But they require large capital investments which have a long gestation period. At the very least, however, they should find a place on the agenda of economic transformation. In the shorter term the distorting effects of the labour tax can be reduced by countervailing taxes.

What has been argued here is to bring as much as possible of the reproduction labour tax on women into market exchange. Tap water and electrification of homes would entail a paid work force in public utilities. Creches mean professional paid child-minders. All this amounts to new sources of officially recorded 'personal disposable income' instead of women's unrecorded burden.

The significance of this should not be lost on governments now trying to reform fiscal practices to raise more revenue. Without any cost it can release women's labour, correct a massive distortion in the labour market and raise revenue through sustainable channels. It would be a nice conclusion to hope that this windfall for government is partly used to invest in the capitalisation of women's present supply of water and domestic power.

As long as the huge real cost of reproduction in terms of resources used escapes market exchange, the value of its output can never be taxed to the benefit of the budget. It can only be recorded on the expenditure side through mounting health bills.

References

Commonwealth Secretariat (1989) *Engendering Adjustment for the 1990s* (London).
Economic Commission for Africa (1989) *African Alternative Framework to Structural Adjustment Programmes for Socio-Economic Recovery and Transformation*, E/ECA/CM.15/6/Rev.3 (Addis Ababa).
Moser, Caroline (1989) 'Gender Planning in the Third World: Meeting Practical and Strategic Gender Needs', *World Development*, vol. 17, no. 11.
Sen, Gita (1985) *Development Crisis and Alternative Visions: Third World Women's Perspectives* (Norway: A.s Verbum).

Part II
Case Studies

5 Adjustment from Below: Low-Income Women, Time and the Triple Role in Guayaquil, Ecuador

Caroline O. N. Moser[1]

INTRODUCTION

Widespread concern now exists about deteriorating standards of living, and the severe erosion of the 'human resource base' of the economy, in many Third World countries, after a decade of crisis from debt and recession, and the resulting stabilisation and economic structural adjustment policies (SAPs). The fact that the 'social' costs of SAPs have been most heavily carried by the low-income population in both rural and urban areas, has resulted in proposals to modify the adjustment process to include 'a Human Face' (UNICEF, 1987), with policies to 'strengthen the human resource base' (Demery and Addison, 1987).

To assist the formulation of policy, the World Bank, in collaboration with UNDP and the African Development Bank, have embarked on an extensive research programme to monitor the effects of SAPs in sub-Saharan Africa, setting up the SDA Project Unit, and undertaking the Permanent Household Survey (PHS), a large-scale structured household interview survey to be undertaken over a 5–7 year period (UNDP, 1987). At the same time a proliferating number of detailed micro-level studies of the effects of SAPs on women have been commissioned (Commonwealth Secretariat, 1990).

Gender Bias in Structural Adjustment Policies

Despite increasing concern with the plight of poor households, fundamental problems remain. Because of gender bias in macro-economic policy formulated to reallocate resources, SAPs often have a differential impact within households on men and women, and boys and girls (UNICEF, 1987; UNICEF, n.d.; Elson 1987; and this volume). Through the analysis of recent research in urban Latin America, the purpose of this chapter is to contribute to the ongoing debate concerning the extent to which SAPs have, even if unintentionally, differentially disadvantaged members of low-income households on the basis of gender. The objective is also to show policy-makers the importance of ensuring that current research methodology, such as the SDA survey, shifts from the household as the unit of analysis, towards a more disaggregated approach with greater capability of identifying intra-household differentiation. In addition, the limitations of research which isolates low-income women, outside of the context of their households, is identified.

A longitudinal case study of an urban low-income community, Indio Guayas, in Guayaquil, Ecuador, between 1978 and 1988, provides the opportunity to examine the relevance of three 'kinds of male bias', which Elson has identified as underlying many SAPs (Elson, 1990, p. 6).[2]

The first is male bias concerning the sexual division of labour, which ignores barriers to labour reallocation in policies designed to switch from non-tradeables to tradeables, by offering incentives to encourage labour-intensive manufactures and crops for exports. Changing household level employment patterns in Indio Guayas are examined in order to assess the extent to which any retraining and transfer of labour has occurred, or whether, as Elson has argued, gender barriers to the reallocation of labour has meant greater unemployment for men displaced from non-tradeables, while for any women drawn into export oriented manufacturing this has meant extra work, as factory work is added to the unpaid domestic work which unemployed men remain reluctant to undertake (Elson, 1990, p. 12).[3]

The second male bias is concerned with the unpaid domestic work necessary for reproducing and maintaining human resources and the extent to which SAPs implicitly assume that these processes, which are carried out unpaid by women, will continue regardless of the way in which resources are reallocated (Elson, 1990, p. 6). This raises the question as to how far SAPs are only successful at the cost of longer and harder working days for women, forced to increase their labour both within the market and the household. Preoccupation has been expressed regarding the extent to which their labour is infinitely elastic, or whether a breaking point may be reached when women's capacity to reproduce and maintain human resources may collapse (Jolly, 1987, p. 4).

In the case of Indio Guayas, gender planning methodology, which identifies that women in most low-income households in developing countries have a triple role, provides the necessary tools for identifying how far the issue is elasticity of time, as Elson argues, or *changes in the balancing of time* (Moser, 1986; 1989). 'Women's work' includes not only *reproductive* work (the childbearing and childrearing responsibilities) required to guarantee the maintenance and reproduction of the labour force, and *productive* work in income generating activities. In addition it includes *community managing* work, undertaken at a local settlement level. With the inadequate state provision of items of collective consumption, and the increasing cutbacks in existing basic services such as water and health services, it is women who take responsibility for the allocation of the limited resources to ensure the survival of their households. Although men are involved in *productive* work, they generally do not have a clearly identified reproductive role. Equally, while they are involved in the community they are generally less involved in the provision of items of collective consumption, but have an important *community politics* role in which they organise at the formal political level, generally within the framework of national politics (Barrig and Fort, 1987; Moser, 1987).

Because the triple role of women is not recognised, the fact that women, unlike men, are severely constrained by the burden of simultaneously balancing their different roles is frequently ignored by policy-makers. In addition the tendency to value only productive work, because of its exchange value, with reproductive and community managing work seen as 'natural' and non-productive, and therefore not valued, has serious consequences for women. It means that the majority, if not all, the work that they do is made invisible and fails to be recognised as work either by men in the community or by those planners whose job it is to assess different needs within low-income communities (Moser, 1989).

In examining the impact of SAPs on low-income women in Indio Guayas, the triple role distinction is used for analysing not only the number of hours worked but also, and more importantly, the changes women have made in their allocation of time between work undertaken in the labour market, the community and the household, because of economic crisis. It assists in identifying the extent to which different work is valued by women and men in the community, as well as policy-makers, and consequently the extent to which women find that paid work and unpaid work are increasingly competing for their time.

The third male bias concerns the household, as the social institution which is the source of supply of labour, and the assumption that changes in resource allocations in income, food prices and public expenditure, accompanying stabilisation and SAPs, affect all members of the household in the same way, because of equal intra-household distribution of resources. (Elson, 1990, p. 6). The notion that the household has a 'joint utility' or 'unified family welfare' function is based on the assumption that its concern is to maximise the welfare of all its members, whether through altruism or benevolent dictatorship, and consequently can be treated by planners 'as an individual with a single set of objectives' (Elson, 1990, p. 26; Evans, 1989). In examining the effects of cutbacks in resource allocations on low-income households in Indio Guayas it is necessary to identify intra-household allocations not only of resources, labour and time but also of decision-making as the household mediates to buffer itself against deteriorating conditions.

Differentiation Among Low-Income Women

While the focus of the chapter is on the impact of adjustment processes on low-income women, it is clear that there are severe limitations in studying women in isolation, as is the case in many recent micro-level studies (Commonwealth Secretariat, 1990). This has resulted in a tendency to identify income as the basis of differentiation, and to treat as similar the 'plight' of all low-income women. In reality, however, low-income women have not all been equally, affected by SAPs for not all have been similarly successful in balancing their three roles. In examining differential responses to crisis by women in Indio Guayas it is important to identify the extent to which 'coping strategies' have been influenced by the nature and the composition of the household in which women are positioned. Three determining factors can be identified as likely to affect women: first, the number of persons in the household also involved in productive work and generating a reliable income; second, the particular stage in the household life-cycle when changes occurred; and third, the composition of the household in terms of the number of other females also involved in reproductive work. Analysis of the situation in Indio Guayas in terms of these three variables is intended to assist in the development of appropriate policy proposals to assist low-income women and their families in conditions such as these.

The Problem of Causality

In fact, for policy-makers, the most important purpose of research such as this relates to the issue of causality, and the identification as to which of the social costs experienced are a consequence of debt or recession rather than of the IMF/World Bank stabilisation/SAP interventions. Of equal importance for them is the question of counterfactuals, and the thorny problem as to what conditions would have been like had SAPs not occurred. At the outset it is critical to recognise the difficult methodological problems in directly answering questions such as these, and therefore the necessity to identify changes resulting from both recession and adjustment generally, with more specific inferences drawn out where ever possible.

Critical, therefore, for such research is the identification of the most important factors affecting low-income households during recession and the process of adjustment. In the Latin American urban context three types of changes are identified as of greatest importance; first, changes in income, through changes in wages, and levels and sectors of employment for employees, and through changes in product prices and product demand for self-employment; second, changes in consumption patterns through changes in prices in important purchases, especially food; third, changes in the level and composition of public expenditure, through government sectoral spending cuts particularly in the social sector, resulting in introduction or increase of user charges for services.[4] Despite the difficulties in identifying the degree to which changes are linked to specific adjustment policy, nevertheless, where possible, inferences to causal relationships are made.

For research which seeks to examine micro-level socio-economic processes in terms of macro-level economic trends, it is necessary at the outset to provide a contextual background. The chapter, therefore, starts by very briefly describing Ecuador, its problems of debt and recession, and the stabilisation and structural adjustment measures implemented by two governments since 1982, before also briefly describing the research community, Indio Guayas. This background provides the basis for a more detailed examination of the impact of recession and SAP on income, consumption patterns and the level and composition of public expenditure, the three main areas of change identified. The way the situation has changed for women is examined in terms of their different roles, and where there is adequate data, the links to particular policies suggested. Finally, preliminary conclusions are reached relating to the capacity of low-income women to cope with change, with a distinction made between women who are 'coping', those who are 'burnt out', and finally those who are 'hanging on'. A number of policy recommendations are suggested which while contextually specific, may have wider applicability to other situations in which low-income women have been similarly affected by adjustment processes.

BACKGROUND TO THE RESEARCH

Ecuador and its Economy

Ecuador, with a population of ten million, is one of the smaller Latin American Republics, divided into three distinct geographical regions: the coastal plain with extensive agricultural zones under banana, rice, shrimp and sugar production and cattle rearing, has 50 per cent of the population and is dominated by the export-oriented port city of Guayaquil; the Andean sierra with 46 per cent of the population, which grows subsistence agricultural production mainly potatoes, maize and cereals, and is the location of Quito, the capital city and administrative and government centre; the Amazon Territory, until very recently sparsely populated and uncultivated, the location of oil extraction since drilling began in 1967.

The wider significance of Ecuador lies in the fact that it is a 'median' country. Until 1970 it was one of the poorest in Latin America, but with the discovery of oil, by 1982 it became one of the middle-income countries of the hemisphere, with per capita income equalling its neighbours Colombia and Peru. As a result of its oil-led economic development during the 1970s (it joined OPEC in 1973), the World Bank in 1984 stated that in terms of social progress 'much of the oil income was well spent'. Between 1960 and 1980 more than ten years were added on to Ecuadorian life expectancy, death and infant mortality rates dropped by 40 per cent, and by 1980 virtually all children attended primary school.

During the past twenty-five years Ecuador has experienced average annual GDP growth of 6.7 per cent, although from 1982 to 1988 the rate was only 2.2 per cent per annum. The fluctuating rates reflect the development and decline of the petroleum and oil industry. Oil exports rose from 0 per cent to 70 per cent of total exports between

1970 and 1983, although with subsequent decline in oil prices since then its share has dropped to about 42 per cent of total exports, below agriculture at 52 per cent.

Public sector revenues and expenditures became heavily dependent on oil receipts and external borrowing during the 1970s when public expenditure grew by 9.6 per cent per year in real terms. High oil prices and availability of cheap international credit for oil exporting nations meant that large public sector deficits could be covered, leading however to a 13-fold increase of the public external debt. While the manufacturing industry sector contributed to growth during the oil boom years, mainly because it was highly protected and catered essentially for the home market, it was neither able to compete in foreign markets nor to cope with the depression associated with the post oil boom. For oil income was involved in current consumption rather than in longer-term productive investments. A strong and appreciating sucre, Ecuador's currency, further undermined export-oriented manufacturing as well as agriculture. During 1970–86 agriculture grew at less than 2 per cent per annum and while it accounted for 16 per cent of GDP in 1980, by 1988 it was down to less than 7 per cent.

Recession, Stabilisation and Structural Adjustment Policies

Since 1982 Ecuador has faced a fundamentally changed world economic environment in which new commercial lending has dried up, real interest rates have risen and oil prices have declined. Within the recession period of 1982–8 two particular crisis periods in the Ecuadorian economy can be identified: first, 1982–3 when the bottom dropped out of world oil prices and Ecuador was suddenly plunged into recession; and second, 1986–7 when oil prices fell further and an earthquake caused cutbacks in oil production. During the 1982–8 period two different Ecuadorian governments adopted eight distinct stabilisation/adjustment packages.

The first measures taken in 1982 were essentially a stabilisation policy to induce adjustment, mainly by controlling demand. A fiscal and monetary programme was introduced, the sucre was devalued (its value fell by 17 per cent in 1982, and 32 per cent in 1983) and controls placed on imports, current expenditure and public investment, while the debt payment was revised. Its purpose to reduce real incomes and thereby domestic demand succeeded in that aggregate demand fell to provoke a reduction in GDP in 1982 of 1 per cent and of 2.8 per cent in 1983. In 1984 a new government intensified demand control measures by a further 30 per cent devaluation of the sucre, and suspension of price controls, the reduction in food, energy and fuel subsidies and other measures to reduce the public sector deficit. It also implemented supply-side SAPs with incentives to private producers through measures to eliminate export taxes, liberalise imports, and more flexible interest rates, to expand and diversify the export base. One success story has been the development of the shrimp industry which in 1986 had become Ecuador's second largest source of foreign exchange earnings (World Bank, 1988).

Despite such measures it proved necessary in late 1985 to devalue the sucre once more. When oil prices halved between 1985 and 1986 from 25 to 12.7 dollars a barrel, the fall cost the country 950 million dollars, equivalent to 8 per cent of the Internal Product. Following the requirements of the IMF, the government reformulated its SAP in 1986, introducing flexible interest rates and an end to treasury foreign exchange control. However, the public sector deficit continued to increase, rising from 5.1 per cent of GDP in 1986, to 10.5 per cent of GDP in 1987, to 12 per cent in 1988, although this was less to satisfy basic priorities than to meet the political demands of powerful interest groups (UNICEF, 1988). By 1986, the economy entered a profound recession with a mere 1.6 per cent growth rate. Further deterioration occurred in 1987, because of both the world global economic situation and the disruption to oil production caused by the March earthquake. By 1988, despite the SAP, Ecuador's economic situation was critical, with the main problems identified as the size of the foreign debt and the acute recession in internal economic activities. Agricultural production for the internal market stagnated together with food processing and textiles as real incomes of the salaried and waged sectors fell. The new government in August 1988 was faced with debt rescheduling, and the necessity to control further the public expenditure deficit.

The Research Community: Barrio Indio Guayas, Guayaquil

Within the Ecuadorian economy Guayaquil is the country's largest city, chief port and major centre of trade and industry. Historically, growth has been linked to the different phases of Ecuador's primary export oriented economy. As an industrial enclave, its population growth has reflected the agricultural sector's declining capacity to retain its population as much as the city's potential to create industrial employment. It expanded rapidly during the 1970s at the time of the oil boom because of very high in-migration rates mainly from the surrounding rural areas. This helped to swell the population from 500 000 in 1960 to 1.2 million in 1982 and an estimated 2 million in 1988.

Guayaquil's commercial activity is focused around the 40 gridiron blocks of the original Spanish colonial city, which in the 1970s were encircled by the inner-city rental tenements. To the north on higher ground are the predominantly middle- and upper-income areas, while to the west and south are the tidal swamplands which provide the predominant area for low-income expansion. Settlement of this peripheral zone, known as the *suburbios* (literally suburbs) occurred between 1940 and 1980 when the low-income population excluded from the conventional housing market invaded this municipal owned swampland.

This research was undertaken in Indio Guayas, the name given to an area of swampland about ten blocks in size, located on the far edge of Cisne Dos, one of the administrative districts of the city. The settlement has no clear physical limits but in 1978 had some 3000 residents, the majority of whom belonged to the Indio Guayas neighbourhood or *barrio* committee. In 1978 Indio Guayas was a 'pioneer settlement' of young upwardly mobile families, who had moved from inner-city rental accommodation and acquired their own 10 by 30 metre plots, to own *de facto* their homes. They incrementally build their first houses of split bamboo and wood on catwalks, relying on irregularly delivered water tankers and pirated electricity. During the late 1970s and early 1980s the residents mobilised and petitioned local politicians and government to provide infill, drinking water and electricity for their community (Moser, 1982, p. 1).

Data from a household survey undertaken in 1978 showed a mean age for both men and women of 30 years. Free unions were the relationship with most households headed by men and having an average household size of 5.8 persons. The community was representative of the lower-paid end of unskilled non-unionised labour. The men were employed as mechanics, construction workers, tailoring outworkers, unskilled factory workers or labourers, while the women were employed as domestic servants, washerwomen, cooks, sellers and dressmakers (Moser, 1981). However, far from being society's casualties, the residents of Indio Guayas were an upwardly aspiring community, struggling through hard work and initiative to improve their standard of living and through better health and education the employment prospects for their children, if not for themselves.

RECESSION, STABILISATION AND STRUCTURAL
ADJUSTMENT AND ITS IMPACT ON LOW-INCOME
HOUSEHOLDS IN INDIO GUAYAS

Changes in Income, Wages and Employment

In examining changes under recession and adjustment, the first fundamental indicator identified is change in income and real resources in cash or kind at the household level. As Cornia *et al* have noted, 'these resources are needed in the area of food, housing, clothing, transport and to an extent health, water sanitation, education and child care' (Cornia *et al*, 1987, p. 37). In an urban context changes in household level income are most directly affected by changes in real wage levels and self-employment rates as well as by shifts in the labour market. In examining trends in Indio Guayas, it is important to relate them to those at national level.

In Ecuador it is estimated that open unemployment increased from 5.7 per cent of the economically active population (EAP) in 1980 to 11 per cent in 1987, accompanied by an 'explosive' growth in underemployment which in 1984 was estimated at 50 per cent for Quito and Guayaquil (UNICEF, 1988, p. 23). This was accompanied by a greater decline in the value of real wages than that of per capita GNP. These changes reflect major features of the IMF 'deflationary' stabilisation measures designed to reduce employment in the public sector, to freeze wages through a stringent wage control policy, as well as a high inflation rate especially of food and drink (ibid, p. 23). The sectors in which wage work declined particularly severely were those in which the EAP was most concentrated, namely agriculture, industry and construction. In agriculture, participation rates fell from 19 per cent to 6.8 per cent; in industry from 31.5 per cent to 11.5 per cent; and in the construction sector from 50.6 per cent to 28.6 per cent (BCE, 1986, p. 139).

In Guayaquil, the decline in oil revenue and attempts at cutbacks in public sector spending have reduced private investment, particularly in the construction sector. Interestingly enough, however, as shown in Table 5.1, in Indio Guayas this has not resulted in a shift out of the construction sector for men, with the number working in this sector remaining very much the same, at 11 per cent in 1988 compared to 12 per cent in 1978. However, with a downturn in demand for labour on large infrastructure and office building projects, most of the men are now employed in the *suburbios* on local house upgrading

Table 5.1 Breakdown of occupational categories 1978–88 (in %)

Census occupational category	Women 1978	Women 1988	Men 1978	Men 1988
Professional				
teacher	1.0	2.9	1.4	0.8
nursing auxiliary	0.0	2.9	0.0	0.0
other	0.0	2.9	0.0	1.7
Managers	0.0	2.9	0.0	0.8
Office workers	1.0	1.4	4.6	4.0
Sellers	36.0	33.8	19.7	21.0
Agricultural labour	2.0	0.0	1.8	.8
Transport	0.0	0.0	8.4	9.0
Artisan/machine operator				
shoes	0.0	0.0	2.3	0.0
dressmakers	14.0	17.6	0.0	0.0
tailors	0.0	0.0	6.6	2.5
mechanics	0.0	0.0	4.7	6.0
skilled construction	0.0	0.0	12.0	11.0
carpentry/lacquer	0.0	0.0	6.0	9.0
other artisan	0.0	0.0	0.0	2.0
Other factory workers	0.0	2.9	9.8	8.0
Labourers	0.0	0.0	9.8	6.0
Personal services	39.0	35.2	6.1	6.1
Other	7.0	0.0	4.6	4.0
Total	100.0	99.7	99.5	99.1
n =	(230)	(131)	(213)	(118)

or the building of extensions. In addition, real wages in the construction sector have declined and are now only worth half to two-thirds of their 1979 value. Most important of all, changes in contractual conditions have occurred, with far fewer skilled men working on fixed-term contracts (with rights to benefits such as social security), and many more increasingly employed, like their unskilled colleagues, on a daily basis. This increased casualisation of work in the construction sector has resulted in greater underemployment and unemployment for periods sometimes as long as six months of the year.

The number of men sellers has remained the same at around 20 per cent. The number of artisans also shows stability, although more shoemakers and tailors were evident in 1978 than in 1988, while slightly more mechanics and carpenters were also found in 1988 than before. A breakdown of factory and labouring work shows the only real area of expansion for male employment has been in sea products, particularly shrimp industry. Around 7 per cent of the male heads of household had jobs in this well-paid sector. With shrimp farms covering an extensive area along the Pacific coast this has resulted in a small but growing male circulatory migration pattern from Indio Guayas in which only one weekend in three is spent at home. For the men in Indio Guayas, therefore, few opportunities to shift from non-tradeables to tradeables in labour-intensive manufacturing have materialised with SAPs. Consequently, it is rural incentives for export crops such as shrimps, biased in favour of male employment, which is proving increasingly attractive for urban men, regardless of the consequences for social relations in urban households.

Women in Indio Guayas have been severely affected by the fact that less men than before are generating a reliable income, and the value of their wage packet is lower than it was in 1980. First and foremost, more women have to work, with female participation rates increasing from 40 per cent in 1978 to 52 per cent in 1988.[5] Although more women are working, the majority have not been able to take up new opportunities in the labour market. No new factory work recruiting female labour has been created, and women have been forced to remain in the traditional areas of domestic service and street selling in which they have always worked. Although gender segregation in the labour market has protected women's employment in the service sector, this has only been achieved at lower rates of pay. As shown in Table 5.1, in 1978 39 per cent of economically active women were domestic servants, cooks or washerwomen, while by 1988 35 per cent were in the same occupations, although the wages of the average worker had fallen to two-thirds of its 1979 value. The same is true of street and front-room selling, probably the most involutionary part of the informal sector given its capability to absorb additional labour without increased productivity. In 1978 36 per cent of women were street sellers, as compared to 33.8 per cent in 1988, with the numbers of dressmakers remaining the same at 14 per cent.

The biggest change has been the increase of those in professional (teachers and nursing auxiliaries) and office jobs, growing from 2 per cent in 1978 to 10.2 per cent in 1988. Comprising mainly younger women, this reflects the slowly increasing differentiation in the socio-economic composition of Indio Guayas as the city's spatial expansion makes it more attractive to higher income groups. Data from the 1988 survey shows that of those households with working daughters, the largest number were employed as shop workers (36

Table 5.2   Changes in the number of economically active within the
household in Indio Guayas, 1978–88 (in %)

Number working	1978	1988
1	49	34
2	32	32
3	11	20
4	6	9
5 or more	2	3
Total	100	98

per cent). Although the majority of them had completed secondary school, they were either on short-term contracts or selling on commission. A further 15 per cent were in professional and office jobs, and over 20 per cent were in domestic service. Although increasing differentiation may continue among the next generation of women, nevertheless the employment opportunities are not commensurate with the increased educational qualifications, and the likelihood is that the majority, once they have their own dependants, will retreat into the residual female occupations of selling and domestic service.

In fact Elson's concerns about gender barriers in the reallocation of *paid* labour do not emerge as a major issue. What is more important than gender barriers is that hardly any new jobs in tradeables have been generated for anyone within the community. No new jobs have been generated for women, and only a few for men, and these in Guayaquil itself.

A second fundamental change resulting from changes in income has been changes in the number of economically active people in the household. As shown in Table 5.2, fewer households can now depend on the income of one earner. There has been a decline in the number of households with one working (from 49 per cent to 34 per cent) and a significant increase in the numbers with three or more working (from 19 per cent to 32 per cent). With more people in the households having to work, it is clear that the strategy of who works, and who stays at home, depends on both the ages of the children, and the number of daughters who may replace their mothers in undertaking reproductive tasks in the home, as further discussed below.

A third change has been in the composition of the household with the number of woman-headed households increasing from 12 per cent to 19 per cent in the past decade. While there are certainly more older widowed or deserted women in the community than there were

Table 5.3   Changes in the composition of the household in Indio Guayas, 1978–88 (in %)

Household type	1978	1988
Nuclear	52	51
Women headed	12	18.3
Extended	25	25
Other	11	5
Total	100	99.3

before 1990, there is also an increasing number of *de facto* women-headed households, as shown in Table 5.3. In some cases men have temporarily migrated to the rural areas to work in agriculture or the shrimp industry, leaving their family in Indio Guayas because of better opportunities for female employment and children's education in the city. Frequently, however, these men soon set up other households in the rural areas, resulting in a declining responsibility to the urban household.

Although the number of nuclear and extended families has re-mained fairly constant (52 per cent and 25 per cent respectively), the composition of extended families has changed. Less now have depen-dent grandparents, while there are more married sons and daughters, and their income earning partners. Young couples are less likely to leave the family home to start their own home than they were before 1980. Two reasons have been put forward to explain this trend: first, households are now more dependent on additional income earners; second, the incentives to replicate the 'pioneer process' are not as great in the current politico-economic context. The process of land invasion and settlement consolidation which was an option in the 1970s, now faces the new reality of bankrupt local and national governments, and public utilities which no longer have the financial capacity to expand already overextended services into more far-flung squatter settlements.[6]

Changes in Consumption Patterns

During the past decade the cost of living has increased for low-income households. One of the principal long-term root causes is the agricultural development policy adopted during the petrol boom period when changes from subsistence basic grains production to export-oriented cash crops provoked a decline in foodstuff production for the home market. Inflationary rises in food prices have also been caused by the removal of subsidies on basic staples and the sucre's devaluations, which have increased the prices of imported foods. With wages frozen while food prices and other essential items such as energy and petrol have risen (with knock-on effects for transport costs), real incomes have fallen. It has been estimated that in 1984 the minimum salary for those with stable wage employment was meeting only 65 per cent of the costs of the family shopping basket. Furthermore it has also been calculated that the purchasing power of informal sector earnings cover only 35 per cent of the value of the family food basket (UNICEF, 1988, p. 3). Price increases in staple food items in Guayaquil during the one-year period June 1987–8, for instance, ranged from 50 per cent increase on milk to 194 per cent on potatoes. Other important changes included 79 per cent on eggs, 55 per cent on fish, 117 per cent on tomatoes, 25 per cent on platano and 93 per cent on rice.

This has resulted in changes in household diet. Sub-sample data for the period July 1987 to July 1988 showed, for instance, that 42 per cent of households no longer drink milk at all, while in those where milk is still drunk, the average consumption has decreased sharply from 4.6 litres per household per week to 1.4 litres. (The corner shop which used to order 36 litres of milk per day now only orders 12.) Similarly the average number of times per week fish is eaten has declined from nearly three to under two, for eggs from an average of 4.9 per week to 2.63. There has been a shift from potatoes to *platano*, and from drinking fresh fruit juice to powdered fruit drink or water. Detailed data on daily menus shows the following: first, a tendency to eat less per meal and thereby stretch the food previously eaten at one meal to cover both midday and evening meals; second, to eat less meals, with first supper and then breakfast cut out. In July 1988 one-quarter of the households were eating one meal a day, with the breakfast cut at times justified on the misguided assumption that 'the children get free milk at school'.

It is also harder to pay for essentials. High inflation during the 1989–1990 has meant that many of the local small shops which used to give credit now are unable to because of losses incurred by bad debts. At the same time the decline in stable household income has resulted in a reduction in monthly or weekly bulk purchases in the centre. Non-perishable food items such as cooking oil, lentils, spaghetti and sugar are now more likely to be bought in small quantities at higher prices at local shops. Another indicator of change in consumption patterns is provided by the number of broken-down refrigerators which were bought during the boom period between 1978 and 1982, and which households are now unable to mend. The lack of a refrigerator in a hot climate means that food has to be prepared on a daily basis, and this has consequences in time spent cooking. It reverses the trend over the 1980s during which women saw their cooking time reduced as they changed from cooking on kerosene or charcoal to gas.

Changes in dietary patterns have resulted in a deterioration in the nutritional status of households, particularly of children. A two-week survey of all children under 12 attending a local health centre revealed that 79 per cent were suffering some level of malnutrition, of which 28 per cent were first-degree, 38 per cent were second-degree and 13 per cent were third-degree. Although this data is not sufficient to indicate a trend, it nevertheless reflects the findings of national-level nutritional status (see UNICEF, 1988; Freire, 1984; 1988). It was also evident from data collected at a qualitative level that women feed themselves last, and eat least, with anaemia a much voiced complaint.

In a situation of personal debt, loans from wealthier kin are increasingly sought after while the sale or pawning of jewellery or other valuables occurs more commonly, as well as borrowing smaller amounts off neighbouring women. A number of community-level self-help saving schemes have also been developed by women within local *barrio* committees. A small amount is put away each week in a savings club to provide a small capital source to help pay school matriculation costs or for new clothes at Christmas. The *cadena* is another initiative introduced since 1985. Forty families pay weekly quotas into a rotating fund which is used exclusively for the purchase of housing materials. Self-help saving schemes are again mainly organised by women.

Changes in Levels and Composition of Public Expenditure due to Changes in Governmental Sectoral Spending

During the oil boom social sector spending benefited considerably. While the total national budget grew at an average of 5.8 per cent during the 1972–82 period, the social sector budget grew on average by 11.3 per cent per year. The social sector share of the national budget rose from 31.7 per cent in 1972 to 39.5 per cent in 1980. With the 1981 adjustment measures it fell to 30.5 per cent by 1985, picking up to 34.2 per cent in 1986. The highest share of the national budget is on education (26.5 per cent), followed by health (6.5 per cent) and social welfare (1 per cent) (World Bank, 1988, pp. 97–8). However, these figures hide per capita shifts, and UNICEF has argued that while the health budget represented 7 per cent of the national budget between 1979 and 1984, its real value per capita declined by 18 per cent between 1981 and 1985 (Suarez y col, 1987, p. 49). In an urban community such as Indio Guayas, the problem with social services relates not so much to lack of provision as to the quality of service provided, and the extent to which it is free or bought. Payment can either be direct, through private sector provision, or indirect, through hidden transfer charges for users in state provision, or through unpaid labour time in non-governmental organisation service provision.

In 1978 in Indio Guayas, the nearest health services were provided by the out-patient departments of the government Hospital Jesus de Maria, and the USAID-supported Hospital de Guayaquil on the edge of the suburbios, together with other city centre private services. The past decade has witnessed a proliferation in the growth of private practices in the sector itself, as much a consequence of the oversupply of professionals as the demand for their services. For instance, within seventeen blocks on the main access road which passes through Indio Guayas there are six general practitioners, two surgeons, three paediatric specialists, four dentists, and an obstetrician as well as three pharmacies and a laboratory. The most important state provision has been a highly overcrowded Primary Health Centre located a bus-ride away, while the only surviving NGO provision is a small health clinic, financed by a foreign religious order, which provides a doctor's surgery and drugs at a subsidised rate.

While data on local health sector spending cuts were unobtainable, there was a general consensus that government-run services had deteriorated, indicated in the survey. Asked which service they would use if a member of their family fell ill, 50 per cent responded that they would go to the state hospital, 35 per cent to a private doctor and 11 per cent to the health centre. Asked where they had gone the last time a member of the family had been ill, 42 per cent said they had used the hospital, 48 per cent a private doctor while only 9 per cent had used the health centre. In the 1987–8 period the doctor at the subsidised NGO clinic said the number of patients had doubled because patients could no longer afford to pay for private services. The picture of health care which emerges therefore is one of

increasing privatisation with costs born by the low-income population, and the failure of most subsidised programmes, such as the
UNICEF-supported Primary Health Care Programme, to survive in
the long term (Moser and Sollis, 1989).

In 1980 the only educational facility in Indio Guayas was a cane-
walled primary school with 70 to 80 children per class. In 1988 the
same school was a large complex operating a three-shift schooling
system, built of cement and bricks, with financial assistance from
Plan International, an international NGO. UNICEF Pre-Escolar
Programme has survived in Indio Guayas since 1984 largely because
of the extensive community-level support, which has included the
building of a community centre. Local members are nominated as
teachers and paid a 'stipend' for their part-time work. The state
primary school, however, has problems similar to those identified at
the national level, with inadequate equipment, low quality of teaching and outdated teaching methods. At the national level primary
schooling extends to 86 per cent of the population, but only 35.7 per
cent are in the appropriate grade for their age. Despite such limitations, increasing competition to enter the labour market has led to an
expansion in demand for formal educational qualifications. In Indio
Guayas there is widespread concern to educate both sons and daughters as long as possible. Low-income families invest considerable
proportions of their income and savings to educate their children.
The survey showed that in 1988, 36 per cent of households had sent
up to five of their children to private fee-paying schools (for a year or
more), in the expectation that it would provide better education than
the equivalent state school. While a quarter had gone to pre-primary
schools, the highest investment was made at primary level, attended
by 65 per cent, with only 12 per cent at secondary level.

Although state education is technically 'free', in reality numerous
charges are transferred to the parents. Over the past decade the
annual school entry 'matriculation' fee, particularly at secondary
level, has become a crippling expense for households who are unable
to save during the year. Matriculation fees, set by individual school
head teachers, together with their executive councils, vary widely
according to the status of the school but can cost up to or more than
one month's salary of a domestic servant. When additional costs such
as uniform, school books and transportation are included, the annual
cost of secondary school per year can reach between one to two
minimum monthly salaries. One more-prosperous parent in Indio
Guayas who paid a 2400 sucre matriculation fee in 1983 is now paying

10 500 sucres, an increase of 337 per cent. The minimum salary in August 1988 was 19 000 sucres per month when the total year's schooling costs were calculated by the same parent as likely to be 40 500 sucres.

The combined effect of the fall in real income due to cuts in wages inflationary food prices and increased expenses on education and health has meant that the majority of households in Indio Guayas are poorer in real terms than they were in 1980, with a marked deterioration in the past two years. The extent to which this has affected all members of the household equally obviously relates to who within the household is making up the shortfall. With men contributing less, or, at times, no cash to the household budget, the crucial question concerns whether it is the women who have had to find more resources. This is most usefully analysed in terms of their triple role.

THE IMPACT OF RECESSION AND ADJUSTMENT PROCESSES ON WOMEN IN INDIO GUAYAS

The Productive Role of Women

The changes outlined above have had a number of important implications for women in their productive role. More women are working in income generating activities than were doing before 1980, in many cases as the primary, reliable income earner. Although badly paid, both domestic service and selling provide more stable and reliable work contracts than do the increasingly irregular day labour available for men.

The main factor determining *which* women are working is the number of persons in the household involved in productive work and generating a reliable income. Some women have always worked. Four-fifths of women in the sub-sample worked during the 1978–88 period. Of those, nearly half (48.14 per cent) have worked throughout the period: because as heads of households they have always been the sole income earner; because the low income of their spouse has meant the household has depended on their income; or because they have chosen to work. The particular stage in the household life-cycle is a second factor that also affects which women work. Those few women not working tended to be in extended or women-headed households where daughters, sons or in-laws are now contributing to household income and the woman's duties are entirely confined to reproductive work relating to household needs. This option also suggests that the size of household can affect its level of income.

When women go out to work depends on factors external and internal to the household. The sub-sample shows that 18.5 per cent entered work during the 1982–3 period, with the same number entering in the 1987–8 period. All stated that they had started working because their household income was not sufficient to cover family needs, with *'no alcanza'* a commonly heard phrase. The certainty that their entry coincided with the two crisis periods when macro-economic measures resulted in declining wages and increased food prices suggests a direct causal link. In particular, inflationary food prices in 1987–8 were identified by women as a direct reason for going out to work. Within the household the other important reason identified was the cost of secondary-level schooling, again exacerbated by inflationary matriculation fee increases since 1988. Households experiencing additional pressure were those with one or two children in secondary schooling.

Where women work depends not only on their skills but also on their level of mobility. Least mobile are those who work from home because of young children or their husband's dislike of their going out to work. The less skilled run highly competitive front-room shops, while the more skilled work as dressmakers. Slightly more mobile are those selling cooked food on the corner of nearby main roads, leaving their children for short periods of time. Laundry women must be able to travel for periods of the day, while the most mobile are domestic servants many of whom leave the house at 6 a.m. in order to cross the city, returning at 8 or 9 p.m. at night. Evidence suggests that among unskilled women there is a correlation between mobility and the amount earned.

It is clear that women are more likely to be making up the shortfall in household income. Not only are more involved in income-earning activities than before 1980, but with the decline in real wages they are also working longer hours. This is most evident in the case of poorer less-skilled women in laundry or domestic service, particularly heads of households, who have always worked. Whereas in 1980 they 'did' for one family or possibly two, the majority are now fitting in two to three families, working as long as 60 hours a week, including Saturdays, in order to earn the same amount as before in real terms.

In addition, women are now forced to seek work when their children are younger than before. Even the poorest women are reluctant to go out to work until their children reach primary school age, while among higher-income families secondary school entry is preferred. The evidence suggests that most women now work once their children are in primary school, with increasing numbers entering the labour force as soon as possible after their last (intended) child is born. Of those in the sub-sample entering the labour market since 1978, all entered prior to their youngest child's tenth birthday, and nearly 80 per cent before their sixth birthday.

A third factor which affects women's ability to work is the composition of the household in terms of the number of other females involved in reproductive work. Although the presence of other adult women able to assist in reproductive activities is sometimes important, it is the number of daughters, and their ages, which most directly determines strategies followed. With a greater number of women both working, and working longer hours, daughters are forced increasingly to dovetail their schooling to their mother's working hours. Although the half-day school shift system makes it possible for daughters to continue at school while taking in reproductive responsibilities, it nevertheless means they have less time for school homework than do their brothers. As a result, girls are often disadvantaged in terms of academic achievement, causing them to fail in school. The future productive potential of daughters, therefore, is increasingly constrained by their present reproductive activities.

The Reproductive Role of Women

In their reproductive roles as wives and mothers, women have been affected by the adjustment process, above all in terms of conflicting demands on their time. Despite the fact that more women are working than in 1978, the cultural norm in Indio Guayas that reproductive work is women's work has not changed with men not taking on new reproductive responsibilities (other than in isolated examples, particularly of household enterprises such as tailoring where men assist in child-care and cooking while women do the daily travelling to the subcontractor). Where Elson's concerns about gender barriers are justified, therefore, is in women's unpaid labour, since men have not taken on more domestic unpaid labour. Increasing pressure for women to earn an income has resulted in less time than before to dedicate to child-care and domestic responsibilities. The sub-sample showed that the average number of children per household as 4.78, indicating the number of years during which close access to the home was necessary.

The capacity of women to balance productive and reproductive work depends on both the composition of the household in terms of other females, and on the particular stage in the household life-cycle. Women with only very young children, who are forced out to work, have no alternative other than to lock them up while away, obviously the most dangerous solutions. The eldest daughter very rapidly assumes responsibility for her siblings but is not put in charge of cooking until the age of ten or eleven. In this situation women start their day at 4 or 5 a.m., cooking food to leave ready for their children to eat during the day, and doing additional domestic tasks on their return. Once daughters are able to undertake cooking, as well as child-care responsibilities, women do not get more rest, but work longer hours outside the home. Those households with more than two daughters make maximum use of the half-day school shift system by sending out different daughters to different shifts thus freeing up the mother for full-time work.

In the sub-sample there were a small but growing number of households effectively headed by daughters who undertook not only all reproductive activities but also attended community meetings on Saturdays and Sundays, thus also fulfilling their mother's community managing role. Despite the fact that women in this situation may still have a number of young children their only real role now is a productive one. In 1980 this phenomenon was not apparent, suggesting that women were balancing better their reproductive and productive activities. The situation is exacerbated in those households headed by women, and has become particularly problematic in those households where men have recently migrated for work reasons. For instance, although only 6 per cent of the male labour force had migrated to work in the shrimp industry, this initiative was the direct result of structural adjustment incentives. Increasing employment opportunities in this rural export-oriented sector, while increasing male income, had indirect costs such as the breakdown of some marital relationships, and a reduction in male economic responsibility within the household.

A reduction in women's time for reproductive activities has a number of important implications for their children. First, young children are receiving less care than before, when locked up unattended, or attended by elder sisters. They are more likely to play truant from school, and to become street children, although not necessarily identified as such, roaming locally, running errands in return for food, and protected by sympathetic neighbours only as long as they remain in the street. Second, young children are suffering additional nutritional problems when not fed by their mothers. Food left for division amongst children is often not fairly divided, and there are often nutritional problems in food cooked by elder siblings. Third, elder daughters forced into reproductive activities at a young age are themselves suffering from less parental care and guidance. Although socialised to assist their mothers with domestic tasks, daughters do not automatically accept responsibilities thrust on them. Resistance causes conflict with their mothers, and can lead them to become irresponsible, neglecting their siblings, sometimes resulting in early promiscuity and even prostitution.

Fourth, a reduction in parental control is detrimental for sons. One of the greatest concerns expressed by women forced out to work was the fact that it reduced their capacity to control teenage sons, who were more than tempted to drop out of school, become involved in street gangs and be exposed to drugs. This problem was exacerbated when the parental responsibility of the father also ceased, for instance due to out-migration. In Indio Guayas it was felt very strongly that the number of street gangs and associated theft had increased considerably since 1985, with the level of drug addiction especially from cocaine paste now a widely perceived problem. The doctor at the local health clinic confirmed that after 1988 men had increasingly been seeking guidance about drug addiction.

Women in their reproductive role have responsibility for household budgeting and ensuring not only that sufficient food is provided daily but also that larger bills such as school costs are paid. However, their control over the allocation of total household income was very limited. The data in the sub-sample showed that joint decision-making or sharing of resources within the household was not common, with most women receiving a daily allowance from their partners. Although in most cases the amount received had increased during the previous year this increase had not kept pace with inflation; men did not necessarily allocate increased income to household expenses, such that the notion that the household had a 'joint utility' or 'unified family welfare' function was not borne out in reality.

Supportive evidence is provided by the clear causal linkage which can be drawn between changes in consumption patterns and increased domestic violence within the household. In the sub-sample, 18 per cent women said there had been a decrease in domestic violence. These were mainly women earning a reliable income, who identified more respect from their male partners as associated with their greater economic independence. While 27 per cent said nothing had changed, 48 per cent said there had been an increase in domestic violence, identifying this as the direct consequence of lack of sufficient cash, and stating that it always occurred when the woman had to ask for more money, in other words when attempting to control how resources were pooled. A distinction was made between those men who became angry out of frustration from not earning enough and those who became angry because they wanted to retain what they did earn for their personal expenditures, identified as other women and alcohol. In both cases, however, the consequence was the same, with men beating their women. Additional problems are emerging with increasing drug addiction, which unlike alcohol is consumed mainly by younger men. While undertaking field work the first suicide known to the community leader occurred when a young male cocaine addict killed himself after a confrontation with his wife over the allocation of most of his income to service his addiction rather than feed his three young children.

Comparative anthropological research shows that the pressure to earn an income is making it increasingly important for women to effectively control their fertility, than was the case before 1980. Although the stage in the life-cycle is an important determinant, nevertheless the 1988 sub-sample showed that while a quarter of women were not using any form of contraception, and a further quarter were using the coil, 42 per cent had undergone tubotamy, at the birth of their youngest child. However, women were not in control of this fertility decision, with their husband's permission required for the operation.[7]

The Community Managing Role of Women

During the late 1970s and early 1980s women played an important community managing role in struggling to acquire infrastructural resources such as infill, water and electricity for the area (Moser, 1987). This centred around popular mobilisation, linked to particular political patronage with intensive activity at election time. Cutbacks in public spending since 1983 has meant that patronage of this type has virtually ceased. In this context NGOs are playing an increasingly important role in service delivery, not only as in the UNICEF education and health programmes but also, for instance, community-level 'developmental' programmes introduced by Plan International since 1983.

This has had important implications for women, who are spending more time than before in their community managing role in order to negotiate NGO participatory delivery systems. These programmes, such as Plan International, are based on the voluntary unpaid involvement of women on a regular long-term basis. Women community leaders are expected to provide access to the community, and along with paid community development workers to supervise the allocation of resources for development programmes. In order to get access to resources families are required to attend weekly meetings and undertake community-level voluntary activities. Other than in leadership roles, participation is almost entirely by women. As an extension of their domestic role women take primary responsibility for the success of community-level projects. In some cases, as in the UNICEF Pre-Escolar, these are managed by the community, while in other cases top-down provision results in participation only in the implementation phase.

The decreasing provision of services by the government has led women to recognise the importance of encouraging the entry, and ensuring the long-term survival, of community-based programmes. Since it is the lack of time which often results in failure, to ensure NGO's continued working with them, women are forced to find the time. In August 1988, for instance, up to 200 women were meeting for three hours every Sunday afternoon in order to get access to Plan International's community-level housing improvement programme. At the same time, women with constantly sick children make it their business to attend the Saturday afternoon health talks run by the NGO health clinic. Even men are gradually beginning to recognise this role. A local carpenter summed it up when he said 'I earn the money, and my wife looks after the children and attends the meetings'.

CONCLUSION: WOMEN, TIME AND THE TRIPLE ROLE

Policy-makers have become preoccupied that recession and adjustment have resulted in an extension of the working day of low-income women. The evidence from Indio Guayas shows that the real problem is not the length of time women work but the way in which they balance their time between activities undertaken in their reproductive, productive and community managing roles. In addition it has become important to differentiate such women's work intergenerationally, so as to identify when the extra time comes from daughters rather than mothers. In both cases the extra demands on time are on the female gender, but the number of women involved has increased considerably.

Over the past decade low-income women in Indio Guayas always have worked between twelve and eighteen hours per day, depending on such factors as the composition of household, the time of year, and their skills. Therefore, the hours worked have not changed fundamentally. What has changed is the time allocated to the different activities undertaken by them. The necessity to get access to resources has forced women to allocate increasing time to productive and community managing activities, at the expense of reproductive activities, which in many cases have become a secondary priority. The fact that paid work and unpaid work are competing for women's time has important impacts on children, on women themselves and on the disintegration of the household.

It is clear that in the case of Indio Guayas, gender bias in macroeconomic policy formulated to reallocate resources has differentially disadvantaged low-income women. Not all women can cope under crisis and it is necessary to stop romanticising about their infinite capacity to do so. At the same time, they do not form a heterogeneous group, and, in terms of their capacity to balance their three roles in the changing situation, fall roughly into three groups.[8]

The first group, women who are 'coping', are those women balancing their three roles. They are more likely to be in stable relationships, with partners who have reliable sources of income. The household income is likely to be supplemented by others working, and there may be other females also involved in reproductive work. About 30 per cent of women are coping.

The second group are women who are 'burnt out'. These are no longer balancing their three roles, and their productive role predominates. They are most likely to be women who head households or are the primary income earners, working in domestic service, with partners who make no financial contribution to the household. They are often older women at the end of their reproductive cycle, physically and mentally exhausted after years of responsibility for a large numbers of dependents. Their inability to balance their roles results in a tendency to hand over all reproductive responsibilities to older daughters who cannot or will not take all the necessary responsibility. The consequence is that their younger still-dependent children drop out of school, and roam the streets. About 15 per cent of women are no longer coping, already casualties and burnt out.

The third group, women who are 'hanging on', are those who are under pressure but still trying to balance their three roles, making choices depending on the composition of the household and the extent to which other household members are providing reliable income. Some are women without partners, who, if they are the main income earners have sufficient support from other females. Others are women with partners who have been forced out to work to help pay for the increased household expenses. These women are using up future resources in order to survive today, sending their sons out to work, or keeping their daughters at home to take over domestic responsibilities. About 55 per cent of women are invisibly at risk, only just hanging on.

Ultimately, only the introduction of a gender-aware planning perspective will change current policy approaches to low-income women such as these. Nevertheless there are also a number of pragmatic changes which can assist them in the short term. Although those women identified as 'burnt out' are an obvious target group for assistance, the group identified as 'hanging on', although less visible are a greater priority in terms of policy prescriptions for human resource development in Indio Guayas. Although policy-makers may not prioritise the problems of these women, account must also be taken of the fact that their daughters are often losing schooling. It is essential, therefore, to ensure that compensatory programmes, designed to 'protect the basic living standards, health and nutrition', target not only the 'burnt out', but also those 'hanging on' (UNICEF, 1987, p. 134).

Too much focus on women as 'victims' of adjustment may undermine their capacity to organise themselves within existing community-level structures and discourage bottom-up, self-help solutions. Meso and sectoral programmes and projects whose priorities include 'expenditures and activities which help maintain the incomes of the poor' (UNICEF, 1987, p. 134) are more likely to succeed when they are planned in collaboration with, and implemented by, community-level organisations, especially those led and organised by women.

For although women are 'victims' of adjustment, they are also a largely untapped resource with their community managing role unrecognised. Yet they are prepared to invest commitment and time in those interventions directly or indirectly likely to benefit their families and children. Local women know community needs, and can identify the particular constraints, often much better than professionals who often neither know the communities, nor have the same level of commitment to project success.

All over the world low-income women are providing voluntary labour in their community managing role, in their productive role, are working below the minimum wage (often for no more than a stipend), at the same time as maintaining and reproducing human resources in their reproductive role. As aid donors and national governments alike seek to find 'sustainable' solutions to the current crisis, failure to acknowledge what is happening before their eyes means that gender blindness has now become inexcusable.

Notes

1. This article was originally written for UNICEF, New York. An earlier, abbreviated version, entitled *The Impact of Recession and Adjustment Policies at the Micro-Level: Low Income Women and their Households in Guayaquil, Ecuador*, was published in UNICEF (1989).

   The 1988 fieldwork and analysis of research data was undertaken in collaboration with Peter Sollis. I should like to acknowledge his important contribution to this article. I should also like to thank Michael Cohen for encouraging me to examine adjustment processes at the micro-level, Richard Jolly for his interest in this research, and Diane Elson for her helpful comments on this article. Without the support and commitment of the *moradores* of Indio Guayas it would not have been possible to do this research. As ever I am indebted to them, particularly to Emma Torres, Rosa Vera and Lucie Savalla, who after ten years are really much better field workers in their own community than I could ever be.

2. Fieldwork for this longitudinal study was first undertaken in 1977–8, and was based on participant observation through living in the *barrio*, and a survey of 244 households of three different block groups, intended to show changes in the settlement and consolidation processes. Further anthropological fieldwork was undertaken in January 1979 and August 1982. A re-study of the *barrio* was undertaken in July–August 1988, based once more on participant observation, and a sample survey of 141 households in the same area (referred to as the survey). A further semi-structured questionnaire was undertaken with a sub-sample of 33 households from the sample survey, selected to be representative of the different household structures in Indio Guayas (referred to as the sub-sample). The purpose of the sub-sample was to examine in greater depth at a qualitative level important processes highlighted in the survey. Analysis of the issues therefore relates only up to the period of August 1988, and not to further changes which may have occurred since then. For a more detailed description of the research methodology, see Sollis and Moser (1990).

3. Elaborating on this issues, Elson argues that:

   taking no account of gender leads to the belief, expressed by the Chief of the Trade and Adjustment Policy Division in the World Bank, that 'it is relatively easy to retrain and transfer labour originally working in, say, construction or commerce, for employment in the export . . of, say, radios or garments' (Selowsky, 1987). (Elson, 1990, p. 8)

4. The changes identified as of greatest importance were selected after useful discussions with Diane Elson and Frances Stewart.
5. Both these figures are much higher than the national average which in 1982 was 18.55 per cent. The differences result not only from the fact that the Indio Guayas sample is biased towards a low-income population but also because of the 'invisibility' of so much of women's productive work in national accounting.
6. I am grateful to Diego Carrion for his analysis of this issue.
7. One resourceful woman, whose husband would not give permission, persuaded the hospital to accept instead the permission of her mother and her brother, arguing that the two together was equal to that of the husband.
8. These provisional estimates as to the size of each group have been made on the basis of conclusions reached as a result of both qualitative and quantitative research undertaken in August 1988.

References

Barrig, M. and Fort, A. (1987) 'La Ciudad de las Mujeres: Pobladores y Servicios. El Caso de El Augustino', *Women, Low-Income Households and Urban Services Working Papers* (Lima).
BCE (Banco Central de Ecuador) (1986) *Cuentas Nacionales no. 8*, (Quito: Banco Central de Ecuador).
Commonwealth Secretariat (1990) *Engendering Adjustment for the 1990s* (London: Commonwealth Secretariat).
Cornia, G., R. Jolly and F. Stewart (1987) *Adjustment with a Human Face: Vol. 1* (Oxford: Oxford University Press).
Cornia, G., R. Jolly and F. Stewart (1988) *Adjustment with a Human Face: Vol. 2* (Oxford: Oxford University Press).
Demery, L. and T. Addison (1987) *The Alleviation of Poverty Under Structural Adjustment* (Washington: The World Bank).
Elson, D. (1987) 'The Impact of Structural Adjustment on Women: Concepts and Issues', paper presented at Institute of African Alternatives Conference, City University, London.
Elson, D. (1990) 'Male Bias in Macroeconomics: The Case of Structural Adjustment', in D. Elson (ed.), *Male Bias in the Development Process* (Manchester University Press).
Evans, A. (1989) 'Gender Issues in Rural Development Economics', Institute of Development Studies, Discussion Paper no. 254.

Freire, W. (1985) 'La Situacion Nutricional en Ecuador', *Revista Ecuador Debate*, no. 9, CAAP, Quito.
Freire, W. (1988) 'Diagnostico de la situacion nutricional de la poblacion ecuatoriana menor de cinco anos, en 1986, Resultados preliminares', CONADE, Quito.
Jolly, R. (1987) 'Women's Needs and Adjustment Policies in Developing Countries', an address to the Women's Development Group of the OECD, Paris.
Moser, C. O. N. (1981) 'Surviving in the Suburbios', *Bulletin of the Institute of Development Studies*, vol. 12, no. 3.
Moser, C. O. N. (1982) 'A Home of One's Own: Squatter Housing Strategy in Guayaquil, Ecuador', in A. Gilbert (ed.), *Urbanization in Contemporary Latin America* (London: John Wiley).
Moser, C. O. N. (1986) 'Women's Needs in the Urban System: Training Strategies in Gender Aware Planning', in J. Bruce, M. Kohn and M. Schmink (eds), *Learning About Women and Urban Services in Latin America and the Caribbean* (New York: Population Council).
Moser, C. O. N. (1987) 'Mobilization is Women's Work: Struggles for Infrastructure in Guayaquil, Ecuador', in C. Moser and L. Peake (eds), *Women, Human Settlements and Housing* (London: Tavistock).
Moser, C. O. N. (1989) 'Gender Planning in the Third World: Meeting Practical and Strategic Gender Needs', *World Development*, vol. 17, no. 11.
Moser, C. and P. Sollis (1989) *The UNICEF/MSP Primary Health Care Programme, Guayaquil, Ecuador: Evaluation of the Cisne Dos Project from a Community Perspective*, report prepared for UNICEF (New York) mimeo.
Selowsky, M. (1987) 'Adjustment in the 1980s: An Overview of Issues', *Finance and Development*, vol. 24, no. 2, pp. 11–14.
Sollis, P. and C. Moser (1990) 'A Methodological Framework for Analysing the Social Costs of Adjustment at the Micro-Level: The Case of Guayaquil, Ecuador', paper presented at Workshop on the Evaluation of Social Development, Centre for Development Studies, Swansea.
Suarez, J. y col (1987) 'La Situacion de la Salud en el Ecuador 1969–85', MPS-INIMMS-OPS-OMS, Quito.
UNDP (1987) Regional Programme for Africa: Fourth Cycle, *Assessment of Social Dimensions of Structural Adjustment in Sub-Saharan Africa*, paper no. RAF/86/037/A/01/42.
UNICEF (n.d.) *The Invisible Adjustment; Poor Women and the Economic Crisis* (UNICEF Americas and Caribbean Regional Office).
UNICEF (1987) *The State of the World's Children* (New York: UNICEF).
UNICEF (1988) *La Crisis: Efectos en Ninos y Mujeres Ecuatorianos* (Quito, Ecuador).
UNICEF (1989) *The Invisible Adjustment: Poor Women and the Economic Crisis*, second revised edition, UNICEF the Americas and the Caribbean Programme.
World Bank (1984) *Ecuador: An Agenda for Recovery and Sustained Growth* (Washington: The World Bank).
World Bank (1988) *Ecuador: Country Economic Memorandum* (Washington: The World Bank).

6 Structural Adjustment and Gender in Côte d'Ivoire
Winifred Weekes-Vagliani

1 INTRODUCTION

The purpose of this chapter is twofold: to identify and describe the impact of adjustment programmes on education, the informal sector in employment, agriculture, gender issues and family/household structure; and to use an existing household survey to get empirical evidence of these relationships in a specific setting.

The approach is based on the current work programme of the Development Centre and work elsewhere in OECD. In particular, eight case studies[1] on Adjustment and Equitable Growth are being undertaken using a multisectoral analytical framework to analyse countries' economic experience and to provide empirical evidence on the consequences of economic crisis and structural adjustment policy.

The Ivorian Economy

In 1980 Côte d'Ivoire was at the top of the list of sub-Saharan countries with a GNP per capita of 1150 US dollars and in the middle range of low middle-income countries (classification in World Bank Development Report 1982, excluding Gabon). This situation was the result of vigorous growth of GNP since Independence in 1960 of about 7.2 per cent a year. This period was also characterised by an opening-up of the country to foreign capital and workers (Africans and non-Africans). There was a concentration on export agriculture and a great deal of State intervention in the economic sector.

In 1987, Côte d'Ivoire was still among the middle-income countries, but at a lower level with a GNP per capita of 740 US dollars. While these figures cannot adequately portray the reality of living conditions in the country, they do illustrate in a dramatic way that the country's economy has changed and this is due to external and internal factors.

117

Adjustment programmes became necessary to combat a number of macro-economic imbalances in the economy (i.e. balance of payments, budgetary deficits and growing indebtedness). (See introduction to forthcoming OECD publication, *Adjustment and Equitable Growth in Côte d'Ivoire*.) Stabilisation and adjustment measures under the IMF (International Monetary Fund) and the World Bank started in 1981. One major thrust of the adjustment measures was to redress the terms of trade between rural and urban areas with measures in favour of comparative advantage crops: cocoa and coffee.

Other adjustment measures sought to reduce government expenditures amongst which were education at the secondary and university level with the abolition of scholarships and transportation subsidies for students.

Adjustment policies in Côte d'Ivoire have been a rather long and complex process which started shortly after the boom in coffee and cocoa in 1977–8 and have continued to the present. Adjustment has not simply been a reaction to external shocks and imbalances of the 1970s, but it has also been accompanied by favourable and unfavourable climatic shocks in the 1970s and by shocks in the world market during the 1980s (see chronology of events in the Annex). Adjustment has been composed of a set of programmes to redress the financial and economic imbalances at the macro-economic and sectoral levels. If austerity is the key word and the response to large-scale investments, which were at times misdirected, it is also a matter of improving the efficiency of the management of public and parastatal enterprises. Spelling out the social implications of equity and poverty reduction are practically absent from the programmes. At best, they are taken into account by assuming that a resurgence of growth due to a reduction in imbalances will be beneficial to everyone (see ch. 3 of the forthcoming OECD publication).

This short chapter in the present volume indicates how socio-cultural factors including gender and family systems have evolved so that women may be affected differently from men by structural adjustment.

Ivorian Society

There are approximately 50 ethnic groups in Côte d'Ivoire with different family and inheritance systems. Although there has been, and still is, considerable animosity between the various groups, there is no clear-cut hierarchy of ethnic groups and the acculturation pattern present in other countries (Weekes-Vagliani, 1985, Chapter 4) is altogether missing, that is, rejection of one's ethnic identity is unheard of even among the most Westernised urban élites.

Most of Côte d'Ivoire's ethnic groups have migrated to the country within the last three centuries (e.g. Agnis, Baules, Abrons, Atties and other Akan groups). The latter groups broke from the Ashanti in Ghana as a result of family quarrels and internecine wars. The Krous, Bété and the people west of Bandama are from Liberia and the Mandes are from the Nigerian central belt (Weekes-Vagliani, 1985, Chapter 5).

Traditionally, Côte d'Ivoire had no large empire with a strong hierarchical hereditary and politico-military structure such as the Mossi of Upper Volta, Benin, the Hausa or the Ashanti. There were some monarchies (Abron, Indenie), but power was diffused and delegated. In general, the land belonged to the village collectivity (Weekes-Vagliani, 1985, Chapter 6). These village communities, each attached to a tribe, were the most important units and the land owned was divided among extended families.

Ecological and economic phenomena are also linked. In the Northern Savannah half of the country, it is impossible to grow the two main export crops in the Ivorian economy. In the forest areas, the cash crops provided high rural revenues and good regional infrastructure has attracted migrants to the regions with rapid urban development.

Methodology and Approach

Existing anthropological and sociological studies have been used to inform our understanding of the restructured household data which includes information on economic level, education level of the 're-spondents', i.e. the household head (male and female) and the spouse, their children and other relatives living in the household, occupations (informal/formal sector), crops cultivated in the rural areas, presence of family enterprises and management patterns, etc. This combination of existing literature and recent household data provides clues to particular problems in this society to be aware of so that new insights may be revealed with this analysis and will indicate additional ground to be covered.

An examination of per capita expenditures was used to classify each household by economic level, using different poverty thresholds for Abidjan, other cities and the three rural regions: the eastern and western forest (the plantation areas) and the northern savannah which is the poorest region in Côte d'Ivoire.

This analysis responds to the need to investigate with empirical data, the question of how women and children have been affected by recession and adjustment. Careful micro-analysis of the impact on women in developing countries has generally been neglected by macro-economists working on the social dimensions of adjustment. Of the eight case studies being done for the Development Centre, only Côte d'Ivoire and Ghana will include a gender-differentiated analysis. The other researchers preparing the case studies for this project in Latin America, Asia and North Africa believed that the necessary data for such an analysis would be unavailable. Indeed the Côte d'Ivoire and Ghanaian household surveys are somewhat unique for these countries because they include crop data.

In fact, we are confronted with a major methodological problem: in the Ivorian permanent household survey, the household was considered as a unit as far as income and expenditures are involved and was not collected with gender differentiation in mind. (The SDA, Social Dimensions of Adjustment, unit at the World Bank is planning to modify the data sets for the other 20 African countries in which they plan household surveys.) The survey does, nevertheless, yield abundant related data. The problem has been how to make it useful for our purposes. It was necessary to restructure the data tape created for other purposes and to develop new typologies, which could penetrate the dense and complex web of human activity and provide answers to the questions of interest here. For example, a family structure household typology was developed from the household roster.

A distinction must be made, however, between the long-term trends of the economy, i.e. the 'results' of the development strategy to date, and the effects of adjustment programmes. In fact, without knowing what the base-line is for the sub-groups concerned, it is impossible to measure the impact of adjustment. Moreover, development objectives may conflict with the goals of adjustment programmes in regard to specific socio-economic groups, as we shall illustrate below.

Hypothesis

Therefore, an umbrella hypothesis which is in fact relevant apart from the issue of gender differentiation is that those development efforts which are not aimed at redressing the inequalities between specific groups tend to reinforce existing inequalities. The first tabulations were examined with these questions in mind: are historical patterns of gender, economic and regional bias persisting or changing – and what is the direction and intensity of the change, if any?

The first step in describing the links between adjustment and gender is to formulate the policy issues related to certain processes we know to be associated with adjustment and find out if these processes affect men and women differently. It is also evident that the objectives of structural adjustment conflict with one another in terms of who benefits and who loses. Evidence from Côte d'Ivoire suggests that one of the major thrusts of adjustment policies in Côte d'Ivoire is aimed at redressing rural/urban terms of trade so as to increase incomes and living standards in rural areas.

These policies are also directed toward the allocation of resources in the agricultural sector to activities with the highest comparative advantage: cocoa and coffee. At the same time, food-crop self-sufficiency was declared a national priority in the early 1980s. But evidence from the literature[2] shows that women have been deprived of land and time to cultivate food crops for their own income needs. They are still expected to feed themselves and their families with shrinking resources. There is a critical gender dimension to the well-established competition between export and food-crop production. Therefore, adequate understanding of how to achieve adjustment goals and food self-sufficiency clearly requires attention to this dimension.

The special contribution of the approach used in the analysis of this micro-data has been to focus on variables which are important for policy especially for the design of poverty alleviating programmes and policies. The following examples indicate the kinds of 'devices' used in our analysis to reveal the significance of adult women in the household and the persistence of certain traditional patterns of solidarity. For example, the *family structure* typology developed from the household roster distinguished: (i) female-headed households, (ii) nuclear family structure (male-head), (iii) extended nuclear (other relatives present), (iv) polygamous, both conjugal and extended. This typology was essential to increase the visibility of women in the sample and its implications for questions which will address the issue of reaching women in different kinds of households and family situations. The family structure typology also improves our understanding of a phenomenon of particular importance in African situations, namely traditional solidarity for poorer members of one's 'community' or ethnic group. There is evidence from this data that such solidarity persists and increases as economic level decreases in both urban and rural areas, thus indicating a change in the traditional pattern of support which until very recently was from the wealthy to the poor.[3] Similarly, an occupational typology developed to examine the informal sector especially in urban areas also revealed interesting patterns of income level for informal sector occupations for men and women which will be presented below.

The Education Variable

Review of educational reforms implemented following Independence in 1960 indicates that Côte d'Ivoire's efforts to promote education are amongst the most impressive in Africa. The goal of universal primary education for the 6–11 age group by 1986, however, has not been achieved. Public schools are free of charge and particular efforts have been made to increase the number of girls being educated. To identify possible gender or economic bias during recession or adjustment, we examined the proportion of male and female school-age children in school by economic level, in each region.

The purpose of gender-differentiated studies is to show that a consideration for women indeed increases the efficient use of resources so that planners will perceive women as part of the solution to the development problems posed to the whole population, such as, lagging food production, development of the informal sector in urban and rural areas, the improvement of family nutrition, etc.

Following this introduction the major findings from the Ivorian Permanent Household Survey for 1985 and their relationship to socio-cultural variables will be presented in section II. Section III will present examples for specific ethnic groups in Côte d'Ivoire to illustrate a gendered approach to planning during adjustment, and section IV will discuss the policy implications for research and the implementation of programmes.

II   MAJOR FINDINGS FROM THE IVORIAN PERMANENT HOUSEHOLD SURVEY FOR 1985

(a) Education, Development and Adjustment

A number of hypotheses were formulated concerning education, development and adjustment, and were related to the reforms car-

Table 6.1(a)   To show the percentage of each age group having obtained a primary school diploma

Regions	20–24	25–29	30–34	35–39	40+	Total in sample
Abidjan	80.0	81.0	73.0	66.0	36.0	294
Other cities	80.0	72.0	79.0	55.0	77.0	308
Eastern Forest	20.0	42.0	12.0	0.0	1.0	199
Western Forest	*	*	*	*	*	
North	*	*	*	*	*	

Table 6.1(b)   The percentage of female heads of households having obtained a primary school diploma

Regions	20–29	30–39	40+	Total in sample
Abidjan	44.0	64.0	30.0	43
Other cities	85.7	30.0	10.5	36
Eastern Forest	*	*	*	9
Western Forest	0	*	*	7
North	*	*	*	9

* No information available from the survey for most of the sample.

ried out in Côte d'Ivoire after Independence. At that time the three major goals of educational policy in Côte d'Ivoire were social, political and economic. The integration of more than 60 ethnic groups present in Côte d'Ivoire became one of the principal tasks of the educational system. 'Education was also perceived by local leaders as an effective means of ensuring social justice.'[4] Economic development was to be fuelled by education.

Education and Development Strategy
The age group 25–29 in 1985 was born between 1956 and 1960, therefore they were of school-age right after Independence in 1960. The hypothesis that a greater proportion of the men and women under 30 years of age, than older people, would have at least a primary school diploma was generally confirmed. However, the intensity of this relationship (between age and education) was not as great as expected (see Table 6.1). This means that the development strategy and the effort made for universal primary education has not been as successful as it should have been given the enormous budgetary effort made by

Table 6.2(a)   Percentage in each age group with at least a primary school diploma

Regions	Age groups 15–24	25–29	30–34	35–39	40+	Total in sample
Abidjan	63.0	58.0	27.0	40.0	12.0	431
Other cities	48.6	47.0	25.0	0.0	16.0	476
East. For.	32.0	13.0	17.0	25.0	0.0	246
West. For.	19.0	12.0	6.0	0.0	0.0	272
North	6.0	7.0	0.0	10.0	0.0	202
'Other members' – female						
Abidjan	56.7	37.8	38.6	60.0 (a)	4.0	345
Other cities	39.5	24.1	23.0	17.0	10.0	449

(a) *N* = 5.

Table 6.2(b)   To show the percentages obtaining a primary school diploma of single women and wives within the same age groups

Spouses	15–24	25–29	30–34	35–39	40+
Abidjan	20.6	40.0	37.0	26.0	12.0
Other cities	22.50	23.0	11.0	4.0	4.0
Single women					
Abidjan	56.7	37.8	38.6	60.0 (a)	4.0
Other cities	39.5	24.1	23.0	17.0	10.0

(a) *N* = 5.

the Ivorian authorities since Independence.

Adjustment measures which started early in 1981 put a break on educational expenditures. The general economic crisis which preceded adjustment has meant that many middle-class families who could afford private schools before have shifted to public schools thus putting a new burden on government-supported schools.[5] The literature for the 1960s and the 1970s reported economic, regional and gender bias in access to education.[6] The correlation between education and economic level in the 1985 survey data does not have the explanatory power expected, i.e. education level does not increase regularly as economic level increases in all regions. Gender bias in education found in Abidjan, other cities and some rural areas was due to poverty. In other words, the tendencies reported in the literature persist; fewer poor school-age boys are in school than the middle-class or rich ones and fewer poor school-age girls than poor

Table 6.3 Proportion of school-age boys and girls in school by economic level and region

Households according to economic group and region	Percentage of school-age children in school		Number of school-age children	
	Boys	Girls	Boys	Girls
Poor				
Abidjan	68.0*	59.0*	146	137
Other cities	72.0*	58.0*	246	208
East. For.	51.0*	42.0	188	141
West. For.	62.0	60.0	130	131
North	28.0*	18.0*	158	99
Middle-income				
Abidjan	86.0*	80.0*	97	105
Other cities	71.0	76.0*	113	113
East. For.	51.0	55.0	80	62
West. For.	48.0	40.0	126	114
North	43.0	33.0	44	24
Rich				
Abidjan	92.0*	92.0*	103	110
Other Cities	88.0*	92.0*	86	59
East. For.	76.0*	59.0	42	54
West. For.	59.0*	46.0	107	69
North	50.0*	38.0*	20	24
Total				
Abidjan	80.0*	75.6*	346	352
Other Cities	75.0*	68.4*	445	380
East. For.	54.0	48.6	310	257
West. For.	56.0	50.0	363	314
North	33.0*	23.8*	222	147

Note: The differences in percentages may seem important, but they are not always statistically significant. This is due to the small number of cases being compared. In particular the differences between boys and girls are not often significant. Those which are will be marked with an asterisk.
* These are cases in which the differences between boys and girls are not significant.

boys are in school (see Table 6.3). When families have to choose they continue to prefer the education of their sons. This refers to the education of school-age boys and girls today.

As far as the parents of these children are concerned, comparisons between men and women in the same age groups show great differences in education according to gender showing long-term trends of gender bias (see Tables 6.1, 6.2(a) and 6.2(b)). In addition, the findings of the 1985 permanent survey suggest that the reduction in expenditures for secondary and university level education is having a negative impact on young women (15–19 and 20–24 age groups). In fact a smaller proportion of these young women have attained secondary level than women 30–39 years of age in Abidjan, for example. However, regional bias is still the most evident: many fewer school-age girls and boys in the North are in school, than in Abidjan, other cities and the two plantation areas.

(b) Agriculture, Development, Adjustment and Gender

Family Structure and Production Patterns
The working hypothesis used in the examination of family/household structure and the proportion of the land devoted to export and/or food crops was based on the literature. As mentioned earlier, studies have shown that polygamous households devoted more of their land to export crop production rather than food production, therefore we expected to find this pattern in the two forest-plantation areas of Côte d'Ivoire. A corollary to this hypothesis is that there would be a positive correlation between the number of female adults in the household and the proportion of the land used for export crops. This was expected to be the case because households with more than one adult female could ensure both family food provisioning and export crop production with this additional female labour. Table 6.4(a), (b) and (c) show the situations in the two plantation areas (coffee and cocoa – comparative advantage crops) and in the North (cash crops cotton and rice). From 1987 to 1989 there was an implicit subsidy to producers of cocoa and coffee. The government maintained prices to producers while world market prices declined, consequently the stabilisation agency incurred losses (Caisse de stabilisation et de soutien pour les produits agricoles (CSSPPA) – the agency which set the prices for agricultural product in Côte d'Ivoire). In 1989 the government reduced the price paid to producers due to the crisis and the drop in the price of cocoa on the world market.

Although polygamy has increased 10 per cent in the two forest areas since the 1978 agricultural census (see Table 6.5) and polygamous households do devote a little more of their land than the other types of households to export crops, most of the land in both plantation areas and for all family/household types is used in food production. Our hypothesis, therefore, is not confirmed. In the North, about 10 per cent more of the land, in all family types, is used for food production compared to the forest areas.

Table 6.4(a)   Proportion of the land devoted to export and food crops by
type of household: Eastern Forest (land scarce region)

Type of household	Percentage export crops	Percentage food crops	Total number of hectares
Female head	38.5	61.5	109
N=9 Average surface cultivated = 12			
Nuclear + Children	32.7	67.3	254
N=40 Average surface = 6			
Nuclear + Children	42.0	58.0	588
+ Relatives			
N=57 Average surface = 11			
Polygamous +	48.6	51.4	1091
Children + Relatives			
N=64 Average surface = 17			
Other: Brothers, etc.	25.0	75.0	64
N=12 Average surface = 5			

Table 6.4(b)   Proportion of land devoted to export and food crops by
type of household: Western Forest (not land scarce region)

Female Head			
N=7 Average surface = 11	39.7	60.3	78
Nuclear + Children	41.4	58.6	476
N=53 Average surface = 9			
Nuclear + Children	38.6	61.4	945
+ Relatives			
N=93 Average surface = 10			
Polygamous + Children			
+ Relatives	43.4	56.6	1030
N=81 Average surface = 13			
Other: Brothers, etc.	44.9	55.1	49
N=9 Average surface = 5			

However, the survey data does not tell us the rationale behind this
utilisation of family resources; ways to fill in this gap in our knowledge will be suggested in section IV of this chapter.

(c) The Urban Informal Sector

In the last two decades, literature on the informal sector has become
extremely abundant, leading to increased recognition of its importance in the development process. Nevertheless, there is still considerable confusion as to the specific characteristics, scale and role of this

Table 6.4(c)   Proportion of the land devoted to export and food crops by type of household: North (land available but labour scarce region)

Type of household	*Percentage export crops*	*Percentage food crops*	*Total number of hectares*
Female head	25.6	74.4	39
N=9 Average surface = 4			
Nuclear + Children	25.9	74.1	232
N=49 Average surface = 5			
Nuclear + Children	31.4	68.6	338
+ Relatives			
N=62 Average surface = 6			
Polygamous + Children	24.1	75.9	406
+ Relatives			
N=60 Average surface = 7			
Other: Brothers, etc.	18.8	81.2	32
N=13 Average surface = 2			

Table 6.5   Percentage of polygamy in each region

	Percentage households polygamous	*Total households analysed*
Abidjan	13	334
Other cities	21	342
Eastern Forest	34	206
Western Forest	35	287
North	29	223

sector. Moreover, there is a lack of clear policy conclusions to enhance its employment potential; in this regard, no systematic assessment has yet been made of macro policies or their effects on employment.

Among the areas which need examination are the institutional and overall economic framework (economic system, sociocultural factors, level of development and development strategy). Another aspect to be studied are the linkages with the formal sector of the economy, in particular, ways and means to strengthen the complementarity between the two sectors.

Structural Adjustment Measures and Their Impact on Employment: Employment and the Informal Sector
Typical structural adjustment programmes involve some combination

of (a) reduced government expenditures, (b) abolition or significant change in controls, regulations and other 'dirigiste' policies and practices, and (c) encouragement of private sector activities and entrepreneurial income. The impact on employment is typically negative (indeed, sharply negative in certain formerly 'protected' areas such as government or parastatal employment) in the short run, with the hope and expectation that as reforms 'bite' so growth and expanded employment opportunities will follow. More specific impact on the informal sector are measures such as devaluation and government expenditure restraint described below.

For example, abolishing food subsidies apparently has no direct impact on employment. But indirect effects could be very important. In fact we should distinguish between measures which influence employment and revenue and those which affect the standard of living of households in other ways. The impact on women may be indirect in the sense that higher food prices for staples may push more poor women into informal-sector employment to 'make ends meet'. Government expenditure cuts in education and health provision may add to the burdens put on women to generate more income to cover the new costs of these services. The push into the informal sector is due to the lower education levels of women to begin with which may be reinforced by the adjustment measure.

Export industries benefit from devaluation as do import substituting industries, including some informal-sector activities. Urban groups are generally hurt more than rural groups for a number of reasons such as the fact that imports form a greater share of urban consumption than rural consumption.

Government expenditure restraint means *inter alia* government investments are cut back; this has a negative effect on the nontradeables sector such as construction where many unskilled and semi-skilled people work. The resulting reduction in wages and salaries of construction workers and others laid off because of this reduction in government spending reduces demand for goods and services produced by both the formal and informal-sector enterprises. Redundant workers may shift into informal-sector activities, thus increasing the supply of informal-sector goods and services in the face of reduced demand, leading to a possible reduction in income per informal-sector enterprise or person.[7] A reduction in public sector employment often results in a cut in lower echelon personnel which increases urban unemployment, and results in increased informal-sector activities in order to survive.

Informal Sector Characteristics

Anthropological studies and ILO investigative missions in the 1960s and 1970s showed that the formally unemployed were undertaking a wide range of economic activities from small-scale manufacture to provision of services which provided an income, albeit frequently minimal.[8] The term 'informal sector' came to designate this area of economic activity; 'much of the data suggested that women rather than men make up the bulk of those involved in the sector'.[9] However, this gender pattern may be different depending on the geographical region and the range of informal-sector activities engaged in. If this is indeed still found to be the case, then it is clear that policies will have to be specifically designed to benefit women rather than men or even families.

The literature on the informal sector is now vast, and while definitional debates continue to some extent, there is a measure of agreement that it relates to situations governed by (a) informal, market and social relationship based contracts or understandings, (b) small-scale micro-enterprise, and (c) enterprise with low cost per workplace, indeed often avoiding the expense of a fixed workplace. As regards the informal sector and gender issues, the conclusions from a still small, but growing literature can be summarised along the following lines: women workers as a potentially vulnerable group often cluster at the low-income end even of the informal sector. This may be reinforced by social barriers that frustrate entry in other apparently easy entry and relatively lucrative activities.

According to Banerjee[10] the informal/formal dichotomy is not based on a classification of economic activities. It is rather a division between workers according to the nature of the labour contracts under which they work. In a labour-surplus economy, the logic of the market place can be kept at bay for some groups which constitute the formal sector. At the same time, some specially vulnerable groups, like the women workers of India, stagnate in the informal sector and form a pool of cheap labour.

Sheila Allen[11] argues that the widespread, though largely invisible labour of people (mainly women) working for wages in their own homes is an essential part of capitalist production, providing a flexible and cheap form of labour for a wide range of manufacturing industry.

Heyzer[12] lists four factors which interact to explain the concentration of women, particularly married women with young children, in the informal sector. The form this work takes is also the result of these four factors: '(1) the changing requirements of the labour process in different branches of production at certain phases of economic reorganisation, (2) differential labour absorption and the creation of an age-specific female workforce, (3) the ideological assumptions which determine the economic spaces allocated to women and the value placed on female labour power, (4) the close interrelationship between the domestic role of women and their position as specific kinds of wage workers.'

Furthermore Heyzer points out that an examination is needed of the interaction of dominant ideologies and economic processes in the structuring and allocation of very specific economic spaces to women.[13]

Education and schooling are used as screening mechanisms which effectively exclude substantial portions of women from stable employment. As Heyzer points out, 'access to schooling in low-income families is often sex-specific'. As mentioned earlier, it is frequently the male child who continues with his education while the female child drops out to substitute work for schooling, or to reduce the financial cost of schooling within the household unit.

Older married women with few education qualifications are most discriminated against in formal employment. Employers in the formal sector seem to prefer males and young single educated women.

Heyzer also finds that women's informal-sector employment differs from that of men's in a number of ways. Most often their activities in the informal sector are compatible with their reproductive roles, particularly child-rearing, and are often extensions of their domestic responsibilities. They are also concentrated in areas with lesser growth potential. Women may be excluded from sectors which need access to skill acquisition, such as learning on the job.

This is borne out by Abdou Touré's brilliant impressionistic study of informal sector activities in Abidjan (see Table 6.6).

Perhaps what is needed is a typology of characteristics of the informal sector, given the wide range and different levels of activities usually included in this sector. It may be useful to categorise activities as to the physical (finance and infrastructure) and human capital necessary to carry them out. More generally, how are socio-cultural structures or elements thereof related to the social organisation of production in the informal sector?

A typology of informal activities might distinguish three or more types of informal-sector activities:

Table 6.6 Occupations of men and women in the informal sector in Abidjan and other cities

Nationalities	Small-scale (Men) occupations	Small-scale (Women) occupations
Ivorians	car guards, windshield wipers, car washers, auto-mechanics, metal & paint repairers, public 'writers' (for illiterates), hairdressers, aphrodisiac sellers, plastic identity-card makers, car licences, etc., carpenters, floormakers, construction workers, house painters, car parking aids, newspaper sellers, etc.	market women, itinerant market women, attiéké sellers, fried banana sellers, shady go-betweens, dress-makers, hairdressers in open air, foot washers (in the market), maids, cooks, care of children.
Voltaiques	house guards, servants, cooks, launderers, gardeners, horticulturalists, tailors, art street sellers, masons, soft-drink street sellers, bricklayers, brochette sellers, chicken sellers in market, egg sellers.	farmers and market women of their produce (tomatoes, cabbage, salad and corn, etc.).
Maliens	house to house sales, masons, metal workers, construction workers, brick-layers, blacksmith, weighers of men, butchers, auto-mechanics, charcoal sellers, record street sellers, book street sellers, auto-mechanics metal auto-repairs and painters, chair renters (for funerals, baptisms & marriages), bridgebuilders (quick impromptu type).	soap makers, kolanut sellers, brochette sellers, hairdressers in open air, cloth sellers, fresh peeled pineapple sellers.

Guineans	destruction of cars, auto mechanics, radio repairs, wallpaper hangers, market men, musicians (popular orchestras).	hairdressers in open air, fast food preparers, cloth sellers, singers in popular orchestras.
Ghananians	travelling tailors, shoe repairs, apothecary, car washer.	street foods preparers, street prostitutes.
Nigerians	shopkeepers, sellers of various objects in the market, butchers, radio repairs, photographers, weighers of men, auto-mechanics, tyre repairs, poor people's banker, chair renters, barbers, porters, itinerant sellers, itinerant manicure & pedicure, cafe owners, launderers, necklace sellers, buyers & sellers of empty bottles, barbers & circumcision practitioners, egg sellers, fruit sellers, art sellers, itinerant and sedentary sellers of grilled meat, fish cleaners in the port, itinerant poultry sellers, shoemakers.	door to door sellers of beauty products, market women, door to door hairdressers.
Senegalese	cloth sellers, itinerant and sedentary art sellers, jewellery makers, café 'criers', restaurant owners.	restaurant owners, sellers of cloth and dresses.

Source: Abdou Touré *Les petits métiers à Abidjan* (Editions Karthala, Paris, 1985).

- activity with minimal need for physical or human capital (e.g. windshield wipers of cars in Abidjan); (see Table 6.6, informal activities of men and women in Abidjan);
- activity which requires some capital or provision of infrastructure but no schooling (e.g. prepared-food sellers need small amounts of capital to acquire the ingredients of their products, cooking utensils, money to buy fuel, etc.);
- activity which has the ability to grow and develop through skill acquisition, expansion of the enterprise, scope for investment, etc.;
- and at the edge of the informal sector, high human and physical capital necessary (e.g. sub-contracting in manufacturing, need for machines and skilled personnel).

Another typology for characterising the informal sector might indicate how such a mixed bag of activities can be 'sorted into those that bear a direct or indirect relationship to international markets and those that have only the most tenuous connection'.[14]

For instance, while some view the urban informal sector as consisting of free-entry jobs with low rates of pay from which people seek to escape into higher-paying positions at the first opportunity, others point to the voluntary movement of workers from the formal sector into jobs in the informal sector which are relatively high paying and which require skills and/or financial capital and which therefore are *not* free-entry.

Gender Issues and Other Considerations

Conventional economics views the household as a homogeneous unit in which resources and income are shared equally by all family members. Available evidence, however, suggests that intrahousehold distribution of resources and income vary by sex and age. There are also differences in the way women use available resources. Most of women's expenditures go back into the household for food and other necessities. Men are reported to spend increased income on consumer goods even when a greater contribution to the family's food supplies would be essential. But even where there is a close integration of women's and men's contribution to urban and rural livelihoods, it would be a mistake to see women and men within the household as a homogeneous human resource perfectly substitutable and experiencing the same opportunity costs and gains in agricultural and urban change.

An analysis of labour markets could reveal effects on women. Labour markets may impose on poor men and women interlocking and cumulative disadvantage. Discrimination in access to skills, lack of mobility and poor health may determine low wage rates for the poor and the type of employment they have.

Gender roles are culture specific; therefore, a gender-differentiated analysis includes knowledge of and respect for indigenous socio-cultural values. There must be an informed understanding of the people concerned. An effort must be made to understand what role family systems and specific cultures play in perpetuating patterns of behaviour which deprive women of full participation in development.

Ethnic origin imposes and determines certain work patterns (e.g. the sexual division of labour). The success of certain adjustment measures may depend on taking these patterns into account.

In order to conduct such gender-differentiated analysis, information is needed about socio-cultural structures, including family systems, which determine:

• relations of economic exchange within households;
• gender division of labour in different tasks and occupations;
• the way different sources of cash income are earmarked (and by whom) for different requirements (for household consumption and other expenditures).

More generally, how are socio-cultural structures or elements thereof influenced by adjustment measures? How are the sub-groups (defined by their socio-economic and demographic characteristics, i.e. age, sex and civil status) affected by adjustment programmes? And what is the relationship of sex, age, and household composition to employment in the informal sector?

Our concern in discovering the links between demographic characteristics of households and poverty is to see if certain sub-groups in the population can be identified in a way that we can see the effects of adjustment programmes on the welfare of these groups. The effects of these programmes may not always be traceable; however, identification of the sub-groups is useful because it points to a dimension of poverty which may otherwise be forgotten. In addition this identification may indicate other measures which must be taken to alleviate poverty in these groups.

This analysis would provide circumstantial evidence in that we cannot say without knowing the rationale behind decisions to change consumption/production patterns, whether participation in the informal sector is in response to specific adjustment measures or rather the result of cumulative causation – a chain of events which has as a result an increase in the informal sector and the number of women employed there. For example, adjustment measures cut government expenditures and the number of jobs under formal government employment, which may in turn increase the number of people in the informal sector, especially women and young people.

The Informal Sector in Urban Côte d'Ivoire
Vijverberg (Weekes-Vagliani, 1989, p. 96) reports that '23.1 per cent of all male workers and 54.9 per cent of all female workers residing in Abidjan and other urban areas are engaged in non-agricultural self-employment'. As Vijverberg also points out, without a better understanding of the role of non-agricultural self-employment, government policy in regard to the self-employed cannot provide the proper incentives (Weekes-Vagliani, 1989, p. 97).

While Oudin ('Population et emploi non structuré en Côte d'Ivoire', brochure n° 51, AMIRA, Paris, juin 1986, p. 2) analyses data for the 1970 to 1980 period just before adjustment programmes began to be implemented, he uses demographic data and analysis of information on employment in enterprises to indicate long-term tendencies in the growth of the informal sector in urban areas of Côte d'Ivoire. According to Oudin (p. 6) informal street and market activities employ most of the people in this sector in Ivorian cities, as well as in the rest of Africa. However, a significant part of the informal sector is located in people's homes. In regard to women in this sector, as pointed out above and borne out in the 1985 survey, the majority are at the lower end of the informal sector (90 per cent of the poor women; see Table 6.7). In Côte d'Ivoire and especially in cities, women were and still are mostly traders, market women or street sellers of prepared foods near offices and factories, as well as selling cooked foods in their own homes (Oudin, 1986, p 29 and Table 6.6).

Oudin concludes from data from 1975 to 1980 (Oudin, 1986 p. 11) and population projections beyond 1980, in addition to statistics on modern enterprises, that without a doubt there has been an acceleration in the growth of informal-sector activities. These activities are responsible for half the jobs created between 1975 and 1980. The majority of these new 'jobs' increase the number of people working in itinerant activities.

One of the problems in using the concepts of employment in

Table 6.7   The proportion of men and women at each economic level in the informal sector

Economic level in household	Abidjan		Other cities	
	Men	*Women*	*Men*	*Women*
Poor	56.0	90.0	36.0°	56.0
Middle-income	42.0	72.0	38.0°°	47.0
Rich	25.0	29.0	32.0	54.0

° 43 per cent of the poor men are in agriculture in other cities.
°° 28 per cent of middle-income men are in agriculture in other cities.

referring to informal activities is that they apply to individuals. However, the behaviour of an individual is determined by his or her membership of a family, residential or lineage group, so that this activity may be motivated by what is advantageous to the group. The current concept of employment ignores this reality and only retains the individual's activity (Oudin, 1989, pp 23–24).

The Informal Sector and the 1985 Permanent Household Survey
Incomes in the informal sector vary a great deal for men and women. Table 6.7 shows the proportion of men and women in the informal sector at each economic level; the percentage of rich men and women in the informal sector in Abidjan and other cities deserves our attention.

The fact that about one-quarter of the rich men and women in Abidjan are in the informal sector and that over half of the rich women in other cities also work in this sector can be interpreted in the light of the typology of the informal sector outlined above and the information on the experience of the women in one ethnic group which will be presented in section III below. In addition, our perception of the significance of the management patterns of family enterprises will be informed by the socio-cultural data as to who appropriates the income from joint labour by men and women and presented below in the following section.

III ADJUSTMENT AND A GENDERED SOCIO-CULTURAL APPROACH TO PLANNING IN CÔTE D'IVOIRE

(a) Socio-Cultural Background

A literature review of family systems in Côte d'Ivoire[15] emphasises economic autonomy for women; in addition, the coping mechanisms for survival in an adjustment period increase the economic responsibilities of women. The different ethnic groups[16] present in Côte d'Ivoire can be categorised according to linguistic criteria into five big groups, which inhabit certain geographical areas.

The family structures of these different groups are very varied. Generally the main distinctions can be described in the following manner: family systems of patrilineal, matrilineal or bilineal descent. These patterns which have most relevance in rural areas, nevertheless persist in urban areas. Generally, it is a fair comment to say that the household cannot be seen as a corporately producing or consuming unit for analytical purposes. One pattern is especially prevalent in systems of matrilineal and bilineal descent. In these families, there is no family/household budget, but two parallel incomes in the same household. Husbands' and wives' incomes are not shared but each is responsible for certain expenditures. In systems of patrilineal descent, the male head has greater control over all the income in the household. This financial autonomy for women in family systems of matrilineal and bilineal descent has important policy implications because the increase in women's incomes is a greater guarantee for improved family nutrition.[17] Matrilineal or bilineal systems concern the majority of the population, and even in patrilineal groups women benefit from a certain growing autonomy due to their close ties to their family of origin.

The general evolution of family structure today has led to the greater economic isolation of women. The dissolution of lineage ties and the traditional system of rights and obligations is responsible for this isolation, especially in matrilineal societies. Simultaneously with this isolation, the economic responsibilities of women are increasing, especially in matrilineal societies.

(b) The Adioukrou Group and the Production of Attiéké (Ground Cassava Meal)

In the previous section an allusion was made to the experience of the Adioukrou ethnic group and the production of ground cassava meal (attiéké). The example presented here shows the importance of taking socio-cultural and gender issues into consideration when informal sector activities are to be enhanced and facilitated.

The Adioukrou ethnic group is one of the groups which inhabits the salt-water lakes area in southern Côte d'Ivoire. In the past, this group was the economic link between other ethnic groups in the north and the south.

The family system of the Adioukrou is bilineal, but matrilineal ties predominate in many instances. The latter system means that children belong to their mother's lineage; however, the family residence is patrilocal and the father has authority over his own children under his roof, but the maternal uncle has the power to 'loan out' these children. In principal a young man begins his life dependent on his father, with whom he works, but one day he will inherit from his maternal uncle, with whom he often resides at a later stage of his life. Therefore, each individual belongs to two lineages and can claim his adherence to either one or both according to his interests.

The Resources of the Adioukrou Group and the Consequences of the Diffusion of Commercial Crops on the Life of the Women of this Group
The Adioukrou group traditionally cultivate palms. The traditional communal palm lands of this group are controlled by the men. Alongside this main 'lineage' crop, food crops are grown and the profits from this production is controlled by women, especially cassava, yams, peanuts and condiments.

After Independence, the number of coffee and cocoa plantations increased rapidly in Adioukrou country; export crop cultivation overtook food production and the Adioukrou planters began to accumulate wealth. The development of these cash crops affected family systems in general and particularly the lives of women. The legal arrangements made in the new Independence era established patrilineal inheritance of land which has made the Adioukrou more bilineal. However, customary inheritance practices still persist and the traditional matrilineal inheritance practices predominate. But these matrilineal ties create conflictual relationships in this transitional period. The newly wealthy father-planters tend to want to leave the cultivation rights to the land to their sons and thus tend to forget their traditional obligations to their nephews.

With the development of cash crops, women have been deprived of their traditional access to land and the possibility of intercropping permitted by the traditional production of palms. Thus changes in traditional practices preceded adjustment. For example, the women of the Adioukrou (Akan group) traditionally cultivated palms for palm oil. The parastatal SODEPALM deprived them of their traditional cultivation and processing practices, so they have turned to producing attiéké (cassava meal) which is a staple of this ethnic group. The production and sale of attiéké is of double interest: it responds to a new urban need and it brings in personal income. They sell attiéké especially to the men of their ethnic group in Abidjan.

The new economic situation created was to the disadvantage of the women, so they turned to this new initiative. But cassava, a traditional crop, became a commercial crop and as such brought about 'commercial' exchanges between women, the producers of attiéké, and men (their spouses, uncles and brothers), the 'owners' of the land on which cassava is grown.

Men and women cultivate cassava together, then the men sell the harvest to the women who produce the attiéké and in turn control the profits from the sale of attiéké. But this 'solution' to their needs for resources to assume their family obligations (feeding the family including their husbands, and school fees for their children) is full of difficulties and problems at a number of levels including production and commercialisation. The production factor comprises the problem of available land, long hard hours of physical labour, and the costs of labour (if they need to hire someone to help cultivate the land). Commercialisation is complicated by the location of the market for attiéké which is essentially sold in urban markets such as Treichville in Abidjan. The women resort to 'middle-men', wholesalers, some of whom are also Adioukrou literate women (the wealthy women in the informal sector referred to above). These 'middle-men' make an enormous profit on the resale of attiéké, reducing the benefits to the producers of attiéké to absurdly low levels.

However, the main need of the poor women attiéké producers is for labour-saving technology so that they could devote the time saved to diversifying their other food production. The Ivorian government has made an effort to support attiéké production but the various 'solutions' proposed have failed to resolve the organisational problems related to this activity.

In any case, according to the economic rationale of traditional societies in Côte d'Ivoire, as cassava becomes a commercial crop – a producer of wealth – it will rapidly be monopolised by men; who, as mentioned earlier, hold the land and can easily control cassava production. The resistance to the feminisation of property rights would be enormous, even in matrilineal territory. According to A. Traoré,[18] this process of appropriation of cassava by men has already begun in certain localities of Adioukrou country.

However, the Ivorian government has intervened in favour of women and the rights to land recently.[19] The innovative role of the government in planning for long-term adjustment and increased food production would be to build on the traditional economic autonomy of women in food production. Government or private intervention could facilitate access to the necessary technology and take measures to facilitate the marketing of attiéké, which would give the benefits to the initial producers instead of middle-men and women.

(c) **Gender Management Patterns in Non-Agricultural Family Enterprises and Socio-Cultural Data**

The 1985 Ivorian Permanent Household Survey provides data on the management patterns in family enterprises and we have examined these patterns in the light of the socio-cultural data available. These management patterns are of interest to our problematic for two reasons:

1. It would be interesting to know if the same socio-cultural rules operate for these enterprises as for food and export crop production, in regard to who appropriates the income. An attentive reading of the appropriation patterns in agriculture indicates that if men and women work together on a crop, the men appropriate the income. If a woman works alone or with other women she/they control the income from this activity.
2. Poor families may have different gender management patterns than middle-income and rich families because the women in the latter classes (at least in cities) may have access to work in the formal private sector or in government/employment, given their education level, mentioned above.

Unfortunately, the survey data does not indicate who appropriates the income from family enterprises, but programmes to encourage small family enterprises should keep these socio-cultural patterns in mind to ensure that poor women are the actors *and* the beneficiaries of initiatives to encourage such undertakings.

The proportion of households with a non-agricultural enterprise diminishes as economic level increases in Abidjan: 65 per cent of the poor, 45 per cent of the middle-income but only 29 per cent of the wealthy have these enterprises. In other cities, the poor and the middle-income are similar: about 55 per cent of each have these enterprises compared to 36 per cent of the wealthy. In the eastern forest, the oldest plantation area in Côte d'Ivoire, it is the opposite: the proportion of households with enterprises increases with economic level; in the two other rural areas the proportion does not vary according to economic level.

More than half of these enterprises in all regions, except the North, are managed by one or more women in the same household. In Abidjan, only 10 per cent of the enterprises in the rich households are managed by a man and a woman; in other cities there is practically no difference in management patterns according to economic level. In the three rural areas about one-quarter of the enterprises in the rich households are managed by a man and a woman.

IV   POLICY IMPLICATIONS FOR RESEARCH AND IMPLEMENTATION OF PROGRAMMES

There must be a concerted threefold effort to improve our ability to do gender-differentiated analysis and to get gender issues into basic macro-planning. This includes: data collection methods; sample composition; and type of data. Data collection should get information on the separate contributions of men and women (not on the household as a unit) and sample composition should include enough people in the categories which are important for policy.[20] Attention must also be paid to the type of information sought in order to get dynamics into what is a static picture, no matter how kaleidoscopic, of one point in time.

For example, although there are not many female-headed households in the Ivorian Permanent Household Survey for 1985, there is every reason to believe that the number of this type of household is increasing. The socio-cultural data indicated marital conflict due to family systems in transition; these conflicts may result in an increase in female-headed households. The geographic distribution of these households and their particular characteristics need special attention. We know from the Ivorian survey that they exist at all economic levels in each region.[21]

Cultures move as a whole: if one of the components is changed then the others are also likely to change in consequence. The traditional economic autonomy of Senoufo, Baoulé[22] and other women is obviously rooted in these systems of family formation. If they are deprived of this autonomy other features of the system such as crop cultivation patterns and food production may suffer, with negative results for development. Development programmes – and in this sense long-term structural adjustment programmes can be equated with development[23] – should encourage and strengthen the traditional economic autonomy of Ivorian women.

Too often 'modernisation' has decreased the capacity of women to provide for themselves and their families, by gearing agricultural extension work and other activities to men instead of providing realistic incentives to both men and women.

The household survey and the socio-cultural data indicate the need to develop programmes which will deal with the problems in their totality, with catalytic entry points that involve the different family members and respect the division of labour and the rationale behind the utilisation of family resources that the people themselves have decided.

However, the complexity of the situation and the rapid changes taking place argue against studies which are too global in scale and where the results are too delayed or far removed for policy-makers to attack the problems in the time available. Action research is needed,[24] small-scale and on the spot. The development problems should be recognised at the national and sectoral level, but the possible solutions to the problems must also take into account the situation at the local level.

ANNEX: CHRONOLOGY OF EVENTS

Principal Events and Measures Taken Between 1977 and 1987

1977–8: Boom in world prices for coffee and cocoa.
1978–9: First austerity measures in the form of annulling or postponing investments. Fiscal measures (increase in value added tax, taxes on tobacco and fuel).
1979: Second oil shock.
1980: The International Agreement on Coffee introduced export quotas.
1981: Adoption of an austerity current expenditure budget (preceding the stabilisation and adjustment programmes sponsored by the IMF and the World Bank – the same year) with limitation on an increase in expenditures of up to 5 per cent in current francs and the following specific measures:

– A 10 per cent increase in the price of petrol.
– Increase in rates:

(a) electricity: + 7.5 per cent
(b) trains: + 9 per cent for passengers
                          + 11 per cent for merchandise
(c) water: + 8.3 and 5.3 per cent in 2 stages
(d) transportation: SOTRA (Société de transport) + 25 per
                          cent; Air Ivoire + 15 per cent
(e) rice: increase in consumer price of 10 per cent;
                          price paid to producers decrease 20 per
                          cent.

– Salary measures: alignment of salaries of public agencies with the
civil service salaries which had been frozen.

1981:   Record harvest with growth in the primary sector of 7.5 per cent.
1981:   Agreements with the IMF (January 1981) on a stabilisation pro-
         gramme between 1981 and 1983 as indicative of a broader mechan-
         ism of the Extended financial facility covering 485 million dollars of
         Special Drawing Rights (SDR) and with the World Bank (Decem-
         ber 1981) on a Structural Adjustment Loan (SAL, of 150 million
         dollars). At the macro-economic management level, these two
         agreements (followed by several agreements which were confirmed
         between 1984 and 1988 and SAL II in 1983 and SAL III 1986)
         overlapping with the following objectives:

         – Reinforcing budgetary discipline and the consolidation of public
         finances including the setting-up of a financial co-ordination and
         control committee for investments.
         – The limitation of foreign borrowing.
         – The limitation of internal credit, including the public sector.
         – At the level of public enterprises and sectoral policies, numerous
         measures were envisaged in SAL I and in part prolonged in SAL
         II and III. We summarise here those measures which were
         actually implemented.

         Management of public enterprises: Closing down of 16 public enter-
         prises (between 1978 and 1982), control of domestic and foreign
         borrowing, auditing of management practices, preparation of reha-
         bilitation plans, implementation of an increase in tariffs, reorganisa-
         tion of the finances of the three major public enterprises in the
         agricultural sector (including paying up arrears).

         Agricultural policy: Incentives for export crops and rice by an
         increase in the price to producers (between 1981 and 1984) for:
         coffee and cocoa (+ 33 per cent) cotton (+ 43 per cent – but at the
         same time abolition of the subsidies for fertilisers used for cotton),
         an increase to small producers of palm oil (+ 35 per cent) rice
         paddy (+ 33 per cent accompanied by an increase in the price of
         rice for consumers of 23 per cent). For small rubber producers – the
         price was put in line with world prices. Privatisation of public
         activities for the processing and marketing of rice.

1982:   Increase of 10 per cent in the minimum wage in the private and semi-public sectors; a freeze in the ceilings for the calculation of social coverage.

1983:   Severe drought.
1984:   Restructuring of foreign debt with the Paris and London Clubs.
1984–5: Confirmation or broadening of austerity measures:

- Limitation of current expenditures to an increase of 1 per cent in 1983 in current francs.
- Reduction in public investment expenditures in real terms for the fourth consecutive year.
- Reduction of recruitment of civil servants (a decrease in the number of new students in schools training for the public sector from 4132 to 2782).
- Reduction of the number of scholarships for higher education of 50 per cent (from 3800 to about 1900) and a 30 per cent decrease for the secondary level (from 58 000 to 41 000).
- Continuation of the freeze in wages in the public sector for the third year.
- Reduction in the housing subsidies given to civil servants and sale of public sector apartments to individuals.

Commercial and industrial policies

- Promulgation of a revised commercial law for investments (1984).
- Increase of reference values on which export taxes for coffee and cocoa were based.
- Increase in customs duties and the specific tax on fuel.
- First phase of customs and tariff reforms – assuring effective protection of approximately 40 per cent for products which represent more than 80 per cent of industrial value added.
- Adoption of a system of export subsidies based on the value-added (applied only 1987) and replacement of quantitative restrictions on imports by a temporary increase in import taxes.
- Increase of 25 per cent in the rates for electricity and water and for public transportation in Abidjan.
- Increase in the price of bread (+ 7 per cent) and petrol (+ 8 per cent).

1986:   Record harvest of cocoa, an increase of 25 per cent in export revenues from cocoa.
1987:   Falling world prices for coffee which caused a decrease in export revenues from coffee of 40 per cent.
          Suppression of interest payments to creditors of the Paris and London Clubs. Confronted with the financial crisis, increase in the customs duties for products bringing effective protection rate to 52 per cent.

Notes and References

1. This work is based on the preparation for the case study of Côte d'Ivoire as a member of a team of researchers. A meeting was held at the Development Centre, 28 and 29 January 1988, where introductory papers on Africa (Côte d'Ivoire, Ghana, Morocco and Egypt), on Latin America (Chile and Ecuador), and on Asia (Srilanka and Indonesia) were presented. A seminar on the Informal Sector Revisited was held at the Development Centre 7–9 September 1988. A seminar was held 18 April 1988. Two background documents were prepared and discussed at the seminar by the International Centre for Research on Women (ICRW, Washington D.C.): Susan Joekes, Margaret Lycette, Lisa McGowan and Karen Searle, 'Women and Structural Adjustment', Part I: 'A Summary of the Issues', prepared for the meeting of the Women in Development Expert Group of the OECD Development Assistance Committee, Paris, 18 April 1988 (ICRW, Washington D.C.); and Part II: 'Technical Document'.

2. See J. Bisilliat and M. Fieloux, *Femmes du Tiers-Monde* (Le Sycomore, Paris 1983). M. Auge, 'Statut, pouvoir et richesse: relations de dépendance et rapports de production dans la société alladian', *Cahiers d'études africaines*, vol. IX, pp. 461–81 (1969). J. Dey, *Système de riziculture* (FAO, Rome, 1983). M. Etienne, 'Rapports de sexe et de classe et mobilité socio-économique chez les Baoulé (Côte d'Ivoire)', *Anthropologie et Société*, vol. II, no. 1, pp. 71–94 (1987). A. Traoré, *L'accès des femmes ivoiriennes aux ressources. Les femmes et la terre en pays Adioukrou* (BIT, Geneva, 1981). W. Weekes-Vagliani, *Actors and Institutions in the Food Chain: The Case of the Ivory Coast*, Development Centre papers (OECD, 1985).

3. J. Bisilliat and M. Fieloux, *Femmes du Tiers-Monde* (Le Sycomore, Paris, 1983). Aminata Traoré et Philippe Antoine, 'Croissance économique et modèles familiaux en Côte d'Ivoire', in *Femmes et politiques alimentaires*, Actes du séminaire international ORSTOM-CIE, 14–18 janvier 1985 (Paris, ORSTOM, 1985) p. 441. François Régis Mahieu, 'African Micro Economy under Rights and Obligations', miméo, Faculté des Sciences Economiques, Abidjan, June 1988.

4. Torsten Husen and T. Neville Postlethwaite (editors-in-chief) *The International Encyclopedia of Education: Research and Studies*, vol. 5, I–L (Pergamon Press, 1985) pp. 2753–9 (Ivory Coast: System of Education by P. T. Seya) p. 2753.

5. Mr Gbayoro, Ministry of Plan, Côte d'Ivoire, personal communication, September 1989.

6. Cahiers Formation Emploi, 'Emploi et formation des femmes en Côte d'Ivoire', nos 3 and 4, 1986, Office National de Formation Profession-nelle, Abidjan. Remi Clignet and Philip Foster, *The Fortunate Few: A Study of Secondary Schools and Students in the Ivory Coast* (Northwestern University Press, 1966). Marie Eliou, 'Scolarisation et promotion féminines en Afrique francophone: (Côte d'Ivoire, Haute-Volta, Sénégal)', in *International Review of Education*, XIX/1973/1. Special number: 'The Education of Women'.

7. Ron Hood, Judith McGuire and Martha Starr, 'The Socioeconomic Impact of Macroeconomic Adjustment', Center for Development Technology International Science and Technology Institute, January 1988. This study was commissioned by PPC/PDPR/RP(USAID), p. ii.

8. Kate Young, Preface to 'Women and the Informal Sector', *IDS Bulletin*, vol. 12, no. 3 (July 1981).

9. Ibid.

10. Nirmala Banerjee, 'The Weakest Link', *IDS Bulletin*, ibid, pp. 36–40.

11. Sheila Allen, 'Invisible Threads', *IDS Bulletin*, ibid, pp. 41–7.

12. Noeleen Heyzer, 'Towards a Framework of Analysis', *IDS*, ibid, pp. 3–7.

13. Ibid, p. 3.

14. Susan Joekes, *Women in the World Economy*, an INSTRAW study (International Research and Training Institute for the Advancement of Women) (New York and Oxford: Oxford University Press, 1987).

15. Odile Vincent, 'Les Structures Familiales en Côte d'Ivoire', review of the literature, prepared for the Development Centre, July 1988.

16. The members of the same ethnic group have a common origin and form a homogeneous cultural and political entity. The degree of this homogeneity varies with each group.

17. Eric Thorbecke *et al.*, personal communication concerning a study conducted in Kenya which studied the food expenditure patterns of female-headed households compared to those headed by men. They found that the women spent more on food than men who headed households at the same economic level. The same pattern is present in the 1985 Ivorian Household Survey.

18. A. Traoré, *L'accès des femmes . . .* (1981) (see note 2 above).

19. Gbayoro, personal communication (see note 5 above); and FAO, 'Projet de Développement Nord-est: Etude Agroéconomique et Socio-économique: an identification of problems of the First Phase of the project' (1988).

20. For example, there are only 43 women-headed households out of 334 in Abidjan, 35 rule 342 in other cities 9, 7, and 9 in the three rural regions (Eastern forest, Western forest and North respectively).

21. See Odile Frank, 'The Childbearing Family in Sub-Saharan Africa: Structure, Fertility and the Future', paper prepared for joint Population Council/International Center for Research on Women Seminar Series on the Determinants and Consequences of Female-Headed Households, October 1988, for ways in which culture can influence demographic behaviour using the 1986 Ivorian Permanent Household Survey.

22. For the Senoufo ethnic group, see J. Dey, *Système de riziculture* (see note 2 above); SEDES, 'Région de Korhogo: Etude de Développement socio-économique', Paris, 1965; and Zempleni, various works. For the Baoulé ethnic group, consult: J. P. Chauveau, 'Notes sur l'histoire économique et sociale de la région de Kokumbo (Baoulé sud, Côte d'Ivoire)' (ORSTOM, Paris, 1979); M. Etienne (note 2 above); and P. Etienne, 'Le fait villageois Baoulé', in *Communautés rurales et paysanneries tropicales* (ORSTOM, Paris, 1976).

23. Cf. Paul Streeten, 'Structural Adjustment: A Survey of the Issues and

Options', *World Development*, vol. 15, no. 12 (1987) pp. 1469–82.
24. See Ingrid Palmer, 'Women's Issues and Project Appraisal', in *Rapid Rural Appraisal, IDS Bulletin*, vol. 12, no. 4 (October 1981) pp. 32–9.

Bibliography

Ancey, G. (1970) 'L'influence d'un centre urbain sur la zone rurale environnante. L'exemple de Bouaké-Brobo (Côte d'Ivoire)', *Cahiers ORSTOM, série science humaines*, vol. VII, no. 4, pp. 49–78.

Atlas de Côte d'Ivoire (s.d.) Abidjan, Ministère du Plan de Côte d'Ivoire (ORSTOM).

Atlas de Côte d'Ivoire (1983) (Ed. Jeune Afrique, Paris).

Auge, M. (1969) 'Status, pouvoir et richesse: relations de dépendance et rapports de production dans la société alladian', *Cahiers d'études africaines*, vol. IX, pp. 461–81.

Berron, H. (1981) *Tradition et modernisme en pays lagunaires de Côte d'Ivoire* (Gan: Ophrys).

Binet, J. (1979) 'La famille africaine', *Etudes scientifiques*, Septembre–Décembre, Le Caire, Editions et publications des pères Jésuites.

Bisilliat, J. and M. Fieloux (1983) *Femmes du Tiers-Monde* (Paris: Le Sycomore).

Blanc-Pamard, C. (1979) *Un jeu écologique différentiel: les communautés rurales du contact forêt-savane au fond du 'V Baoulé' Côte d'Ivoire* (Paris: ORSTOM).

Ceccaldi, P. (1974) *Essai de nomenclature des populations, langues et dialectes de Côte d'Ivoire* (Paris: Centre d'Etudes Africaines).

Chauveau, J. P. (1979) *Notes sur l'histoire économique et sociale de la région de Kokumbo* (Baoulé sud. Côte d'Ivoire) (Paris: ORSTOM).

Clignet, R. (1963) 'Tradition et évolution de la vie familiale en Côte d'Ivoire', Paris, Texte dactylographié, thèse de 3rd cycle.

Coulibaly, B. (1984) 'Impacts socio-économiques du projet nord-est et des forages sur les activités de la femme', Mémoire de fin d'études d'agronomie approfondie, CIDT, Ministère de l'agriculture, ENSA, Montpellier.

Deluz, A. (1970) *Organisation sociale et tradition orale. les Gouro de Côte d'Ivoire* (Paris-La Haye: Mouton).

Dey, J. (1983) 'Système de riziculture: Etude de cas concernant la riziculture pluviale stricte et la riziculture de bas-fonds marécageux' (Rome: FAO).

Dozon, J. P. (1979) 'Impasse et contradictions d'une société de développement: l'exemple de l'operatin "Riziculture irriguée en Côte d'Ivoire"', *Cahiers ORSTOM, série sciences humaines*, vol. XVI, no. 1–2.

Dozon, J. P. (1985) *La Société Bété: histoire d'une éthnie de Côte d'Ivoire* (Paris: karthala-ORSTOM).

Dozon, J. P. (1986) 'En Afrique. La famille à la croisée des chemins', in A. Burguière, C. Klapisch-Wuber, M. Ségalen and F. Zonabend (eds), *Histoire de la famille* (Paris: Armand Colin, T. II).

Etienne, M. (1987) 'Rapports de sexe et de classe et mobilité socio-économique chez les Baoulé (Côte d'Ivoire)', *Anthropologie et société*, vol. II, no. 1, pp. 71–94.

Etienne, P. (1976) 'Le fait villageois Baoulé', in *Communautés rurales et paysanneries tropicales* (Paris: ORSTOM).

Evans-Pritchard, E. E. (1971) (1965). *La femme dans les sociétés primitives, et autres essais d'antropologie sociale* (Paris: PUF).

Fieloux, M. (1980) *Les sentiers de la nuits. Les migrations rurales Lobi de la Haute-Volta ver la Côte d'Ivoire* (Paris: ORSTOM).

Janvier, G. (1973) *Bibliographie de la Côte d'Ivoire*, T.II: Sciences de l'homme (Abidjan: Université d'Abidjan).

Kacou, M. H. (1987) 'Commerce féminins à Abidjan', Communautés, *Archives de sciences sociales de la coopération et du developpement*, Janvier-Mars, pp. 78–86.

Meillassoux, C. (1964) *Anthropologie économique des Gouro de Côte d'Ivoire. De l'économie de subsistance à l'agriculture commerciale* (Paris-La Haye: Mouton).

Monnier, Y. (1969) 'Il était une fois à Ayérémou . . . un village du sud-baoule, *Annales de l'Université d'Abidjan'*, Série G, T.I., fasc. I.

O.E.C.D. (Forthcoming) 'Adjustment and Equitable Growth in Côte d'Ivoire', Development Centre Case Study, OECD, Paris.

Osmont, T. (1978) 'Généalogies familiales et stratégies de promotion sociale', Formation et destructuration des familles en milieu urbain; formation des groupes en ville. Rapport d'activité 1978–1979. Mission de la recherche urbaine. EHESS: 146–167.

Oudin, X. (1986) *Population et emploi non structuré en Côte d'Ivoire*, Paris brochure No. 51, AMIRA.

Paulme, D. (1962) *Une société de Côte d'Ivoire hier et aujourd'hui, les Bété* (Paris-La haye: Mouton).

Rambaud, C. (1980) *Elements sur l'emploi féminin et la formation des femmes en Côte d'Ivoire* (Abidjan: Ministère de la condition féminine).

Rambaud, C. (1980) *Les femmes et le circuit de l'attiéké en Côte d'Ivoire* (Abidjan: Ministère de la condition féminine).

Rambaud, C. (1981) *La restauration de rue dans les zones industrielles et tertiaires modernes d'Abidjan* (Texte dactylo).

S.E.D.E.S. (1965) *Région de Korhogo. Étude de développement socio-économique* (Paris).

De The, M. P. (1968) 'Participation féminine au développement rural dans la région de Bouaké', République de Côte d'Ivoire, Ministére du Plan, Abidjan.

Toure, A. (1985) *Les petits métiers à Abidjan. L'imagination au secours de la 'conjoncture'* (Paris: Karthala).

Traore, A. (1981) *L'accés des femmes ivoiriennes aux ressources. Les femmes et la terre en pays Adioukrou* (Genève: BIT).

Weekes-Vagliani, W. (1980) *Women in Development: At the Right Time for The Right Reasons* (Paris: Development Centre Study).

Weekes-Vagliani, W. (1985) *Actors and Institutions in the Food Chain: The Case of the Ivory Coast* (Paris: Development Centre Papers).

Weekes-Vagliani, W. (1985) *The Integration of Women in Development Projects* (OECD Development Centre Papers).

7 Women, Authoritarianism and Market Liberalisation in Chile, 1973–89

Georgina Waylen*

INTRODUCTION

This chapter will examine the impact of market liberalisation (ML) on women in Chile after the imposition of a military government in 1973. It takes as one of its fundamental premises that it is impossible to understand the impact of market liberalisation on Chilean women's lives by looking at the economic policies in isolation from the political project of the military government. Unlike many Third World governments, the Pinochet regime adopted what was an essentially conventional programme of structural adjustment voluntarily rather than at the behest of international institutions such as the IMF and World Bank. It can be argued that these policies were implemented because they appeared to offer a way of achieving political aims: the demobilisation of the working class following a period of high politicisation was to be brought about by restructuring the economy and society away from an industrial base and an interventionist state. So while Chilean economic policies closely resemble the majority of structural adjustment packages, market liberalisation was attempted somewhat earlier in Chile and for different reasons.

The Chilean military government was therefore characterised not only by its adherence to neo-liberal economic policies but also by its authoritarianism. This meant widespread political repression, the banning of trade unions and political parties, and a far-reaching crusade against the evils of communism and subversion which resulted in the imprisonment and death of many. Authoritarianism and ML were linked in two ways. Much of the military was favourably disposed to the implementation of market liberalisation because these economic policies aided the demobilisation of the popular sectors and the defeat of communism. At the same time, this authoritarianism enabled market liberalisation to be pursued more thoroughly, and arguably contributed to the economic 'success' which was apparent in the late 1980s. However, adherence to the military's particular brand of authoritarianism and conservative social ideology was also in direct contradiction to some of the implications of its economic policies. Nowhere can this be seen more clearly than in the case of the impact on women and gender relations, as we shall see below.

As other contributions to this volume have outlined, the move towards liberalisation and the creation of an economy dominated by comparative advantage and the working of the free market, has particular implications for women bóth in their participation in paid employment and for their unpaid activities in the household. The aim of the present contribution is to explore the effects of ML on women when it takes place in a politically authoritarian context. An investigation into the impact of ML on women in Chile has to take into account two central features of the Chilean experience, derived from the distinctive combination of authoritarianism and ML outlined above: first, the thoroughness of the implementation of ML and its 'success', and, second, the contradictions which arose between the conservative social ideology of the military and the implications of the free market policies.

'Successful market liberalisation' and structural adjustment is implicitly premised on the elasticity of women's unpaid labour, which will only stretch so far.[1] It is therefore important to explore what successful market liberalisation looks like in practice, looking firstly at the ways in which the reduced role of the state affects different groups of women both as providers and consumers of services, and secondly at the role women have as workers in the rest of the restructured economy. It is then possible to examine the relative weight of those factors pushing women into the labour market – for example, the need to generate an income – and those drawing them in – for example the creation of new forms of women's employment.

At the same time, the contradictory features of the Chilean experience are striking. While the economic doctrines of market liberalisation talk in terms of the supposedly genderless individual, which obscures important effects on women, the Chilean military espoused a much more overt ideology of the proper role for women in both the public and private spheres, springing more from ideas underpinning their authoritarianism than from their economic doctrines.[2] The promulgation of these views sometimes coincided and sometimes conflicted with the implications of market liberalisation for women. The Chilean military government therefore attempted to implement a contradictory project, the nature of which has been reflected in its diverse outcomes. Analysed as a whole, the different elements have sometimes worked in concert and sometimes in opposition to each other. In order to unravel this, it is necessary to provide the context by examining the overall impact of the neo-liberal economic policies between 1973 and 1989. Having established this background, it is possible to look at the effects of both market liberalisation and authoritarianism on women's lives, showing that no easy generalisations are possible because of the need to disaggregate the impact according to women's class position. Finally, it is important to remember that women are not passive victims of these processes. The concluding section of this chapter will therefore describe some of the organised responses of Chilean women to authoritarianism, political repression and market liberalisation.

MARKET LIBERALISATION: MIRAGE OR MIRACLE?

By the late 1980s Chile was being heralded as an example of successful adjustment. It is argued that through the early implementation of stabilisation and adjustment through privatisation, market liberalisation and adherence to the doctrine of comparative advantage, the Chilean economy has emerged from periods of necessary recession and restructuring as a thriving concern capable of competing on the world market and paying back its foreign debt. While evidence can easily be found to support this view, the picture is not so simple.

The military government which took power in 1973 had no clear economic plan, and the neo-liberal ideas of the so-called Chicago Boys soon found favour.[3] These ideas seemed to provide the policies which would result in the demobilisation of the working class through deflation, unemployment and the individualisation of the labour market following the extreme levels of political polarisation and economic chaos of the Allende period. The effects of the new policies were felt fairly quickly. Public expenditure was cut by 27 per cent in 1975 and GDP fell by 16.6 per cent in the following year, hitting the industrial sector particularly hard and resulting in a huge increase in unemployment which reached 21.9 per cent (including those on emergency programmes) and disproportionately affected low-income households.[4] The 'shock', as it became known, was also used to accelerate the longer-term process of restructuring the economy through freeing the market. Subsidies and price controls were removed, state enterprises were privatised at knock-down prices. Much of the land expropriated during the Allende period was either returned to former owners or sold. By 1979, Chile had become one of the most open economies in the world, tariffs had been reduced to 10 per cent and practically all restrictions on the contraction of foreign debt had been lifted.

The restructuring was not just confined to the economy. Increasingly, attempts were made to push the burden of welfare provision in the spheres of housing, health, education and social security on to the individual and the family, with important repercussions for women. A new labour code was introduced in 1979 to institutionalise the weakened position of workers already eroded by unemployment and falling real wages. Trade-union activities were restricted and strikes carefully controlled. Prior to 1973, Chile had one of the most progressive labour legislations in Latin America, including maternity leave. This was extended under Popular Unity to include a provision that all employers with more than twenty women workers should provide a creche or subsidise the costs of childcare, although it was rarely enforced or implemented. These gains were lost after the military took power.

A short boom in the late 1970s was followed by a deep recession and financial crisis in the early 1980s when the unemployment rate peaked at 31.4 per cent in 1983. This was brought about partly as a result of government policies. The pegging of the exchange rate at the unrealistic level of 39 pesos to the dollar, combined with the low tariff rates, led to a flood of imported consumer goods which was largely paid for through the contraction of a huge foreign debt. The flood of imports also had the effect of devastating Chilean industry producing for the domestic market, while the overvalued exchange rate made Chilean manufactured exports uncompetitive on the world market. Insufficient regulation of the financial sector and the workings of the privatisation process led to the emergence of new financial empires which collapsed in the early 1980s, necessitating government intervention into several banks and resulting in the government taking control by default of many economic assets (since reprivatised).

It is, however, the mid- and late 1980s which are now seen as providing evidence of the Chilean economic miracle.[5] In 1988 GDP grew by around 7 per cent following growth rates of 5.7 per cent in both 1986 and 1987. Chile is now considered to be a model debtor: by 1988 the debt service ratio had declined to just below 30 per cent from a peak of 58.5 per cent in 1984. Chile has therefore maintained good relations with the IMF and World Bank and has as a result received short-term finance, three structural adjustment loans and assistance from the World Bank's International Finance Corporation to help its pioneering debt-for-equity swap schemes.

An important part of the explanation for the fall in the debt service ratio in the late 1980s was the dramatic increase in the volume of exports, which increased four times between 1973 and 1988. The value of Chilean exports increased by 32 per cent in 1988 alone. While some of this was caused by the rise in copper prices, dependence on the export of copper has fallen, so that by 1988 copper formed around 45 per cent of exports, a significant reduction from the peak of 70 per cent. The growth in exports has been achieved through diversification into non-traditional exports along the lines of comparative advantage; this is heralded as one of the major successes of the Chilean model.

Agriculture in particular has experienced considerable growth, led by the expansion of non-traditional crops for export. Fruit, particularly apples and grapes, have provided the basis of this growth. By 1988 fruit provided 12 per cent of total exports. Women's labour, as we shall see below, has played a crucial role in creating this symbol of the successful Chilean model. Forestry is another area where significant growth has been achieved, alongside the promotion of fish and shellfish products. The late 1980s has also seen some recovery in the ISI industries such as textiles which were devastated in the 1970s and early 1980s.

However, these impressive figures do not tell the whole story. The economic success is less spectacular and less solidly based than is often claimed. Taking the average growth rates since 1973, the economy had only grown by 2 per cent per annum. Furthermore, critics argue that the Chilean economy is still over-dependent on the export of primary products even though some are now new. There is a danger that the world market will become saturated with these new non-traditional exports, resulting in protectionist measures and falling prices. The other side of the coin is that the Chilean economy is now more than ever dependent on the import of manufactured goods. In the context of the overheated economy which became visible in the late 1980s, this puts a considerable strain on the balance of payments.

Despite the problems just outlined, the Chilean economic miracle can be seen overall as a success in its own terms. However, it is the social costs which, although an intended consequence, provide a searing indictment of neo-liberal policies in terms of poverty, unemployment and suffering. In 1988, despite a rise of 7 per cent in real wages over the previous year, it was estimated that average real wages were still between 7 and 11 per cent less than they were in 1980.[6] The impact of falling real wages was exacerbated by the decline in the social wage in terms of housing, health, education and social security; for example, the economically active population covered by social security; for example, the economically active population covered by social security fell from 79 per cent in 1974 to 63 per cent in 1980.[7] So despite the rise in real wages and the fall in unemployment, it has been estimated that in 1988 20 per cent of the population was living in extreme poverty and 50 per cent were living in poverty. This has been accompanied by a tremendous increase in the concentration of income. It is claimed that the top 10 per cent saw their income increase by 87 per cent in the ten years up to 1988. So the standard of living of one in five has risen hugely, while the standard of living of four in ten has declined.[8]

The restructuring of the economy and the impact of neo-liberal policies on the distribution of wealth provide one dimension of the context in which Chilean women's experience under Pinochet's rule has to be considered. We now turn to the ideological context of authoritarian rule and the role of conservative social thinking in shaping the regime's policies towards women.

THE IMPACT OF ML AND AUTHORITARIANISM ON CHILEAN WOMEN

The Military's Discourse on Women

As stated above, it is impossible to understand the apparent 'success' of market liberalisation in Chile without looking at the ways in which women's labour has facilitated this. This is incomplete without examining the specific ways in which women were considered by the military government which acted both in concert and contradiction to the effects of market liberalisation. The military government initially expressed its gratitude to the women of Chile for the part they had played in the build-up to the military coup. Mobilisation by mainly middle- and upper-class women on behalf of the right played a very important role in the opposition movement against the Popular Unity government and its eventual downfall.[9] Among the best known is the first 'march of the empty pots' which took place on 1 December 1971 when a large number of women took to the streets to protest at the shortages and rising prices. This was one of the first large-scale demonstrations of opposition to the government. The actions of women mobilising in support of the right were soon co-ordinated by organisations like El Poder Feminino (EPF) which took direct action in the public sphere using very 'unfeminine' methods in the name of defending motherhood and womanhood against the evils of communism.[10]

The installation of the military government was followed by attempts to both demobilise women (often fiercely resented) and control women's organisations, perhaps reminiscent of events in Germany after the Nazis gained power.[11] Right-wing women, primarily from the middle and upper classes, were organised in the SNM, the National Secretariat of Women, under the leadership of Pinochet's wife, in a highly ideological organisation which aimed to enable women 'to better carry out their roles as mothers, wives and housewives'.[12] In 1979–80, the SNM claimed to have 10 000 (uniformed) volunteers; and it has been estimated that between 1973 and 1983 more than two million women were involved in its activities.[13] The SNM has worked closely with another organisation also headed by Lucia Hiriat de Pinochet. The military government also took over the CEMAs, the Mothers' Centres which had been set up in the 1960s so that women could meet, gain the means to generate an income and become involved in community affairs. After 1973 these were often staffed by middle-class volunteers and used as a way of incorporating poorer women into a framework supporting the government in competition with more broadly oppositional organisations often established under the auspices of the Vicariate of the Church, for example by also setting up artisanal workshops.[14] In 1983 CEMA Chile had around 230 000 members, 6000 volunteers and over 10 000 centres.

Obviously these attempts to both demobilise and incorporate women do not fit into the broader tenets of neo-liberalism but are more reminiscent of an authoritarian and corporatist project. While Pinochet praised the heroic role played by women in the fight against socialism, he argued that 'nevertheless the most important labour of women is motherhood', and 'the Chilean woman is beautiful, an indomitable defender of her home, an unselfish, self-sacrificing loyal wife. Her nobility and dignity are not obscured by poverty and hardship.'[15] Indeed, the government attempted to increase the Chilean population and limited access to birth control, after contraception was first sanctioned by the Christian Democrats in the 1960s and extended under Popular Unity.[16] The military government therefore elevated motherhood as a woman's primary role and stressed women's charitable and self-sacrificing role in both the private and public sphere. Women therefore were seen as having a profoundly important role in society as the upholders and defenders of traditional values and as tireless volunteers.

This conception of the proper role for women does dovetail in some areas with the conception of women implicit in the doctrines of ML. For the implementation of ML to be effective in its own terms, it depends on the elasticity of women's unpaid labour within the household, for example to replace welfare services which have been cut and to make ends meet at times of recession, falling real wages and high inflation. This ties in with the notion popular among the military that women's place is in the home caring for husband and children. However, some of the effects of market liberalisation run contrary to parts of this discourse. Women have been pushed into the labour market in greater numbers than ever before and the new economic policies have created new 'women's' jobs, now without the benefit of enforced provision of maternity leave.

The Impact of Market Liberalisation

In attempting to assess the impact of market liberalisation on women in Chile, I will consider several areas: first, some general discussion on the impact of recession on women, followed by an examination of the impact of cuts in state expenditure on women as consumers of state services. I shall conclude with a discussion of the changes in women's role as producers outside the household by looking at paid employment since 1973, using a more detailed discussion of women's employment in the agricultural export sector to highlight some of the contradictions arising out of the Chilean experience. It should be borne in mind that the impact of ML and women's responses have to be disaggregated, for example by examining women's class position and the nature of the household that they are part of: that is, whether there is a male partner, whether he is working or unemployed, whether the household is composed of a nuclear or extended family, whether there are daughters around to perform extra household tasks. All these factors will have an impact on the survival strategies undertaken by individual women and their households.

PICKING UP THE PIECES?

Women have traditionally been responsible for household management in Chile. Therefore in periods of recession it is women who have carried much of the burden of 'making ends meet', in other words trying to maximise household consumption in the face of high levels of unemployment, falling real wages and rising prices. It is estimated that inflation has been consistently higher for poor households. The official index increased by 67 per cent between September 1981 and September 1984, while the consumer price index for the poor increased by 105 per cent.[17] It is poor women who spend extra time looking for bargains, very often in the context of the poor housing conditions of many shanty towns. In the absence of services and amenities, domestic labour takes longer than in better-off households.

The more general effects of recession have been exacerbated by the impact of cuts in social and welfare services, ending almost five decades of expansion of the Chilean welfare state. By 1983, per capita spending on public social services had fallen to 83.1 per cent of its 1970 level. This figure hides a sharper decline to 71.2 per cent of the 1970 level in 1975, a relative increase occurring only in certain areas such as social security and workfare type programmes like PEM (minimum employment programme) and later POJH (programme for heads of households) introduced to ease unemployment at the expense of other services such as health, education and particularly housing.[18] The introduction of PEM and POJH has, however, had a more complex impact on women as they are able to participate in the programmes and receive the same remuneration as men thereby forming an important source of income for poor women. This has been a particular bonus for female-headed households trying to survive in the context of the large wage differentials which exist between men and women in paid employment.[19]

The decline in welfare spending has affected many women in their role as paid providers of welfare services. Within the public sector women's employment has declined. Between 1983 and 1987 the percentage of the labour force employed in the government and

Georgina Waylen 159

financial sector declined from 17 per cent to 9.7 per cent of the total, and as will be seen below, it is clear that employment in the financial sector increased over this period leaving a large absolute decline in state employment.[20]

This decline in public sector employment has had an important impact on the opportunities available for professional women (predominantly from the middle and upper classes). Women have made up a high proportion of professional and technical workers in the post-war period, forming 48.6 per cent in 1970, with around 10–12 per cent of the female labour force falling into this category. However, as a consequence of the concentration of women in higher education in 'female' subjects, women have congregated in the so-called caring professions considered suitable for them.[21] In 1982 almost all social workers and 93 per cent of nurses were women, and nurses comprised 23 per cent of all professional women. A similar pattern can be seen in teaching, where two-thirds of teachers were female and teachers made up 57 per cent of professional women. In the period from December 1986 to April 1987, between 6000 and 8000 teachers were dismissed following the transfer of the control of education to the municipalities (and the Minister of Education claimed that there were still too many teachers). It has also been claimed that women taken on PEM have been carrying out activities which previously would been done by properly salaried employees, generally women. Razcynski argues that this has happened at the Open Centres which provided care for children from extremely poor households, when untrained and unqualified PEM workers have replaced qualified staff.[22] A large number of middle-class professional women have seen their employment opportunities in the state sector reduced, as they tended to congregate in precisely those sectors of the welfare state which have been cut most, and some have been forced to move into the growing private sector.

Women, in their role as consumers of welfare services and as managers of access to public services liaising with education, health and welfare services for other members of the household, have also been particularly hard hit by these cuts. These have significantly increased the amount of unpaid labour women have to expend in the face of reduced or abolished services when the need is growing, i.e. because of poverty and recession. Poor women have had to try and make ends meet in the face of reductions in the contributions to household subsistence coming from public programmes such as maternity subsidies, family allowances, housing programmes and health benefits. The 1986 Health Act introduced charges and ended free ante- and post-natal care and the free family planning available to women. As Stewart has described elsewhere in this volume, it is clear that women lose out when user charges are introduced. According to the Women's Rights Committee, in a reversal of some of the gains made under Allende and Frei, daycare facilities were only available to 12 per cent of the pre-school population by the mid-1980s. After 1973, women took on much of the burden in replacing those services which either became unavailable or households were unable to afford, such as healthcare.

So far, we have seen how the conservative social ideology dedicated to reinforcing the notion of women's proper role has coincided with the effects of cutbacks in the welfare state: the unpaid labour of women in the home has intensified. The declining birthrate, however, can be seen as a response by women to ML which contraverts the military's ideology. Some have argued that the government has avoided extreme hardship through its successful meso-policies which have targeted benefits to the most vulnerable groups, for example through special feeding programmes aimed at those mothers and children identified as vulnerable, mirroring UNICEF's concept of Adjustment with a Human Face. Evidence marshalled to back this up includes declining infant mortality and malnutrition rates.[23]

However, without providing a critique of the whole notion of targeting, there is evidence that part of the explanation for the fall in infant mortality rates can also be found by looking at the decline in the birth rate evident since 1973. Live births per thousand fell from 27.2 in 1973 to 21 in 1986. First, this frees both household and state resources for the remaining births, and more importantly, if these figures are disaggregated, it can be seen that the sharpest decline in the birthrate has taken place among those women most at risk from infant mortality. Births have been concentrated among older mothers – those aged between 20 and 24 – and those with higher levels of education, i.e. among the higher income groups.[24] Therefore despite the government's population policy, which aimed to increase the birthrate, many poor young women postponed the decision to have children as a complex response to contradictory effects of ML, due both to increased poverty which forced them to intensify their income generating activities and to the opportunities provided by the expansion of paid employment for women.[25] High levels of illegal abortion can be seen as further evidence of this. In 1979, for every two women giving birth, one was admitted to hospital with abortion complications.[26]

RESTRUCTURING WOMEN'S LABOUR

Perhaps the clearest area where military ideology and the implications of market liberalisation policies have collided is in the impact on labour market participation. Since 1973 women have been drawn into the labour market, very often as part of survival strategies to deal with poverty, recession and unemployment, particularly of a male partner. In the recession of the early 1980s, women's and men's paid employment was differentially affected: contrary to the experience of some other countries, women's paid employment declined by only 6.6 per cent between 1980 and 1982 whereas men's paid employment declined by 10.9 per cent over the same period.[27] In both periods of recession, the numbers of women seeking work for the first time also increased substantially, implying that women were newly entering the labour market.[28]

In the post-war period up to 1973 women made up approximately 22 per cent of the labour force. By 1976, this figure had increased to 25.2 per cent of all women aged over 15; by 1985 this had reached 28.2 per cent.[29] However, it is clear that the size of the female labour force has been consistently underestimated, particularly in the agricultural and informal sectors, and therefore different sources give different figures.[30] As a percentage of the total labour force, women increased their relative share from 27.6 per cent in 1976 to 34.6 per cent in 1985 in the face of a decline in male activity rates (the ILO put women's share of the labour force at only 30 per cent (29.97 per cent) in 1987).[31] However, the ILO figures do show the number of women in paid employment increasing by 32.3 per cent between 1982 and 1987 (from the low point in 1982, the worst year of recession in the early 1980s), while the male paid workforce increased by 38 per cent over the same period. However, the total number of women considered to be economically active increased by 36 per cent between 1982 and 1987, from 959 400 to 1 394 500, while the increase in the number of economically active men was only 12 per cent over the same period, implying that many men had simply moved from the informal to the formal sector. It is clear, therefore, that there has been a huge expansion in the size of the total economically active female population since 1973.

Women have been drawn into the labour market both through necessity, particularly in the period up to 1983, and through the creation of opportunities for waged work. This has been primarily a result of the structural changes which have occurred in the Chilean economy since 1973, but it has been most apparent since 1983. This contradiction within market liberalisation (relying on expanding women's unpaid labour in the household while also drawing women into the labour market) results in increased burdens on women and is in direct contradiction to the military ideology that women should remain within the domestic sphere and not enter paid employment in larger numbers. It remains to explore which women have moved into the labour market, when, and in what occupations and sectors they have congregated.

In order to get a fuller picture of the changes in women's labour market participation it is necessary to disaggregate the figures. If women's participation is looked at in terms of social class, it can be seen that in 1975 during the period of the 'shock' there was an increase in the participation of working-class women from 22.2 per cent of the total classified as belonging to the 'lower social stratas' in Greater Santiago in 1972 to a figure of 38.1 per cent in 1975.[32] This was accompanied by a decrease in participation on the part of women defined as belonging to the 'upper social stratas' from 69.7 per cent in 1972 to 56.8 per cent of the total in this group in 1975. These women have traditionally had much higher participation rates. These trends were reversed somewhat during the mini-economic boom of the late 1970s.[33] It would appear therefore that poorer women entered the labour market in increased numbers in the face of severe recession which hit them disproportionately hard, and better-off women withdrew.

There is some disagreement over the relationship between women's participation, their age and the number of children they have. Suzana Prates examined women's economic participation by age group during the 1970s. While participation rates increased for all ages, she discovered that the increase was highest for those women aged between 20 and 35 (see Table 7.1). This is the age group with the highest number of dependent children. Indeed, a study of the activity rate of this strata among the low-income groups found a positive correlation between the number of children and participation in the labour force, especially among women with five or more children (a group with historically low participation rates in paid employment). Among the upper stratas, however, an inverse correlation was discovered between the number of children and the economic activity rate, implying that better-off women are not forced so much by economic necessity into the labour market but instead exercise greater choice.[34]

Table 7.1 Economically active women by age

Age	% 1982	% 1986
15–19	14.0	11.3
20–24	33.3	39.6
25–29	35.1	41.1
30–34	32.6	40.0
35–39	30.8	43.3
40–44	28.8	40.0
45–49	26.0	36.4
50–54	21.9	28.7
55–59	16.2	21.8

Source: *ILO Employment Statistics Yearbook, 1988*.

The issue of childcare obviously affects women's participation. Upper-class women can rely on domestic servants, who often live in, to free them from domestic chores and childcare. This provides one explanation for their higher activity rate. Of living-in domestic workers 90 per cent are employed by the top income quintile, who also employ 75 per cent of the living-out servants as well.[35] It is claimed that poorer women in extended families have higher activity rates, presumably because other family members are available to take on domestic tasks. The same pattern is visible for women with older children, where daughters take over household tasks and childcare. Despite low levels of male income and high rates of male unemployment acting as a spur for many women to go out and generate additional income to increase household resources, there is evidence to suggest that the sexual division of labour within the household remains largely unaltered. This forces many women to take on the 'double day' or get their daughters to take their place – thereby reducing the latter's life chances.[36]

Having established that market liberalisation has had a differential impact on women's labour market participation, and that many poor women have intensified their income generating activities in the face of poverty, recession and unemployment particularly in the period up to 1983, it is possible to analyse what kinds of activities women engage in, focusing on the new opportunities for women created by the restructuring of the economy.

Chilean commercial agriculture, particularly for export, provides an interesting case study of the importance of women's labour in ML, and as such is worth discussing in some detail. In 1970, women formed only around 3.3 per cent of the accredited workforce in the agricultural sector (only 3 per cent of the total employment). This was the result of a long-term decline in women's paid employment in agriculture. The number of remunerated permanent women workers declined sharply after 1935, when women formed 20 per cent of the total (nearly 10 per cent of the total female labour force). By 1965, as a result of modernisation and mechanisation, women formed only 10 per cent of the permanent workforce. Many women were displaced to become unpaid family labour or migrated to look for work in urban areas. This process was exacerbated by land reform measures which were enacted by the Christian Democrats in the 1960s and Allende and Popular Unity in the early 1970s. Both recognised only heads of households and primarily permanent workers as potential beneficiaries from land reform measures; this generally excluded women as they were not generally either permanent workers or regarded as heads of households and so gained only indirectly from land reform, i.e. by being members of households which benefited.[37]

While the total number of people economically active in the agricultural sector is now relatively small, the numbers employed rose from 529 700 in 1980 to 837 400 in 1987, an increase of 58 per cent. This has included a very significant increase in the number of women, although the figures are notoriously unreliable where casual and temporary workers, who are so often women, are concerned. The recorded number of women workers rose from 26 900 in 1980 to 65 900 in 1987, an increase of 145 per cent.[38] The change in women's employment therefore showed a much greater proportionate increase than did men's employment (although by 1987 the female agricultural workforce still only comprised 5.6 per cent of the total recorded number of women in paid employment).

Chilean agriculture changed substantially over the period of military government, becoming, as many argue, more efficient, productive and modern as a result of neo-liberal policies which initially removed subsidies and price controls.[39] In a reversal of the policies of Frei and Allende, some expropriated land was returned to former owners and some sold. Of the land purchased by peasants, half has now been resold, leading to the emergence of a number of large-scale capitalist enterprises, a peasantry and a large group either with no land or not enough to guarantee their survival. The latter are then dependent on wage labour, often living in the rural shanty towns which have grown up particularly in the fruit-growing regions of the Central Valley.

Rural women's participation in agricultural production, both paid and unpaid, has increased substantially. The nature of this participation has been very dependent on the productive region – i.e. whether it is producing for export or domestic consumption, whether the agriculture is peasant-based or capitalist – and the class position of women. Women have either increased their participation on family plots, diversified their activities, for example, into handicrafts, or entered the paid labour market.[40]

Chilean export agriculture has become increasingly characterised by a small permanent labour force which is predominantly male, and a increasingly large temporary seasonal work force which is comprised almost entirely of women. This incorporation of a female labour force on a large scale has proved to be a very significant change and has also occurred in export agriculture in other parts of Latin America, e.g. Colombia and Mexico.[41]

There are several explanations for this development. In the mid-1970s, new technologies such as hormones, fertilisers, hybrid plants and new fruit management techniques were introduced which required a more specialised and skilled labour force. Women were considered to have the appropriate skills which are utilised over much of the fruit-growing cycle, particularly thinning the blossom and later the young fruit, and harvesting and packing, a vitally important task when the apples and table grapes are being exported over long distances for relatively long periods of time. Many women therefore work for periods of four to six months, often for different enterprises over this period. For the rest of the year, many of the women undertake other income-generating activities, e.g. handicraft production and domestic service in Santiago, or enrol on PEM. Hojman claims that many of them become 'permanent' temporary labourers, returning to the same agricultural jobs year after year.[42]

Which women make up this labour force? In her study, Campana discovered that the majority of the temporary workers came from landless households.[43] Lago also argues that, in general, those who enter paid employment of this nature come from households which do not have sufficient land.[44] Many are immigrants to the fruit-growing regions, either from other rural regions or even from the urban areas, and they often congregate in the rural shanty towns. The majority of women studied by Campana were aged between 20 and

34, half were married, and were often working in the context of the unemployment of their male partner, if they had one.[45] It is therefore not surprising that many of them supplied between a third and a half of the household income.

The temporary women workers are paid relatively high wages seen as commensurate with their skills. Campana records that in one fruit-growing region in 1984, employers raised wages and provided transport for their women workers in the face of a severe labour shortage.[46] However, despite the relatively high wages (often paid on a daily basis), the work is temporary, seasonal and involves working very long hours late into the night with no employment rights for part of the year and the prospect of little or no income for the other half of the year. Women also face high non-wage costs in the form of poor or non-existent amenities and services in the rural shanty towns.

Chile has therefore seen a combination of neo-liberal economic policies and agricultural modernisation which has incorporated certain women into paid employment which is considered skilled and which is relatively well paid, albeit on a temporary basis. This has occurred in the context of high male unemployment and obviously runs contrary to the military's overt ideology of returning women to the home.

It has been postulated that another impact of the increase in women's employment in export agriculture is a decrease in the availability of women for service sector employment, particularly domestic service in the urban areas.[47] Migration by women from the rural areas initially increased after the coup, then declined because of the impact of severe recession which led to a reduction in income generating opportunities in the urban areas. The economic boom in the late 1970s caused numbers to expand as migrants were drawn to Santiago by the increased levels of micro-economic activity. This trend was reversed during the recession of the early 1980s and then increased, but only slowly, during the rest of the decade. Hojman argues that the emergence of rural shanty towns, i.e. increased rural to rural migration, and the increase in women's agricultural employment from 1983 onwards have contributed to this phenomenon.[48]

The service sector absorbs many female migrants and has provided the livelihood for a large proportion of Chilean women since 1973. The term 'service sector' spans both the so-called formal and informal sectors. The number of women roughly estimated to be in paid employment in the service sector (category 6 of Table 7.2) increased from 758 400 in 1980 (79 per cent of the total employed females) to

Table 7.2   Women's employment by industry (in thousands)

	Total	Agric.	Ind.	Comm.	Fin.	Ser.
1980	959.3	26.9	149.1	224.6	26.8	507.0
1981	955.5	21.4	134.6	233.8	31.9	512.5
1982	895.4	22.6	102.1	192.0	37.6	522.3
1983	989.2	24.3	111.3	207.6	30.3	594.2
1984	1005.9	30.6	126.2	229.0	36.8	559.9
1985	1099.7	43.6	120.8	248.5	45.6	619.1
1986	1156.7	52.1	134.0	255.4	50.5	636.3
1987	1184.4	65.9	155.4	269.9	56.4	608.4

Source: *ILO Employment Statistics Yearbook, 1988*, p. 404.

934 700 in 1987 (78.9 per cent of the total), an increase of 23.2 per cent, while the numbers considered to be economically active in these three categories, i.e. also including those in the informal sector in so far as they can be quantified, increased from 709 700 in 1982 to 1 001 000 in 1987.[49]

It is clear that the number of women involved in the 'formal' segments of the service sector increased in precisely those sectors which often expand during economic restructuring along neo-liberal lines. The number of women involved in the financial sector increased by 110 per cent, despite the crisis it experienced in the early 1980s, absorbing 4.7 per cent of the economically active female population and forming 32.5 per cent of the total economically active in this sector (the number of men increased by only 62.9 per cent).

Commerce (both wholesale and retail), restaurants and hotels increased their female paid workforce by 20 per cent between 1980 and 1987 (men by only 15 per cent). Women formed 39 per cent of those economically active in this category and the commercial sector absorbed 22 per cent of the total economically active female population. In line with the emphasis on and expansion of consumption by those who could afford it, one of the symbols of Chile's experience of neo-liberalism has been the 'caracol' (a spiral-shaped shopping arcade), where women have found employment as shop assistants.

The number of women employed in communal, personal and social services steadily increased by a total of 20 per cent from 1980 (while the numbers of men had fallen by 1978 after wild fluctuations), and in 1987 women formed 54 per cent of the total recorded as both employed and economically active in this category and 51.4 per cent of the employed female workforce and 50 per cent of the economically active population. Within this, the proportion active in personal and domestic services increased.[50]

Women form around 97 per cent of the total number of domestic workers. Domestic service has long provided many women, particularly migrants from rural areas, with a wage and accommodation, while requiring little formal education and training, but all too often it entails unprotected, unregulated and non-unionised conditions. Around 25 per cent of the economically active female population were domestic servants throughout the 1960s. In 1987 it was estimated conservatively that there were at least 150 000 domestic servants in Chile.[51] It has been claimed that in 1978, domestic servants formed 26.16 per cent of the actively employed female population which had fallen to 20.1 per cent in 1982.[52]

Hojman has argued that demand for domestic service has fluctuated with economic activity, falling at times of slump and increasing at times of boom. Because the employment of domestic workers is so concentrated in the top quintile any increase in the income of the rich is likely to increase the demand for servants. Hojman claims that a tight labour market (caused by an expansion of alternative female employment at a time of economic growth) in the middle 1980s resulted in the wages of domestic workers rising faster than wages in any other sector of the economy.[53]

Informal-sector activities in general have, it is argued, provided many poor women with the means to earn some kind of an income, either within their own household so as to be compatible with domestic tasks, or outside of it. Clarissa Hardy states that by 1980 the informal sector made up 26.5 per cent of the labour force whereas in 1960 only 19 per cent had been occupied in this way. Of the 494 200 people falling into this category in 1982, 51.8 per cent were women and 22.7 per cent of the total were young people aged between 12 and 24 years.[54] Many women have therefore taken in work at home such as sewing, knitting and washing in order to survive or have provided goods and services such as prostitution on the streets. Hardy argues that these kinds of 'commercio marginal' (marginal commerce) and all personal services including domestic service experienced the largest growth in the late 1970s and early 1980s, and within this part of the informal sector, women comprised 72.3 per cent of the labour force and the young formed 28.8 per cent of the total.

Marginal informal-sector activities such as street selling and prostitution are the most difficult to quantify and to include in labour force statistics. In addition to prostitution, 'commercio ambulante' (street selling) is also illegal, so women face the additional hardship of raids by the police, confiscation of goods, and fines.[55] This is a very precarious way to make a living.

The share of manufacturing in providing women's employment declined steadily after 1973. In the post-war period around 20 per cent of the female labour force were employed in the industrial sector, primarily in the import substituting consumer industries such as footwear, textiles and leathergoods. These suffered badly in the late 1970s and early 1980s and were only just beginning to show significant recovery in the late 1980s. In 1980, 15.5 per cent of the employed female workforce worked in manufacturing industry; by 1982 this figure had fallen to 11.4 per cent and had only returned to 13.1 per cent of the total by 1987 (an absolute increase of only 4.2 per cent). Men's employment in manufacturing as a proportion of total male employment was not so badly hit, standing at 16.3 per cent of total male employment in 1980, falling to 13.2 per cent in 1982 and recovering to 16 per cent of the total in 1987. This represents an absolute increase of 20.6 per cent over the seven-year period. The discrepancy between levels of male and female employment in the industrial sector is due to the fact that the greatest industrial expansion has taken place in the refining and processing of raw materials, such as wood processing, industrial chemicals, and mineral products, industries where male labour has traditionally predominated. In contrast to some other Third World countries, Chile has not encouraged the development of Free Trade Zones, which have tended to include types of manufacturing such as electronics, and more recently data processing, which have often provided employment for women. Chile's economic restructuring has therefore not favoured manufacturing, and within this, women's share of manufacturing employment has also declined.

Women have therefore moved into the labour market in substantial numbers since 1973. They have increased their participation in paid employment in those sectors which have expanded as a result of economic restructuring brought about by ML. This has occurred particularly in export agriculture and commerce. Women have also intensified their income generating activities in the informal sector. This expansion of women's income-earning economic activity has occurred both because of the need to generate resources in the face of high levels of poverty and because the economic restructuring has created an increased demand for women's labour particularly after 1983.

WOMEN'S COLLECTIVE RESPONSES

Having examined women's individual responses, this section will consider women's collective responses to the effects of market liberalisation and authoritarianism. These cannot be seen separately as the two have worked in concert and many seemingly solely economic responses have important political dimensions. Most marked has been the re-emergence of the Chilean feminist movement which has influenced many of the other developments both directly and indirectly, and the re-emergence of collective organising in the poorer urban areas, predominantly by women. The military government has therefore failed in its attempt to depoliticise and individualise many women and Chilean society in general.

There have been attempts to increase the unionisation of women workers and to make sure that the trade-union movement has defended the interests of women employees. From 1982 onwards, some women involved in the agricultural export industry began to join the rural labour unions. In addition to workplace issues, these women's sections have raised more general women's issues, for example child care, the double day and the local organisation of International Women's Day.[56] Lago claims that the new generation of female union leaders have themselves been influenced by the feminist movement and urban women's community organisations.[57] There have also been attempts to organise unions of domestic workers and street sellers. A women's department of CNS, the national trade-union co-ordinating body, was formed in 1976 and went on to hold conferences for women delegates; it organised the 1978 International Women's Day protest, the first large-scale demonstration to be held after the imposition of military rule.

In addition to the organisation of women as workers, there has been an increase in urban community-based organisations operating collective forms of survival strategy. Organizaciones Economicas Populares (OEPs) have been established in poor and so-called marginal neighbourhoods. In June 1985, 1125 OEPs were recorded in the metropolitan region.[58] Hardy has identified four types of OEPs, and women dominated in the two most numerous types (43 per cent of the total number of OEPs were women-only). In 1985, 32.8 per cent of OEPs were Organizaciones Laboral-Productivas, i.e. they produced goods and services for exchange in the market and therefore generated income. Other studies have shown that over 50 per cent of these were artisanal workshops (for example, workshops making

Arpilleras (embroideries, made by women, sometimes under the auspices of the church, which depict scenes from Chilean life and often bear an oppositional message) and 10 per cent were communal bakeries. Of the Organizaciones Laboral-Productivas, 62 per cent were women-only and 65 per cent of the total number of workers employed were women.[59]

The second major type of OEP, Organizaciones Consumo Alimentario (organisations centred around the consumption of food) made up 48 per cent of the total number and can be seen as, in part, a response to cuts in welfare services. These included the Ollas Communes (communal soup pots) providing hot meals collectively and the Comprando Juntos (buying committees) allowing women to purchase goods more economically. In addition, a smaller number of OEPs were set up to provide social services, and women again dominate in the 'grupos de salud' (health groups). In the face of economic hardship, poor women have extended their roles as home managers and social organisers into new collective community organisations. However, it has been argued that to regard these organisations as simply economic would be to ignore their role as important forums for the development of self-awareness and political organisation.[60]

Military repression and human rights abuses, particularly the disappearances, have been the spur for other forms of collective organisation. The Agrupacion de Familiares de Detenidos–Desaparacidos (the group of relatives of the detained–disappeared) grew up soon after the installation of the military government in late 1974/5. It was founded primarily by women who kept meeting each other trekking round the prisons and government offices trying to discover the whereabouts of their relatives. The organisations are comprised mainly of women, who argue that they are neither primarily politically motivated nor feminist.[61] They held demonstrations outside the Moneda Palace every Friday afternoon, and the participants carried photographs of their missing relatives.[62]

The third collective response consists of those activities which can more easily be termed 'feminist', either self-consciously or because of the nature of the activities engaged in. The military dictatorship has seen the emergence of a new feminist movement, heir to the struggles and organisations of those which arose earlier in the century. A predominantly middle-class feminist movement existed in Chile in the first half of the twentieth century and an active campaign for women's suffrage existed in the interwar period.[63] After gaining the vote, the women's movement entered a period of 'feminist silence' according to Julietta Kirkwood, as politicised women moved out of women's organisations and entered into mainstream politics and joined other political parties, but with few visible results. By 1973 only one of the 200 senators and three of the 400 elected deputies were women.

Military rule and authoritarianism has also contributed to the re-evaluation many Chilean women have undertaken of the lack of democracy in their own lives – hence one of the slogans of the new women's movement, 'Democracia en Chile y en la casa'. This, combined with the experience of increased material burdens and the double-day, helped to lead women once again to begin organising as women. Other developments also fed into this re-emergence: the relative reduction in the level of repression after 1977; and the 'renovacion politica' (political renewal) which occurred on the left and led to the emergence of broader definitions of the political which were more likely to include women's struggles. The Circulo de Estudios de la Mujer was set up in 1977, and this was followed by the emergence of several different women's organisations in the early 1980s.[64] A number of umbrella organisations, MEMCH83 and Mujeres por la Vida, also emerged to co-ordinate the openly oppositional activity which became increasingly common during and after 1983. In addition to protesting, feminists have also been engaged in analysing the position of Chilean women. Julietta Kirkwood, in particular, has looked at the links between authoritarianism and patriarchy and the implications of this for the creation of a truly liberating form of democratic politics.[65]

Many of the responses outlined above overlap; indeed there are often considerable links between them. The Arpillera workshops, for example, combined protests against human rights abuses with an income generating strategy for women who are often without any other source of income. Feminists have also taken part in organising in the poorer districts of Santiago and in the trade-union movement. The experience of women organising together around basic needs issues has also been a deeply politicising experience for many of those involved.

CONCLUSION

In conclusion, Chile provides an interesting case study when examining the impact of market liberalisation on women. Chile has seen 'successful' market liberalisation enforced as part of a contradictory package by an authoritarian government. The success of the economic policies has therefore depended on both authoritarianism which helped its implementation and an increase in both women's paid and unpaid labour.

The conservative social ideology of the military, one part of its authoritarianism, had an uneasy relationship with market liberalisation. The two worked in concert with regard to some policies towards the welfare state. Cuts in service provision and the doctrine of 'a woman's place is in the home' are very compatible. Women, as both consumers and producers, have been differentially affected by all the cuts in state welfare provision. Poor women and their households are less likely to be able to pay for private sector services; while middle- and upper- class women have seen professional employment opportunities in the state sector decline. At the same time, however, some meso-level policies such as employment programmes have provided poor women with an important subsidy.

The effects of market liberalisation, however, diverge from the tenets of the ideology with regard to women's remunerated labour. Women's economic activity rates have increased sharply over the period of military rule. Again, women have been affected differentially. Poorer women particularly, have intensified their income generating activities, often in the informal sector. This occurred most markedly in the 1970s and early 1980s in the face of severe hardship, falling wage levels and male unemployment. Since 1983 the demand for women's labour has increased substantially, particularly in those sectors which have experienced high growth during this period of restructuring along neo-liberal lines. The increased demand in the agricultural, commercial and financial services sectors has reduced the supply of labour for the more traditional female activities such as domestic work. Market liberalisation, therefore, while increasing hardship, also increased employment opportunities for some women.

Contrary to the aims of the military's project, the combination of authoritarianism and market liberalisation contributed to a new phase of women's collective organising. This has taken various forms: the OEPs, the urban community organisations, human rights groups, and a new wave of feminist activity. The authoritarian project of controlling and depoliticising women clearly failed. So while the political ideology of the military has contributed to the apparent success of market liberalisation, the ideological project itself has not been so successful in the longer term.

Notes and References

* I would like to thank Liz Harvey, Ruth Pearson and Paul Cammack for their helpful comments on earlier versions of this work.

1. See D. Elson, 'The Impact of Structural Adjustment on Women: Concepts and Issues', in B. Onimode (ed.), *The IMF, the World Bank and African Debt*, vol. 2 (Zed Press, 1989); and P. Antrobus, 'Consequences and Responses to Social and Economic Deterioration: The Experience of the English Speaking Caribbean', Paper prepared for the Workshop on Economic Crisis, Household Survival Strategies and Women's Work, Cornell University, 2–5 September 1988.
2. For a discussion of the philosophical underpinnings of this brand of new right thinking, see G. Waylen, 'Women and Neo-Liberalism', in J. Evans *et al.*, *Feminism and Political Theory* (Sage, 1986) pp. 85–102.
3. See, for example, P. O'Brien and J. Roddick, *Chile: The Pinochet Decade* (Latin America Bureau, 1983). P. O'Brien, 'Authoritarianism and the New Orthodoxy: The Political Economy of the Chilean Regime 1973–82', in P. O'Brien and P. Cammack (eds), *Generals in Retreat: The Crisis of Military Rule in Latin America*, pp. 144–183 (Manchester University Press, 1985). A. Valenzuela and J. Valenzuela, *Military Rule in Chile: Dictatorship and Oppositions* (Johns Hopkins University Press, 1987).
4. Raczynski argues that in Greater Santiago blue-collar workers experienced twice the unemployment of white-collar workers, and that heads of household in the bottom 20 per cent were laid off at three times the rate for better-off heads of household. See D. Raczynski, 'Social Policy, Poverty and Vulnerable Groups: Children in Chile', in A. Cornea, R. Jolly and F. Stewart (eds), *Adjustment with a Human Face*, vol 2 (Oxford University Press, 1987) p. 61.
5. Most of the figures in this section come from either the *The Economist Intelligence Unit Country Profile* (EIU CP) or the *Economist Intelligence Unit Quarterly Report* (EIU QR) for Chile, 1988–9 or from the *Latin American Regional Reports: Southern Cone* (LARR SC) or the *Latin American Weekly Report* (LAWR) for 1986–9.
6. LARR SC, September 1988.
7. Quoted in D. Razcynski, 'Social Policy, Poverty and Vulnerable Groups: Children in Chile', in *Adjustment with a Human Face*, vol. 2 (see note 4 above) p. 64.
8. See LAWR, 12.10.1989.
9. See E. Chaney, 'The Mobilization of Women in Allende's Chile', in J. Jaquette (ed.), *Women in Politics* (Wiley, 1974) pp. 267–80. While the 'peaceful transition to socialism' did hold out the prospect of profound change favourable to women, it can be argued that the Allende government, despite its need to improve its standing among the female electorate, did not achieve as much as it could have done both in terms of the inclusion of women in government and the implementation of concrete measures to improve women's lives. It is argued that this failure to provide an emancipatory alternative is partly responsible for the opposi-

tion that many middle- and upper-class women expressed towards the UP government.
10. See M. Crummett, 'El Poder Feminino: The Mobilization of Women against Socialism in Chile', *Latin American Perspectives*, vol. 4, no. 4 (1977) pp. 103–13. M. Mattelart, 'Chile: The Feminine Version of the Coup D'Etat', in J. Nash, (ed.), *Sex and Class in Latin America* (Bergin, 1980) pp. 279–301.
11. See Claudia Koonz, *Mothers in the Fatherland* (London: Jonathan Cape, 1987).
12. Quoted in P. Chuckryk, 'Protest, Politics and Personal Life: the Emergence of Feminism in a Military Dictatorship, Chile 1973 to 1983', PhD dissertation, York University, Toronto, Canada, 1984, p. 234.
13. See X. Bunster, 'Watch Out for the Little Nazi Man that All of Us Have Inside: Mobilization and Militarization of Women in Militarized Chile', *Women's Studies International Forum*, vol. 11, no. 5 (1988) p. 487.
14. See M. Agosin, *Scraps of Life* (London: Zed Press, 1988).
15. Quoted in P. Chuchryk, 'Protest, Politics . . .', p. 235.
16. See *Military Ideology and the Dissolution of Democracy-Women in Chile*, Change International Reports: Women and Society (London, 1981) p. 8; and *Somos Mas Chile: Women's Delegation Report*, Chile Solidarity Campaign (London, 1986).
17. Quoted in D. Raczynski, 'Social Policy . . .', p. 64.
18. Women formed 18.4 per cent of PEM in 1976, rising to 52.5 per cent in 1982, presumably caused partly by many male heads of household moving on to POJH: see Chuckryk, PhD, table 29, p. 475.
19. Wage differentials between men and women by level of education:

		Women's as a % of men's
1974	low	66
	middle	59
	specialised	47
	university	56
1982	low	60
	middle	55
	specialised	67
	university	49

low: no education or elementary education
middle: secondary education
specialised: technical, non-university education
university: university education, not necessarily completed.

Source: Dept of Economics, University of Chile, quoted in Chuckyrk, PhD, p. 472.

20. EIU CP 1988/9.
21. While the percentage of women in the annual university intake reached 41.5 per cent in 1974, very few women study science and engineering,

and are highly concentrated in education and health sciences, thereby having an important impact on the opportunities for many middle-class women in the labour market.

22. See D. Raczynski, 'Social Policy . . .', p. 74–5.
23. See D. Hojman, 'Neo-Liberal Economic Policies and Infant and Child Mortality: A Simulation of a Chilean Paradox', *World Development*, vol. 17, no. 1 (1989); and Raczynski, 'Social Policy . . .', p. 76.
24. See A. Foxley and D. Razcyinski, 'Vulnerable Groups in Recessionary Situations: The case of Children and the Young in Chile', *World Development*, vol. 12, no. 3 (1984) pp. 223–6.
25. It has been claimed that Pinochet believed that Chile was underpopulated and therefore attempted to limit women's access to contraception in order to increase the birthrate. See Somos Mas (note 16 above) p. 14.
26. P. Chuckryk, 'Protest, Politics . . .', p. 180.
27. See *ILO Employment Statistics Yearbook* (Geneva, 1988) p. 404.
28. See *ILO Employment Statistics Yearbook*, 1988, p. 655.
29. See A. Leiva, 'Las Desigualdades en el trabajo de hombres y mujeres', *Coyuntura Economica*, 14 (1987) p. 10, cited in P. Chuckryk, 'Feminist Anti-Authoritarian Politics: The Role of Women's Organisations in the Transition to Democracy', in J. Jaquette (ed.), *The Women's Movement in Latin America: Feminism and the Transition to Democracy* (Unwin Hyman, 1989) pp. 149–84.
30. The ILO put the female activity rate at 20.6 per cent and the male rate at 50.2 per cent in 1986.
31. Leiva, 'Las Desigualdades . . .', p. 187.
32. The definitions of upper and lower social stratas are those used by Rosales, quoted in Chuckryk, Phd, table 12, p. 460.
33. P. Chuchryk in her PhD quotes one explanation which is that upper-class women wished to purchase the consumer goods which were flooding into Chile and therefore attempted to move back into paid employment. See Chuckryk, PhD, p. 199.
34. S. Prates, 'Women's Labour and Family Survival Strategies under the "Stabilisation Models" in Latin America', paper prepared for the Expert Group Meeting on Policies for Social Integration, Centre for Social Development and Humanitarian Affairs, United Nations, Vienna, 1981, p. 35.
35. Figures quoted in D. Hojman, 'Land Reform, Female Migration and the Market for Domestic Service in Chile', *Journal of Latin American Studies*, vol. 21, no. 1 (1989) p. 111.
36. Walker mentions the unwillingness of male partners of the women involved in the Maria Goretti 'olla comun' to take on household tasks in their absence. See H. Walker Larrain, 'Transformation of Practices in Grassroots Organisations: A case study in Chile', PhD, University of Toronto, 1985, pp. 90–100.
37. See P. Garrett, 'Women and Agrarian Reform: Chile 1964–73', *Sociologia Ruralis*, 22 (1982). See also D. C. Deere, 'Women and Agrarian Reform', in C. D. Deere and M. de Leon (eds), *Rural Women and State Policy* (Westview Press, 1987) pp. 165–90.
38. The figures are based on the fourth quarter of every year, a time when a

high number of women are employed in the agricultural sector. The figures come from the *ILO Employment Statistics Yearbook*, 1988, p. 404.

39. Although faced with a sharp decline in the production of crops for domestic consumption, the government was forced to intervene and restore some of the protective measures which it had initially removed.
40. See M. Lago, 'Rural Women and the Neo-Liberal Model in Chile', in Deere and de Leon, *Rural Women and State Policy*, pp. 26–7.
41. See M. Crummett, 'Rural Women and Migration in Latin America', in Deere and de Leon, *Rural Women and State Policy*, p. 247.
42. D. Hojman, 'Prospects for Rural Employment and Wages under Neo-Liberal Policies: The Case of Chilean Agriculture', *Bulletin of Latin American Research*, vol. 8, no. 1 (1989) p. 118.
43. P. Campana, 'Peasant Economy, Women's Labour and Differential Forms of Capitalist Development: A Comparative Study in Three Contrasting Situations in Peru and Chile', PhD thesis, University of Durham, 1985, p. 112.
44. Lago, 'Rural Women and the Neo-Liberal Model', p. 26.
45. See Campana, 'Peasant Economy . . .', pp. 112–18.
46. Ibid, p. 119.
47. In 1978 it was estimated that 90.7 per cent of domestic servants were employed in urban areas. Source: P. Alonso, M. R. Larrain and R. Salidad, 'La Empleada de Casa Particular', in Corravabias (ed.), *Chile Mujer y Sociedad* (Santiago, 1978).
48. See David Hojman, 'Land Reform Activity Fluctuations, Female Migration and the Market for Domestic Service in Chile', *Journal of Latin American Studies*, vol. 21, no. 1 (1989).
49. See *ILO Yearbook*, 1988, pp. 70–71, 404. All the statistics in this section come from this source.
50. Of the total workforce (men and women) between 1983 and 1988, 11.9 per cent were employed in communal and social services and the numbers employed in personal and domestic services increased from 12.6 per cent to 13.3 per cent. Source: Banco Central, quoted in EIU CP, 1988/9.
51. David Hojman, 'Domestic Servants in Santiago, Chile: Research Note', *Bulletin of Latin American Research*, vol. 6, no. 1 (1987) pp. 65–7.
52. See Alonso *et al.*, 'La Empleada . . .', for figures for 1978; and Chuchkryk thesis for 1982 figures (drawn from INE).
53. Hojman, 'Land Reform, Female Activity Rate . . . . . .', *JLAS*, p. 129.
54. Clarissa Hardy, 'Organizadas de Subsistencia: los sectores populares frente a sus necessidades en Chile', PET, WP no. 41, 1985.
55. For a description of this process, see *Somos Mas Chile: Women's Delegation Report*, published by the Chile Solidarity Campaign, London, 1986.
56. See *Somos Mas*, ibid, for description of a meeting.
57. Lago, 'Rural Women and the Neo-Liberal Model', p. 32.
58. Figures quoted in Clarissa Hardy, 'Estratagias Orginazadas de Subsistencia: Los Sectores Sociales frente a sus necessidades en Chile', PET, WP 41, Chile, 1985.

59. See Clarissa Hardy, 'Los Talleres Artisanales de Conchali: La Organizacion, su recorrida y sus protagonistas', PET, 1984.
60. H. Walker Larrain, 'Transformation of Practices in Grassroots Organisations: A Casestudy in Chile', PhD, University of Toronto, 1985.
61. Quoted in J. Schirmer, '"Those Who Die For Life Cannot Be Called Dead": Women and Human Rights Protest in Latin America', *Feminist Review*, no. 32 (1989) p. 21.
62. This essentially personal emphasis has been used in other ways. For example, the testimonies of the families of 57 missing women and children were published together with their life-histories, details of their disappearance, their photographs and poems by them. See the Agrupacion de Familiares de Detenidos–Desaparacidos, *Donde Estan: Mujeres Chilenas Detenidas–Desaparacidas* (Santiago, 1986).
63. See J. Kirkwood, 'Women and Politics in Chile', *International Social Science Journal*, 35 (1983) p. 634.
64. CODEM – Comite de Defensa de los Derechos de la Mujer; MUDECHI – Mujeres de Chile; and MOMUPO – Movimiento de Mujeres Pobladoras. For further details, see P. Chuchryk, 'Feminist Anti-Authoritarian Politics: The role of Women's Organisations in the Chilean Transition to Democracy', in Jaquette (ed.), *The Women's Movement. . . .*
65. Her best known work in English is 'Women and Politics in Chile' (see note 63 above).

8 The Christian Churches and Women's Experience of Structural Adjustment in Nigeria

Carolyne Dennis

INTRODUCTION

Existing accounts of the impact of structural adjustment programmes[1] on the populations of the countries affected have focused, understandably, on their effects on such vital indicators as infant mortality, enrolment in education and decline in real incomes.[2] This emphasis has been expanded to provide gendered analyses of adjustment programmes which have derived their significance from their ability to explain the impact of such programmes on households and their differential impact on household members.[3] There is another significant dimension to the construction of a sufficient account of structural adjustment programmes which has so far been relatively neglected. Those who have endured adjustment programmes may have had little control over the causes of the crisis or the content and implementation of the adjustment programmes but they have constructed explanations of the situations in which they find themselves. The construction of such explanations has become increasingly problematic as governments implementing adjustment policies have assumed greater political powers in order to silence opposition to these programmes.[4]

There are signs in literature and popular music of the search to express one of the central experiences of the past decade: the impact of economic crisis and adjustment programmes and the groping towards survival strategies by individuals and households. Many of these songs and stories express the threat to human identity posed by such unremitting hardship. Others invoke resistance at either a political or individual level to the assumption that the present experience is inevitable or an appropriate punishment for past behaviour. Nigeria is a striking example of the production of such 'resistance' in

179

the songs of Fela Anikulapo-Kuti and the stories of Ben Okri, for example, in spite of the hostility of the Federal Military Government to such expressions of opposition.[5]

In the majority of countries enduring structural adjustment programmes, especially in sub-Saharan Africa, explanations at the individual level for traumatic events are customarily constructed in religious terms. Any religious cosmology contains within it the potential to explain the 'causes' of disastrous or unexpected occurrences at the individual or social level. The 'claim' of organised religion to provide explanations of crises is reinforced by the constraints on the range of political explanations of the adjustment which are acceptable to the governments of the countries concerned.[6] Such explanations also offer a method of either coming to terms with or avoiding such disasters in the future. In societies in which religion provides such an important focus for constructing social cosmologies and a framework for social existence, and confronted with the long-term uncertainties and, in many cases, daily hardship, associated with structural adjustment, one would expect religious observance and explanation to undergo significant shifts and modifications in order to address this dominant reality of everyday social and economic existence. Since all religious cosmologies also contain an ideology of gender, these shifts and modifications could be expected to have implications for women.

In this chapter the interrelationship between the experience of a structural adjustment programme and the construction of religious explanations of a traumatic and rapidly changing reality and methods of coming to terms with the results of that experience, will be explored in terms of the recent history of Nigeria. It will begin with a brief account of the most important characteristics of the Structural Adjustment Programme (SAP) in Nigeria and its impact on particular categories of Nigerian women, followed by a discussion of the significance of religious explanations of social and individual 'tragedies' and the rituals by which people 'cope' with these crises. This will be explored further in relation to the most important trends in Nigerian religious affiliation and observance. This analysis provides the basis for an account of the effects of the SAP on religious explanation and observance in Nigeria, focusing on the recent experience of the Christian churches and its significance for Nigerian women. The experience of the SAP in Nigeria has taken place against the background of the long-term issue of the legitimacy of the Nigerian state and its arrangements for distributing power and resources, and the short-term project of the Federal Military Government to secure a return to a form of civilian rule it regards as acceptable. The political context will not be directly addressed in this chapter except as it has influenced the increasing political significance of religious affiliation.[7]

THE STRUCTURAL ADJUSTMENT PROGRAMME IN NIGERIA

The SAP in Nigeria, as in all the other countries undergoing 'adjustment', was preceded by a severe economic crisis. The nature of these crises differed from one economy to another. The Nigerian crisis could perhaps best be characterised as an extreme example of the 'oil exporting economy crisis'. The 1970s were characterised by high levels of public investment, especially in large infrastructure projects such as roads and popular social programmes such as the introduction of Universal Primary Education[8] financed by the rise in the world price of oil in 1973. It was also characterised by substantial increases in income for particular sections of the population especially those people who were able to secure a living unofficially from the public sector. Levels of corruption and rent seeking increased dramatically.[9] In this 'buoyant' economy the economic crisis at the end of the 1970s came as a shock. An explanation was required which identified the cause of the crisis or those people who had caused the emergency and thus suggested its solution. This need to explain the economic crisis had important implications for Nigerian women, particular groups of whom were perceived as contributing to the crisis and the hardship created by the subsequent adjustment programme.

The Structural Adjustment Programme implemented in Nigeria has similar characteristics to structural adjustment programmes being implemented elsewhere in sub-Saharan Africa and Latin America. The Nigerian SAP, while it has been introduced in response to an economic crisis which has characteristics common to the economic situation which preceded adjustment in other countries, like them also has a particular history and has resulted from a specific relationship between the political process and its impact on economic policies and priorities. The structure of the political economy of Nigeria, filtered through the constraints of the period of 'adjustment', has also determined the manner in which the SAP has been implemented and which groups within Nigerian society have borne the costs of its implementation. One of the superficially distinct characteristics of the Nigerian SAP is that it was introduced by the Federal Military Government in Nigeria without direct overt IMF intervention although it bears a remarkable resemblance to programmes in other countries which have been introduced with 'formal' IMF conditionality. This would appear to have been influential in creating the clear self-identification of the members of the Federal Military Government with the SAP they have introduced and also the confidence and bravery required and demonstrated by the critics of the adjustment programme.[10]

The SAP in Nigeria has consisted of measures to 'stabilise' the economy by taking steps to reduce the budgetary and foreign exchange deficits primarily by reducing 'non-productive' government expenditure and a series of devaluations. This has been followed by successive measures designed to 'liberalise' foreign exchange and internal markets, the privatisation of parastatals and an absolute reduction in government expenditure and its shift from 'non-productive' to productive sectors.[11] This has led to the floating of the naira through the mechanism of the Second-tier Foreign Exchange Market (SFEM). The short-term cuts in foreign exchange availability and longer-term increase in its price have reduced access to essential imports and increased their price. It has also had the effect of reducing supplies to factories which are working under capacity and which has led to the retrenchment of the labour force.[12] The reductions in public expenditure have also led to large-scale retrenchment of the public sector labour force.

The freeing of markets, retrenchment of parastatals and the abolition of subsidies has been implemented with the greatest enthusiasm in agriculture. The raising of farm-gate prices has led to increases in agricultural production.[13] It is not yet clear from the available evidence which groups in Nigerian rural communities have been able to take advantage of these price incentives, although comparative evidence from other countries and anecdotal evidence from Nigeria would suggest that it is those farmers who are able to use their access to political power to secure access to the necessary resources of land and credit. This would be consistent with evidence of the impact of earlier agricultural development policies. There are indications that the privatisation of marketing of cash crops, especially of cocoa, has raised problems of the quality of this produce on international markets. The problem of the appropriate emphasis and allocation of resources between the cash crop and food crop sectors is also unresolved. This focus on internationally traded crops has important implications for the ability of Nigerian women to provision their households.

One of the most important components of the Nigerian SAP, as with many other adjustment programmes, has been the cuts in government expenditure on 'non-productive' sectors such as health and education. This has happened because of a lack of government funds and a deliberate cutting of government expenditure in these sectors and the imposition of fees and charges in hospitals and schools as a method of 'cost recovery'.[14] The raising of the price and reducing the availability of these social services, at the same time as incomes, especially in urban areas, have been falling and the basic provisioning of households has become more difficult, has had important consequences for the Nigerian population. In the longer term, the fall in investment in education and the reimposition of charges has severe implications for the development of human resources in Nigeria. In the short term, the risks to nutritional status, especially of low-income groups, and the strain imposed by the survival strategies created in response to the SAP, makes the withdrawal of health provision of central significance. This chapter focuses on one response to the withdrawal of access to health facilities in a period of increasing vulnerability to ill health: the turning to religious remedies.

THE STRUCTURAL ADJUSTMENT PROGRAMME AND WOMEN IN NIGERIA

There are two aspects to the impact of the SAP on Nigerian women which are most relevant to this chapter: the role played by women in the search for scapegoats to explain the origin and 'cause' of the crisis; and the impact of the crisis and the SAP on Nigerian women as a consequence of their household responsibilities. The 1970s are now regarded as a period in which 'normal' social, political and economic structures and processes were overturned. It is likely that the groups chosen as scapegoats will be those who are identified as having diverged from socially acceptable behaviour. In addition there has been since 1983 a military government in Nigeria which has used the rhetoric of renewal, discipline and reform first to conduct a War Against Indiscipline (WAI) and then the National Orientation Movement (NOM) which have operated by searching for social groups who do not appear to be fulfilling their appropriate role within the social and economic structure. Attention has been focused on groups who are not perceived as contributing to the development of 'modern', efficient cities such as beggars, small traders on unauthorised sites and wage earners who are not 'productive'.[15]

A special place in this demonology has been reserved for particular categories of women: women who do not fulfil their duties to bring up their children with the correct values and thus threaten social order and control; and women who do not adequately perform the work for which they are paid because they are trading or concentrating on their domestic responsibilities. There is a third category of women who were identified as being responsible for national decline and indiscipline: the women who live by prostitution who both create problems for urban administrators and planners by acting as a focus for criminals and, in a more general sense, 'cause' a decline in national morality by tempting men into criminal and immoral ways of earning money. It is difficult in the context of southern Nigeria to insist on an exclusively domestic role for women in a society in which they are customarily expected to contribute materially to the household but public moral exhortations of this period were notable for their insistence of the exclusive responsibility of women for domestic management and child rearing. This is an endorsement of the 'natural' appropriateness of the 'double day' for women.

The economic expansion of the 1970s created opportunities for at least two groups of Nigerian women. The first is the small proportion of urban women with access to the educational qualifications for formal sector occupations. The second group is that group of women with the financial resources or the ability to exploit their sexuality in order to pursue activities in the informal sector or as 'sole' agents for government contracts. These groups are closely related to the particular groups of women selected as being one of the 'causes' of the Nigerian economic crisis.

If a particular social group is identified as the cause of an economic crisis and its aftermath, the question arises as to why this group has been selected as a scapegoat. It has already been stated that the source of the identification of women as the cause of the crisis lies in the fact that particular groups of women are perceived as taking on socially unacceptable roles in the preceding period. This assumes that it is particularly important for social stability and the 'health' of a society for women to conform to acceptable forms of behaviour. It also assumes that 'acceptable' forms of behaviour for women does not involve competing with men on the labour market or controlling their own sexuality and using it for financial gain. The source of these ideas of acceptability and appropriateness are likely to lie within the dominant forms of religious beliefs in Nigeria.

It has been very difficult to systematically monitor the impact of the SAP on households and on women in particular. However, the knowledge which exists of the structurally and ideologically defined domestic responsibilities of Nigerian women together with the evidence which is available, suggests that the impact of the SAP on urban households is experienced by women as increasing their responsibilities to manage their households at the same time as reducing the resources to which they have access in order to meet these responsibilities. The reduction in public and private sector wage employment has affected women wage earners and the wives of male wage earners. The rise in the price of essential commodities and the reduction in their availability has increased the investment of money and time required to provision a household. At the same time, the availability has decreased and the cost has increased of publicly and privately provided services such as education and health. As has been stated above, the availability of health facilities has a special significance in a period of increased health risk due to falling nutritional standards and lack of access to education facilities reduces the potential ability of children to enter a problematic labour market.[16]

The analysis of the effect of the economic crisis and the subsequent SAP on Nigerian women, especially low-income urban women, needs to be located within an understanding of their domestic and non-domestic work. In general terms, it is most fruitful to understand these responsibilities within the framework established by Moser, that women in developing countries have triple obligations for reproduction, production and for community management.[17] The assumption that it is 'natural' for women to have these triple responsibilities means that in situations of economic crisis it is common for these obligations to be widened and deepened and redefined as the duty to 'manage' the crisis. A woman who is head of her own household obviously has this responsibility. For a woman in a male-headed household, this duty to manage the crisis could be defined as making the crisis minimally evident to the male head of household in terms of provisioning and obtaining access to socially provided facilities such as water, health and education.[18] To move beyond this general framework of analysis of women's work, it is necessary to examine how the household structure and dominant definitions of women's socially expected role operate in particular societies; to acknowledge the differences between women's experience as well as its general character.

In Nigeria, this differs markedly from one region to another, influenced by economic variations, differences in household structure and interpretations of religious doctrine. A characteristic of the responsibilities of Yoruba women derives from the expectation that they will not only manage the consumption of resources within the household but will play a large part in procuring those resources. This is true for many women in sub-Saharan Africa but in Yoruba communities the expected or preferred way of doing this is through trade or petty commodity production rather than through agricultural work. This potentially leads to women having access to separate sources of money from their husbands. Translated into the conditions of the current economic crisis in Nigeria, this means that Yoruba women are responsible for providing the necessary additional money to provision the household in a period of falling real incomes, to manage the investment of time necessary to secure necessities which are intermittently available and to take upon themselves the responsibilities for securing the health and education of their children which were formerly, at least in part, the responsibility of the state.[19] This requires both more time and money. Under the conditions of the SAP, it is unlikely that there are great differences between the manner in which women's responsibilities are defined in various parts of Nigeria, except insofar as they are perceived as having differential access to income generating activities and thus differential responsibility for generating an income.

This brief analysis of the impact of the SAP in Nigeria has focused on the manner in which women, or particular groups of women, have been identified as one of the major causes of the crisis. This has important implications for the behaviour of women which is perceived as being appropriate to avoid or resolve the crisis. It is a crisis which is experienced at the level of the household, and therefore gender divisions of responsibilities and resources are crucial in determining the nature of this experience for women. Socially dominant definitions of women's responsibilities mean that the SAP has become an extension of women's obligation to manage the household and a 'test' of their commitment to being a wife and mother, in a situation in which women's social behaviour has become a matter of public debate and control. In order to explore, first, the origins of the ideas about appropriate behaviour for women and the relationship between women's behaviour and social and economic crisis, and, second, the manner in which women attempt to 'cope' with the strains of managing the SAP at the household level, the significance of particular religious explanations and organisations will be discussed.

THE NIGERIAN RELIGIOUS CONTEXT

In terms of the focus of this chapter, there are two fundamental aspects of religious systems which are especially relevant. All religious systems provide a cosmology – an explanation of the appropriate relationship between men, men and women and between human beings and the natural world. This cosmology provides the basis of the explanation of 'crisis' and women's responsibility for it which has been identified as an important component of the Nigerian SAP. Religious systems are also institutions which insist on the necessity to constantly observe rituals to reinforce the prescribed meaning of relationships and as the concrete expression of the priorities of its cosmology. The observance of ritual and the establishment and reinforcing of social relationships within a religious context provides one of the most significant mechanisms by which women 'cope' with the strain of being responsible for managing the economic crisis and the impact of the SAP.[20] But the manner in which the cosmologies and rituals are selected, reinforced and reinterpreted depends upon the historical experience of particular societies. The recent religious experience of Nigeria will be outlined before the significance of religious cosmologies and observance in the present period of adjustment is analysed.

The different societies indigenous to Nigeria each had their own dominant religion prior to Islamic and Christian evangelisation and conquest. These religions vary as much as the social and political systems of the societies concerned. They do, however, have some characteristics in common. These religions were associated with particular places and localities and explained the 'meaning' of human society and history and the appropriate relationship between people and the natural world within that particular physical environment.[21] Under specific circumstances they did transcend this geographical specificity; notable examples are the manner in which African religions adapted to the new circumstances created by slavery in south and central America.[22]

In West Africa, the first widespread movement of particular groups of people outside the boundaries of these religious systems is associated with the expansion of Islam. Before the jihads of the nineteenth century, Islam in West Africa in general and in Nigeria in particular was carried by the conversion of long-distance traders travelling far from their own societies and requiring an explanation of the world and a code of ethics and behaviour which focused on the universality of its prescriptions and their applicability under all circumstances and in relationship to all people or at least all men.[23] Given the causes of widespread conversion to Islam in the period before the nineteenth century, it was primarily an experience of men who dominated long-distance trade. There were notable women Moslems, renowned for their learning, holiness, etc., but they were often members of royal houses associated with the spread of Islam. The majority of women, like the majority of men, remained in one specified geographical area and continued to be closely associated with indigenous forms of religion such as spirit possession and divination, even when these were defined as unacceptable by an expanding militant Islam.

If the available evidence historical evidence and the present-day practices of these indigenous religions is examined, it appears that in most of them women occupied a subordinate but essential place. The association of belief and ritual with the continuity of a given society and thus the material basis of that survival meant that they centred around the need to ensure rain, the fertility of the soil, the level of rivers and the continued availability of natural resources. This was often associated with the relationship between female fertility and the survival of a society. Thus female gods and the female priests associated with them were prominent in these religious systems.[24] They often contain beliefs concerning special powers associated with women which can be used for good or ill. These beliefs provide the space for women to assume extraordinary roles within the religious system. They also provide the basis for the social control of women, as a woman who behaves in a socially unacceptable manner who is not defined as 'extraordinary' will be accused of witchcraft.

It is striking how in societies such as Yorubaland in which women may have an important economic role but are not expected to play a role in the public political arena, particular women play a significant role as religious virtuosi and there are a wide range of religious rituals addressed to what are perceived as female concerns, usually concentrated on the need to secure fertility and social peace. Yoruba cosmology is also distinguished by the existence of an *orisa* or god associated with the worship of the human head. The function of this *orisa* is to enable the worshipper to find their own destiny. It is often consulted by those, both men and women, who have reason to feel that they need to change some aspect of their lives, their marriage, their occupation or their *orisa* and thus provides a space for women to change unsatisfactory lives.[25]

Although there were differences in the position of women in the indigenous religious systems of West African societies, it appears that the spread of Islam is associated with a change in the socially accepted behaviour of women at least in towns in which Islamic influence was strongest. The spread of Islam in the societies of the savannah was accompanied by the denunciation of the social and religious practices of Moslems and 'pagans' with particular ferocity being reserved for Moslems who were perceived as combining Islam with indigenous religious practice. One of the areas of greatest condemnation was in religious practices regarded as inconsistent with the practice of Islam. For example, in many West African savannah societies, there were and are cults of spirit possession such as the Hausa *bori* cult which were regarded as particularly abhorrent by the representatives of the 'purified' Islam of the Fulani rulers and teachers of late-nineteenth-century northern Nigeria. These unacceptable religious practices such as *bori* often gave an important place to extraordinary women religious practitioners and were used by women to 'resolve' problems, such as fertility and barrenness, and those encountered in a polygynous marriage.[26]

The cyclical campaigns to purify Islam have had as one of their central foci the perceived need to ensure that women were brought under the control necessary for an Islamic society to exist. One measure of that control was the condemnation of these survivals of indigenous religious practice. The ability to control women's access to public space according to particular interpretations of Islamic law has always been problematic in a region which is largely dependent upon agriculture and in which labour has been scarce. The most successful examples of the 'enclosure' of women took place among the wives of wealthy men living in large urban centres.[27]

The spread of Christianity in West Africa in general and in Nigeria was related closely to European commercial penetration and later political domination. The regions in which the expansion was greatest were those in which European traders were most active and where colonial administrations had the greatest impact. Thus, in Nigeria the areas of greatest Christian conversion by the middle of the twentieth century were the south and south-east of the country and the Yoruba south-west.[28] The religious position in the Yoruba south-west was particularly complex as, in addition to a complex indigenous religious system, it was an area of Moslem evangelisation and Christian missionary activity often within the same communities and affecting members of the same families. It was also, in the latter half of the nineteenth century, an area of physical insecurity and periodic war. Thus from this period, Yoruba communities have had a wide variety of religious activities and explanations available within them and there is evidence of considerable movement by individuals and households between the various forms of religious observance available.[29]

The historical records show that there has always been considerable concern within the missionary churches to denounce indigenous religious activities such as spirit possession, divination and healing ceremonies in which women played an important role. However, one of the distinctive characteristics of the development of Christianity in West Africa has been the emergence of indigenous churches which have sought to establish a different relationship to the indigenous religious and social structure from the missionary churches. This has led to their acceptance of polygyny. In terms of religious beliefs, the indigenous churches exhibit considerable variety but often demonstrate an acceptance of the priorities of indigenous religions combined with a vehement denunciation of their specific practices. This process has been especially significant in Yorubaland. In the early twentieth century, a series of Christian sects were established in this region, usually called *aladura*, or healing churches, which have consistently both attacked indigenous religious practices with great ferocity and developed the same religious priorities of addressing 'this worldly' issues of health and the need for worldly prosperity.[30] They have also been associated with giving women high status and position within the churches and are regarded as being especially appropriate for women to consult on matters which especially affect them, such as fertility, health and the need for money. Thus, when one examines the possible impact of the economic crisis of the 1980s on religious observance, it is necessary to distinguish the missionary churches from the *aladura* churches with the expectation that the latter might be perceived as being especially significant to women confronted with the problem of 'managing' this crisis.

Religious cosmologies provide an explanation which gives meaning to an otherwise chaotic world: 'an area of meaning carved out of a vast mass of meaninglessness, a small clearing of lucidity in a formless, dark, always ominous jungle'.[31] Religious explanations of 'nature' and society and the appropriate relationship between them always incorporate an explicit explanation of the appropriate relationship between men and women and the 'natural' status of women in society. Within Christian cosmologies this has conventionally been interpreted as deriving from the weakness and fragility inherent in women by virtue of their role in physical reproduction, combined with an assumption that the bodily functions associated with physical reproduction create a degree of impurity in women which can only be resolved by religious ritual. There is an alternative emphasis of the place of women in the natural and social world developed by Fatima Mernissi in relation to Islam which focuses on the potential danger which derives from women's imperfect incorporation into the social world because of the special link with 'nature' created by their reproductive functions and their sexuality.[32] It is this type of ideology which acts as the justification for the mechanisms which have been developed to control women through the legal system, religious ideology and the limitation of their social space, regarded as being necessary to preserve men from the harm they can do. This second approach would appear to have an application wider than Islamic society. The potential power of women based on their ability to summon up natural forces is a significant part of many indigenous African religions.

This religious concern with the potentially dangerous and uncontrollable forces associated with female sexuality and reproduction means that the 'control' of women is closely linked with concepts of what is socially appropriate and 'normal'. Circumstances in which women do not appear to be controlled in what are regarded as 'traditional' ways, or appear to be taking on inappropriate social roles, are regarded as abnormal and a sign of the disintegration of the key structures of society. This also has the implication that if an unforeseen calamity strikes a society, the cause must be sought in wicked or socially unacceptable behaviour by members of the society concerned. The socially circumscribed roles open to women and the assumption that this limitation is necessary to maintain social order means that the unacceptable behaviour of women provides a particularly relevant explanation for social or natural catastrophe and women provide an especially appropriate scapegoat. The explanation also provides the basis for the necessary response to traumatic events. One element of the resolution of the crisis has to be the return by women to what are defined as being the 'traditional' or religiously prescribed roles for women in that society.

In Nigeria in the 1980s, there has been a public consensus that inappropriate behaviour by women has been one of the causes of the crisis. There also appears to have been a consensus as to which categories of women were responsible. In the 'world turned upside down'of 1970s' Nigeria, there were identifiable categories of women who were occupying 'inappropriate public space'. As has been stated above, these were women who were able to use their educational qualifications to take advantage of an expanding public sector and women who were able to take advantage of an expanding sector fulfilling public sector contracts. Using a different set of criteria but often targeted at the same women, it was women who were defined as neglecting their domestic duties especially in relation to socialising children and women who used their sexuality for economic gain.[33]

In a context in which religion provides the most pervasive social cosmology, it also provides a guide to appropriate action especially in the face of the unforeseen and uncontrollable. Religious ritual and especially continuous, habitual ritual provides a means of atoning for and coming to terms with uncontrollable events. This is true for individual tragedies such as infertility and bereavement as well as for major social catastrophes such as epidemics and economic crises. Not only have religious institutions provided a series of explanations for such crises but widespread social crises have provided the background for the emergence of new forms of religious observance and even new religions which are perceived as addressing the new problematic situation. In Nigeria, for example, the emergence of the *aladura* churches is associated with the catastrophic results of the influenza epidemic in 1919.[34] Particular prophetic forms of Islam developed in response to the crises created by the imposition of colonial rule and, more recently, with the insecurity for Koranic teachers created by the replacement of Islamic forms of education with Universal Primary Education in the early 1980s.[35]

If we understand religious observance as providing not only a means of developing an explanation of a crisis but also as a means of developing a form of social existence to 'cope' with it, it is clear that the crises in women's lives are frequently accompanied by intensified religious practice and attachment to religious institutions. The significance of religious observance and membership of religious organisations for the 'resolution' of the problem of infertility was mentioned above. Crises of illness, death and desertion are all addressed by many religious institutions which claim to provide both an explanation of and a means of transcending the problems particularly associated with the responsibilities customarily borne by women. The 'transcendence' of personal tragedy is often accomplished by increased religious observance and the opportunity for social recognition and personal fulfilment which arises from membership and holding an official position within religious organisations. Thus, those religious institutions which provide for the possibility of high and increasing levels of ritual observance by lay members and for the possibility of office-holding and the exercise of responsibility by women, might be regarded as most likely to address the needs of women faced with unforeseen crises or personal tragedies.

Given the type of crisis for individuals and households presented by economic crises and Structural Adjustment Programmes, there are three ways in which the possible relationship between religious belief, observance and institutions and women's response to the emergency might be constructed. The first is the manner in which dominant prevailing religious beliefs and the way in which compliance to them is enforced has led to the identification of scapegoats, including particular groups of women, who are explained as being the 'cause' of the crises through their behaviour or, rather, misbehaviour. Second, confronted with a deepening crisis of provisioning households, the management of which is regarded as women's responsibility, for women who operate with religiously based cosmologies and as members of religious organisations, it would be logical for them to look to religion for support and consolation for the burden they bear. This is likely to be manifested by a search for religious institutions which are identified as having the possibility of providing this support and also of increasing the intensity of religious observance in order to elicit greater support in bearing everyday burdens. Third, one project of structural adjustment programmes has been to reduce state social sector spending. This has recently been expanded into a search for organisations to assume the responsibility for health, education and 'community' projects previously defined as being the responsibility of the state. The non-governmental organisations are increasingly regarded as being the repository of the resources of materials, money, labour and organisational capacity to replace state social provision.[36] In many developing countries the NGOs with a local base are likely to be religious in origin. This is intensified in the case of women for whom religious organisations often provide the only socially acceptable network other than those of their own and their husbands' relatives. The following discussion will focus on the first and second aspects of this situation. The third does not as yet appear to be a significant component of the Nigerian SAP, in comparison, for example, with Ghana.

STRUCTURAL ADJUSTMENT, RELIGION AND WOMEN IN NIGERIA

In the Nigerian situation, the potential importance of religious explanations, rituals and institutions in the present period of crisis is made more complex by the fact that this is a period in which the significance of political identities based on religious affiliation has intensified for reasons which are in some ways related to the imposition of the SAP and in some ways are independent of it. It is therefore necessary to discuss briefly the significance of developments within Islam before focusing on developments within Christianity.

The analysis of the recent rise in significance of religious explanations of the social and economic world both as the basis for social and political action and a source of private security and strategy for 'coping' with crisis, has been more systematically developed in relation to Islam than Christianity. It is necessary to draw on the insights of this body of work both to illuminate the interface between Moslem and Christian communities in Nigeria and to begin the process of understanding the characteristics of the parallel but distinct process within Christianity. The growing significance of a particular strand of Islamic explanation and social action usually categorised as 'fundamentalism' is often located in the political imperative of governments wishing to control their populations and at the same time provide a 'radical' alternative to socialist ideas and organisations.[37] This becomes especially important in periods of economic difficulty and crisis in which 'fundamentalist' explanations provide both a causal explanation and a scapegoat and a solution to the problem in terms of the supposed results of observing the prescribed interpretation of Islamic practice. Both these imperatives have considerable significance for women. The exercise of political and social control centres predominantly around the need to regulate and limit the acceptable activity of women. The extent of the regulation and limitation of women's behaviour acts as a benchmark for indicating the success of the project of introducing fundamentalist interpretations of Islamic law and practice. Periods of economic crisis and adjustment which are experienced particularly intensely at the level of the household, create particular burdens for women, as does the decline in observance of social obligations associated with rapid social and economic change. Women are often also regarded as being one of the most important causes of such crises because of the way in which they have increasingly deviated from religiously and politically acceptable behaviour. The new religious movements both present them as the cause of the present crisis who need to be 'punished' and controlled, and also provide them with a means of coping and managing the acute stresses of rapid social change and, more particularly, of economic crisis and the implementation of structural adjustment programmes.

Within Nigerian Islam, 'fundamentalism' is important as the manner in which both political differences between different regions and the competition for resources provided by the state are articulated. This increasing emphasis on the significance of a 'purified' religious observance is also a response to the intensification of inequalities of power and resources and, more specifically, the conditions created by the present economic crisis and the policies of the SAP. Within Nigeria the differences between north and south have customarily been articulated in religious terms, stressing the Moslem identity of the 'true' north, in spite of the fact that there are large communities of Moslems in western Nigeria. The present political debate and manoeuvring is not created by the economic crisis although this tends to intensify its bitterness. The political distinction between north and south which has always been formulated to some extent in religious terms is now increasingly understood in these terms. This has led to intensified religious evangelisation by both Moslem and Christian organisations often heavily dependent upon foreign resources, and to the emphasis upon the political dimensions of religious identity, particularly in opposition to the other religious communities.[38] Within Nigerian Islam there is a long tradition of renewal and tension focused on the decline in religious observance associated with the rich and powerful which was given its most spectacular expression in the jihads of nineteenth-century Hausaland. There is also a long history of religious movements associated with the poor and dispossessed putting forward radical social programmes heavily influenced by the Mahdist tradition derived from Sudan. The most recent major phenomenon of this kind was the Maitatsime rebellion in Kano in the late 1970s.[39] In the early period of economic crisis and the SAP the specific scapegoating of women, reinforced by particular interpretations of religious prescriptions concerning women's public behaviour, were documented as an important response to the crisis in Nigeria.[40]

The history of Christianity in Nigeria is associated with the second phase of European penetration: the imposition of administrative control, after the penetration by trading firms. In south-west and south-east Nigeria in the second half of the nineteenth century, the expansion of Christian influence and the increase in the number of Christian converts is related to the spread of educational facilities associated with the missions. This became especially important in the period following the 1914–18 war, when the numbers of clerical positions in the public and private sector, dependent upon the possession of educational certificates, increased. The 'missionary' churches have always been associated with the upholding of 'western' forms of behaviour, whether in marriage or work, and of the monitoring of individual self-improvement associated with nonconformity. These churches have always also acted as evangelists for particular 'appropriate' forms of behaviour for women. In the past they developed activities appropriate to a conception of women as 'housewives', for whom improvement was related to the ability to accumulate domestic skills and thus run a home with 'civilised' accomplishments such as cake-making and piano-playing. The evidence suggests that in Yorubaland where women have always generated an income, these skills were eagerly sought not as domestic accomplishments but because they could also be used in order to generate income.[41] More recently, the missionary churches have been associated with the provision of educational facilities, especially the most prestigious private schools and have also as the mode of public prayer especially appropriate for the educated bourgeousie.

In the past few years there has been an additional stream of Christian evangelisation which although it is related to the long-established missionary churches has different implications for Nigerian society and is better analysed as being structurally distinct. There has been a significant growth in the evangelising activities of Protestant sects, usually but by no means exclusively American. They are characterised by the availability of large sums of money for the provision of free literature and facilities, and by a focus on the need for individual repentance, reformed behaviour and the identification of external or internal enemies such as Communism, but in cases such as Nigeria, also militant Islam. Their emphasis on the appropriate behaviour for women developed in opposition to what is perceived as prevailing 'sinful' behaviour, poses a distinct alternative model of women's role which although it is not perceived as being as constrained as that of fundamentalist Islam also has a similar emphasis on blaming women for what are identified as the sins of men.

It is clear from the available evidence that the 'new' missionary churches and organisations have established themselves quickly and effectively in the universities. Much of the recent sectarian unrest has originated in conflict on university campuses between Moslem and evangelical Christian students.[42] The reason for this may lie in the recent tendency to articulate social identities in Nigeria in terms of religion to a greater extent than before, and these organisations have resources to support their activities in a situation of greatly reduced resources for any activity. But evidence prior to the economic crisis tends to suggest that women students perceived themselves to be under great pressure from the male students' desire both to treat them as sexual objects and to abuse them for any assertive behaviour.[43] Visible commitment to one of these sects acts as a release from the contradictory pressures of being a young woman in an educational institution in conflict with men and can thus be compared to the retreat into Moslem fundamentalism by other women.

It is not evident that there is any correlation between the rise in membership of evangelical organisations such as those prevalent on Nigerian university campuses and the conditions created by the economic crisis and the SAP. However, the character of the political debate which has accompanied the SAP and which has coincided with the preparation of Nigeria for the return to some variety of civilian rule, has increased the potential attraction of this type of religious organisation to young women. A very unstable and insecure situation has been created in which women's public behaviour, especially that of young, educated women operating in 'male' territory, has been increasingly subject to pressure and criticism. This assessment of the limited relationship between fundamentalist Christianity and the conditions created by structural adjustment may be specific to Nigeria and probably reflects the availability of other Christian explanations of the crisis and the appropriate response to it which will be discussed below. It appears in evidence from Ghana and other African countries.[44] This type of foreign-financed evangelical activity is increasing and has significant political implications for the countries concerned. It bears some similarity to the situation in Latin America where the fundamentalist Protestant churches have invested large resources to spread a message of great social conservatism and individualism combined with a social support system which replaces the decline in state provision to some extent.

The origins of the praying or *aladura* churches in the early 1920s in Yorubaland has been mentioned above. They developed in the period of great uncertainty and hardship in western Nigeria after 1918 which was intensified by the Spanish influenza epidemic. This had a particularly devastating effect in West Africa as people had no form of immunity to the disease. These churches are characterised by a focus on 'earthly' needs for health and money which also provide the basis for Yoruba indigenous religion. At the same time, they advocate extreme hostility and rejection of indigenous strategies for addressing such concerns as praying to specific *orisa* and resorting to divination. In terms of their organisation, they are marked by the extent to which all members of congregations are given the social recognition of holding office. They are also remarkable for the prominent role played by women in ritual and the organisational structure. They are conventionally regarded as being the form of Christian religious expression associated with the low-paid urban wage earner as opposed to the 'missionary' churches' identification with the educated middle classes.

The manner in which the *aladura* churches have been identified as having a special relevance to women and women's needs has been mentioned above. It has been discussed in work on women's health, for example, by Pearce. In recent years our understanding of this process has been extended by research into particular circumstances in which women may be drawn into consulting and becoming members of the *aladura* churches. Uyanga's work suggests that it is women who have fertility problems, who are 'barren' or potentially barren, who tend to become members of *aladura* congregations. This is consistent with the emphasis on the duty of a wife to provide her husband's family with children and especially sons in a society which favours polygyny.[45] In such a situation, the status of a wife within her husband's family depends in the first place upon her reproductive performance.[46]

The focus of the *aladura* churches on the health and economic preoccupations of their members is paralleled by the 'spiritual' churches of Calabar in which these concerns are also central. Some of these churches have been founded by women.[47] They also share with the *aladura* churches the characteristic of being essentially concerned to provide individualistic solutions of individual problems. These individual solutions take place within communities, the strength of which varies according to the permanence or fragility of the churches concerned. This means that in spite of the fears of governments in the past and present as to the potential political significance of these churches, collective political activity does not suggest itself as an appropriate way of extending the effectiveness of the solutions they offer. The 'privatised' character of the solution to secular problems presented by these indigenous churches contrasts with the very interventionist relationship with the political structure adopted by militant Islam.

The theology of the *aladura* churches is both simple in its written form and quite complex in its assumptions. Thus the written literature of these churches stresses the need for believers to live in a moral fashion, which is often defined as *not* following the practices of indigenous Yoruba religion, and committing themselves to a time-consuming and regular routine of prayer involving daily attendance at long church services. The reward of following this routine is that the specific practical, everyday worries of the members of the congregation will be seriously addressed by the pastor, especially if they involve the desire for better health or more money. Second, the requirement that the congregation spend a great deal of their resources of time within the church provides a support group and social recognition within lives which are perceived as being problematic and characterised by failure. Both the available research and common sense and anecdotal evidence in Nigeria suggests that women form a large proportion of *aladura* congregations. These churches do not appear to demand the conformity to strict and limited forms of behaviour as do the fundamentalist Moslem and Christian forms of religious observance, although the wearing of white uniforms and incessant attendance at church services acts as a highly visible sign of a particular religious commitment. It provides a socially acceptable form of identity for men and women who cannot obtain the social recognition which derives from the possession of education or money. *Aladura* churches require the investment of time and emotion from their members rather than material resources.

The 'practical' orientation of the *aladura* churches would appear to be especially appropriate in a period of continuous uncertainty concerning the potential source of money for urban households confronted by the possibility of retrenchment of industrial and administrative labour forces and the consequent effect of this on the informal sector. The relevance of the *aladura* emphasis on measures to ensure the achievement of higher standards of health for the individual *is also evident* to a situation in which health standards are threatened by the rise of food prices and lack of availability of food, falling access to wage employment and income generation and the increasing cost of formal health care. For women who have the responsibility of 'managing' the economic crisis there is an additional source of stress over which they have very little control or ability to predict and understand. The *aladura* churches' specific addressing of the problems faced by women at the level of explanation, ritual and social support system is relevant not only as a strategy for the individual tragedies of poverty or infertility but the individual tragedies created by sudden economic catastrophe.

CONCLUSION

One characteristic of African countries in the grip of structural adjustment programmes appears to be a rise in religious observance. Although there is as yet little quantitative evidence, the expansion in the number of churches and the increase in the time devoted to religious observance and its visibility has been noted by many observers.[48] The form which this rise in religious observance takes varies from one country to another. The rise in certain forms of religious observance within Islam, usually defined as 'fundamentalism', has been subject to increasingly sophisticated analysis, especially from the perspective of its implications for women in these communities. The parallel process of a rise in particular forms of Christian religious observance also associated with the onset of economic crisis and subsequent adjustment policies has been less subject to this type of systematic analysis. It appears to be a more diffuse process with less direct political relevance which tends to reduce its visibility. However, in the Nigerian situation where religious affiliation has at present a direct political relevance, it is clear that there is a systematic process of Christian evangelisation taking place. In the case of the massively funded evangelical churches based in North America, this process has significant implications for the young women who become the adherents of such churches, especially in terms of the definition of acceptable behaviour for women which they propagate. The form taken by this turn to religious forms of explanation and support in the situation created by the economic crisis and the imposition of adjustment policies varies from one region to another. In the case of south-west Nigeria it is suggested that one form of religious organisation, the *aladura* churches, in terms of their stated priorities and the manner in which they define the religious capacities of women, appear to have an 'elective affinity' with women confronted with the problem of managing the Nigerian SAP in their own households. It is less clear in this case what are the implications of this process for the construction of socially accepted female roles or the social control of women's behaviour, as these forms of religious organisations derive their belief systems and organisational structure from examples other than those of the European and American based missionary churches.

Notes and References

1. In this chapter the following terminology will be used: 'structural adjustment programmes' for adjustment programmes following IMF and World Bank conditionality; and 'Structural Adjustment Programme' (SAP) for the adjustment programme being pursued by the Federal Military Government in Nigeria.
2. For example, G. Cornia, R. Jolly and F. Stewart, *Adjustment with a Human Face* (Oxford: Clarendon Press, 1987).
3. D. Elson, 'The Impact of Structural Adjustment on Women, Concepts and Issues', Women and Development programme, Commonwealth Secretariat, 1987; and D. Elson (ed.), *Male Bias in the Development Process* (Manchester University Press, forthcoming).
4. *Review of African Economy*, no. 47 (issue on The Price of Economic Reform).
5. See Chinua Achebe, *Anthills of the Savannah* (London: Anchor Press, 1988); B. Okri, *Stars of the New Curfew* (London: Viking, 1989).
6. In 1989 three critics of the SAP were detained for a considerable period in Nigeria: Dr Tai Solarin, Chief Gani Fawehinmi and Chief Michael Imodu. See *West Africa*, 26 June–2 July 1989, p. 1065.
7. B. Beckman, 'Neo-Colonialism, Capitalism and the State in Nigeria', in H. Bernstein and B. Campbell (eds), *Contradictions of Accumulation in Africa* (Beverly Hills: Sage, 1985); H. Beinen, *Political Conflict and Economic Change in Nigeria* (London: Frank Cass, 1985).
8. A. Olukoshi, 'World Bank/IMF Structural Adjustment Programmes and the African Working Class', 'Conference on the Impact of IMF and World Bank Policies on the People of Africa', Institute for African Alternatives, City University, London, 7–10 September 1987.
9. See C. Dennis, 'Constructing a "Career" Under Conditions of Economic Crisis and Structural Adjustment; The Survival Strategies of Nigerian

Women', in H. Afshar (ed.), *Women, Development and Survival in the Third World* (London: Longman, forthcoming).

10. The relationship between the Nigerian Military Government and its SAP can be compared with that of the Chilean military government and market liberalisation, discussed by Georgina Waylen in her chapter.

11. A. O. Phillips and E. Ndekwu (eds), *Structural Adjustment Programme in a Developing Economy: The Case of Nigeria* (Ibadan: NISER, 1987) ch. 2; World Bank, *Nigeria: Macro-Economic Policies for Structural Adjustment*, Report no. 4506, UNI 15, August 1983.

12. Y. Bangura, 'Crisis and Adjustment: The Experience of Nigerian Workers', 'Conference on the Impact of the IMF and World Bank Policies on the People of Africa', Institute for African Alternatives, City University, 7–10 September 1987.

13. Phillips and Ndekwu, *Structural Adjustment Programme*, 15–16. G. Williams, 'Marketing Without and With Marketing Boards: The Origins of State Marketing Boards in Nigeria', *Review of African Political Economy*, no. 34 (December 1985) pp. 4–15 for the background to the development of parastatal marketing; and G. Williams, 'The World Bank in Rural Nigeria Revisited: A Review of the World Bank's Nigeria; Agricultural Review 1987', *Review of African Political Economy*, no. 43 (1988) pp. 42–67. For a discussion of the situation in Ghana, see E. Hutchful, 'From "Revolution" to Monetarism: The Economics and Politics of the Adjustment Programme in Ghana', in B. Campbell and J. Loxley (eds), *Structural Adjustment in Africa* (London: Macmillan, 1985) pp. 92–131.

14. Phillips and Ndekwu, *Structural Adjustment Programme*, 2; Cornia, Jolly and Stewart, *Adjustment with a Human Face*, ch. 2; C. Dennis, 'The Economic Crisis in Africa and Women's Health: Constructing its Effects on Nigerian Women', African Studies Association UK Conference, 17–19 September 1986.

15. C. Dennis, 'Women and the State in Nigeria: The Case of the Federal Military Government 1984–1985', in H. Afshar (ed.), *Women, State and Ideology* (London: Tavistrock, 1987) pp. 13–27.

16. The impression of increasing reliance on an expanding source of unqualified medical advice is reinforced by one report suggesting that there are 10 000 'quack' doctors in Lagos alone: *West Africa*, 10–16 April 1989, p. 547.

17. C. O. N. Moser, 'Gender Planning in the Third World: Meeting Practical and Strategic Planning Needs', *World Development*, vol. 17, no. 11, 1989.

18. See Winifred Weekes-Vagliani's and Caroline Moser's chapters in this book; and C. Dennis, 'Constructing a "Career" Under Conditions of Economic Crisis and Structural Adjustment: The Survival Strategies of Nigerian Women', in H. Afshar (ed.), *Women, Development and Survival in the Third World* (London: Longman, forthcoming).

19. See A. Bamisaiye and M. A. Oyediran, 'Female Labour Force Participation and the Care of Pre-School Children: A Survey of Mothers Employed at LUTH/CMUL', 'National Workshop on Working Mothers

and Early Childhood Education in Nigeria', NISER, Ibadan, 13–16 September 1981.
20. The phenomenon of increased religious observance and its modification under conditions of economic crisis and adjustment in sub-Saharan Africa has been the subject of much anecdotal comment. It is true not only of Nigeria but of countries such as Zambia and Ghana.
21. E. Isichei, *History of the Igbo People* (London: Macmillan, 1976); N. Fadipe, *The Sociology of the Yoruba* (Ibadan University Press, 1939).
22. P. Verger, *Flux et Reflux de la Traite des Negres Entre le Golfe de Benin et Bahia de Todos Os Santos du XVIIe au XIXe Siecle* (The Hague: Mouton, 1968).
23. R. Horton, 'African Conversion', *Africa*, 41 (1971): P. Clarke, *West Africa and Islam* (London: Edward Arnold, 1982).
24. R. Abiodun, 'Women in Yoruba Religious Images', *African Languages and Cultures*, vol. 2, no. 1 (1989) pp. 1–18 for a discussion of the significance of the goddess Oshun.
25. P. Morton-Williams, 'An Outline of the Cosmology and Cult Organisation of the Oyo Yoruba', *Africa*, vol. 34, no. 3 (1964); K. Barber, 'How Man Makes God in West Africa: Yoruba Attitudes Towards the Orisa', *Africa*, vol. 51, no. 3 (1981) pp. 724–45.
26. C. Dennis, 'The Role of Religious Ideas in Social Change', in S. Afonja and T. O. Pearce (eds), *Social Change in Nigeria* (London: Longman, 1984) pp. 139–57; W. Onwujeogwu, 'The Cult of the Bori Spirits Among the Hausa', in M. Douglas and P. Kaberry (eds), *Man in Africa* (London: Tavistock, 1969) pp. 279–306.
27. R. Pittin, 'Marriage and Alternative Strategies: Career Patterns of Hausa Women in Katsina City', Ph.D thesis, University of London, 1979; E. Schildkrout, 'Dependence and Autonomy: The Economic Activities of Secluded Hausa Women in Kano', in Oppong (ed.) *Female and Male in West Africa* (London: Allen & Unwin, 1983) pp. 107–26.
28. K. Dike, *Trade and Politics in the Niger Delta 1830–1885* (Oxford: Oxford University Press, 1956); E. A. Ayandele, *The Missionary Impact of Modern Nigeria, 1842–1914: A Political and Social Analysis* (London, 1966); M. E. Noah, *Old Calabar: The City States and the Europeans 1800–1885* (Calabar, Nig.: Scholars Press, 1980); C. Dennis, 'Role of Religious Ideas . . .'.
29. D. Aronson, *The City is Our Farm: Seven Migrant Ijebu Yoruba Families* (Cambridge, Mass.: Schenkman, 1978); J. D. Y. Peel, *Ijeshas and Nigerians: The Incorporation of a Yoruba Kingdom 1890s–1970s* (Cambridge University Press, 1983).
30. J. D. Y. Peel, *Aladura: A Religious Movement Among the Yoruba* (London: Oxford University Press, 1968); R. I. J. Hackett (ed.), *New Religious Movements in Nigeria* (Lewiston: Edwin Mellon Press, 1987).
31. P. Berger, *The Social Reality of Religion* (London: Penguin University Books, 1973) p. 33.
32. F. Mernissi, *Beyond the Veil: Male and Female Dynamics in a Modern Muslim Society* (Cambridge, Mass.: Schenkman, 1975).
33. See Dennis, 'Women and The State in Nigeria'.

34. Peel, *Aladura*.
35. Clarke, *West Africa and Islam*.
36. For the latest World Bank thinking on this issue, see World Bank, *Sub-Saharan Africa: From Crisis to Sustainability* (Washington, 1989) p. 86.
37. See Haleh Afshar's chapter in this book. For an analysis of the significance of this phenomenon in the Nigerian context, see R. Pittin, 'Women, Work and Ideology in a Context of Economic Crisis: A Nigerian Case Study', Institute of Social Studies', ISS Working Paper No. 11, The Hague, 1989.
38. Jibrin Ibrahim, 'The Politics of Religion in Nigeria', *Review of African Political Economy*, 45/46 (1989) pp. 65–82.
39. Clarke, *West Africa and Islam*.
40. 'Women in Nigeria Press Release', *Review of African Political Economy*, no. 31 (December 1984) pp. 104–6.
41. B. Awe, 'Formal Education and the Status of Women: An Historical Perspective', in A. Ogunsheye, K. Awosika, C. Dennis and C. M. Di Domenico (eds), *Nigerian Women and Development* (Ibadan: Ford Foundation, 1982).
42. Jibrin Ibrahim's article in *ROAPE*, 45/46 (1989) focuses specifically on this dimension of Moslem–Christian relations.
43. See O. Peters, 'Female Students in Residence: Attitudes and Aspirations of Undergraduates at Queen Elizabeth Hall', in Ogunsheye *et al.*, *Nigerian Women . . .*, pp. 510–17.
44. Tensions in Ghana between missionary sects and Government are described in *West Africa*, 26 June–2 July 1989, p. 1068. See *African Concord*, vol. 4, no. 47 (19 March 1990) pp. 20–21, for a discussion of foreign Christian evangelism in Uganda.
45. T. O. Pearce, 'Role Strain and the Health of Women in Contemporary Nigeria', 'Conference on Nigerian Women and National Development', Institute of African Studies, Ibadan University, June 1985; and J. Uyanga, 'The Medical Role of Spiritual Healing Churches in South Eastern Nigeria', *Nigerian Behavioural Sciences Journal*, vol. 2, nos. 1 and 11, pp. 48–52.
46. See C. Dennis in D. Elson, *Male Bias . . .* (forthcoming).
47. See R. I. J. Hackett, 'Women as Leaders and Participants in the Spiritual Churches', in R. I. J. Hackett, *New Religious Movements in Nigeria* (Lewiston: Edwin Mullen Press, 1987).
48. For example, one phenomenon has been the development of lunchtime Christian prayer meetings in govenment offices in Ghana (Verbal communication, Lynn Brydon, July 1990). One sign of the attractiveness of spiritualist church rituals under present circumstances has been the adoption by the established missionary churches of rituals and ceremonies characteristic of spiritualist or 'healing' churches such as speaking with tongues or spirit possession.

9 Women and Work: Ideology Not Adjustment at Work in Iran

Haleh Afshar

INTRODUCTION

The chapters in this book have concentrated on the explicit adjustment policies initiated by governments in response to the international financial restrictions imposed largely by western donors, or credit agencies. But it is important to note that both in these explicit terms and elsewhere there is a central ideological theme at work which helps render women's work invisible and class them as unemployed, and obligated to perform domestic services.[1] The contention of this chapter is that such ideological constraints can, and do, impose limitations on women's work which may be as restricting, if not more so, than economic ones. Female employment in Iran is a clear example, where despite a decade of war, massive carnage of young men and general call-up of all males over the age of twelve, there has been no rise in female employment and both in absolute and relative terms fewer women are participating in the labour market now than were fifteen years ago. This is all the more surprising since a stated policy of gender segregation at all levels should, at least in theory, have resulted in doubling employment opportunities for women working in the public and private sectors.[2] Furthermore, contrary to the Third World trend, delineated in the previous chapters of this book, both the health and education sectors have been expanding their total employment and their proportion of female employment. But the general post-revolutionary recession has been severely exacerbated in Iran by the eight years of war. This had already created in Iran the constraints that obliged other governments to restrict their welfare expenditure and engage in the implementation of adjustment policies.[3] Thus the combination of ideological and economic factors has resulted in a marked worsening of the employment situation for women in Iran, despite the absence of foreign lending agencies at the macro-economic levels.

WOMEN AND POLITICS

Although the Islamic Republic sees women as the very reflection of its integrity and has espoused the veil as the public statement of its religiosity,[4] politically women's activities have been contained at the margins. As Zahra Rahnavard, leading ideologue and wife of the previous Prime Minister Mir Hosein Mousavi, told a reporter: 'Women have been active and present, at times in larger numbers than men, in all our public demonstrations. But when it comes to political appointments, they are pushed aside.'[5]

The situation has shown no sign of improvement despite some public statements by figures such as President Rafsanjani who declared that no religious impediment existed to the election of women, and asked: 'who can quote a Qoranic verse stating that there should only be 4 women members in the Majlis?'[6] The protest fell on deaf ears and at the next election only three women gained access to the Majlis (Parliament). Once there, the women find themselves excluded and outmanoeuvred, as MP Maryam Behrouzi explains: 'Women are never selected to chair committees, the Majlis merely reflects the male chauvinism that is rampant in our society.'[7] Furthermore they are expected to behave modestly and according to the silent image that the ideology dictates. Thus MP Azam Taleqani explains: 'Women's natural modesty prevents them from saying too much in the Majlis.'[8]

Underrepresented and silenced, women have achieved little in terms of Iranian politics. Their lack of success in turn has led to much discontent expressed by the public at large about their ineffectiveness. Politically women remain a mere reflection of the perceived honour of the Islamic Republic, which in terms of policies and practice has done much to sustain patriarchal controls at all levels.

EDUCATION

The ideological confinement of women to the domestic sphere and their inability to change discriminatory policies has resulted in the creation of a second-class form of citizenship for women in Iran. Their access to both education and employment has been restricted by the assumption that at all times they will remain dependent on a male breadwinner to whom they will show respect and for whom they will provide domestic comforts. Such obligations, however, do not require arduous formal education and as a result a form of bantu education has been deemed suitable. Only the wealthy have been able to circumvent the educational prescriptions of the Islamic Republic for their daughters.

In the first instance the segregation of educational establishments has resulted in a shortage of qualified teachers in certain specialities, such as mathematics and physics and chemistry. Very few secondary girls' schools teach mathematics;[9] and those that do, happen to be private ones situated in the prosperous quarters, often by-passing the laws and employing male teachers. The rapidly increasing population has done little to improve the situation. Even though the sex-ratio in Iran favours men and fewer girls survive to get to school age,[10] still there are not enough girls' schools to accommodate those who wish to attend. In the poorer sectors of the cities schools have to work in shifts, and children can go mornings or afternoons. Even then they may find that there are no teachers or, worse still, that the landlord has thrown the school out of its buildings.

In the classrooms overcrowding is such that most teachers find it difficult to move, let alone teach: 'Since the beginning of the year I have not been able to get to the back of the classroom, to see what the pupils are up to. I have 60 pupils stacked up against one another with no room to move.'[11] Yet despite all the problems, and the intense competition which allows only 10 per cent of the candidates to gain access to tertiary education, year after year young women top the universities' entrance exams in maths, and experimental sciences, as well as arts and humanities.[12] Universities, however, have, since the 'cultural revolution', at the inception of the revolution, barred women from many of the faculties.[13] Initially, areas such as agriculture, engineering and some experimental sciences were completely closed to women. After much protest they were given limited quotas to enter some areas. They were not allowed to enrol for 64 per cent of the subjects offered in maths and experimental sciences, were excluded from 17 per cent of the areas offered in applied sciences and have had to face quotas ranging from 20 to 40 per cent in environmental health, law, health and safety, dental techniques and health care and physiotherapy. In humanities, accounting, psychology, and medical and nursing schools, they face a 50 per cent quota, and midwifery and family health care are exclusive domains for women, with no male students.[14] Sahar Qahraman, in her review of the Islamic government's educational policies,[15] notes that the pre-revolutionary educational policies, barred women from entry to the

Mining School of the Tehran Polytechnic and required them to wear the veil to attend a couple of religious schools and be single and childless to enrol for some nursing schools. Since the revolution women have been barred from enrolling in 54 per cent of the subjects taught at tertiary level.[16]

In the first year of the revolution there was a half-hearted attempt to have segregated technical colleges, and in October 1979 the only women's technical college was set up to teach electrics, electronics ceramics and construction. Within three years construction was closed down, for 'not being physically suited to women',[17] and subsequently electrical was also closed. Finally in 1986 the college was ordered not to take any more students. When the head of the college, Ameneh Masoumian, who is an electronic engineer herself, went to the Ministry of Education, she was told by the Minister: 'This college should have been closed long ago. The reason that it has stayed open so long is that I was not at this post earlier.'[18] Further probes also indicated that the Ministry disapproved of the women working in the all-women potteries of the college 'not wearing the proper full Islamic veil'.[19] Eventually it transpired that the Minister was of the view that women were 'not good at such subjects' and should not attempt to study them.

But even in appropriate subjects, such as art and architecture, women face the ideological barrier and its practical constraints. Thus an architecture student at the same college explains:

> Our society does not allow women to sit and draw a building which is in the process of construction . . . We can't sit and draw anywhere except inside the college yard's walls. We've drawn the buildings that we can see from the yard so often that we could reproduce them in every detail without ever having to see them again.[20]

As to Arts, the Islamic Republic has a very ambivalent attitude to the field as a whole. The Faculty of Music was closed at the very beginning of the revolution, since Islam, it was said, did not approve of music. Other art subjects are under a greater or lesser degree of suspicion, but are regarded on the whole as 'suitable' for women.[21] But in this field there is a critical shortage of qualified university lecturers. As Mrs Sepehri, Deputy Head of the Faculty of Art at El Zahra University, explains:

Universities require post graduate and doctoral certificates from their lecturers . . . But we did not have a doctoral course in Arts before the revolution and do not have any senior level expertise in the field . . . As a result we do not have the possibility of offering post graduate courses.[22]

The continuing success of young women at the entrance-exam level combined with the continuing pressures, have since the end of the war led to a review of the official position on university quotas. The result has been interesting. Officialdom has been arguing that there are no actual quotas, but that rather it is a matter of decision by the faculties themselves. Faculty representatives have been saying that women would themselves not choose to do 'dirty', 'disagreeable' subjects. At the same time they have been emphasising the domestic roles of women. If women are homemakers, then it is a waste of money to educate them. So, for example, the head of the Faculty of Agriculture in Hamadan, Dr Eqbali, while announcing the removal of some of the barriers, said:

Agriculturalists have to work in the dirtiest and smelliest of places; they have to clean stables and deal with animal droppings . . . Women are suited by their nature to raise flowers or maybe chickens, but not to go into the countryside.[23]

His views were echoed by others:

It is reported that a woman who graduates in agriculture cannot go to the villages and work there.[24]

You see, there are some works which are based on physical strength and these are beyond women . . . we cannot deny that men are physically stronger. There are some works, like agriculture, that women cannot do.[25]

It was therefore decided to allow women to study animal husbandry, gardening, botany and environmental studies.

In this context it is interesting to glance at reality for a moment. At the same time that women were barred from reading agriculture at university level, the government was running a 'cultivator of the year' contest for women. Women of all ages and differing degrees of

'physical strength' won each year. Although normally the winners
were rice-cultivators from the northern provinces, there were also a
number of educated woman agriculturalists who won in different
fields such as tree-planting, bee-keeping or market gardening, etc.
Some were pre-revolutionary graduates of schools of agriculture,
others engaged in agriculture as a hobby, and all worked in the
undesirable context of the Iranian countryside.[26]

There are a number of interesting anomalies, which do not fit the
prevalent stereotypes. In education as elsewhere there are still
women who were recruited before the revolution and have retained
their posts. So, for example, in the Faculty of Physics of Tehran's
prestigious Technical University, there have been no promotions
within the academic ranks since the revolution. Thus, after the
advent of the cultural revolution, the faculty is headed by a research
fellow, but the only professor in the Department is a woman who has
held her chair for more than ten years and is irreplaceable in terms of
knowledge and expertise.

But of course the exclusion of women from large areas of education is not based on reality, or even law, but rather on the ideological definition of women as domestic and dependent beings. Hence
the President Hashemi Rafsanjani explains:

> These decisions don't have a legal basis . . . they are based on
> practical research . . . that is an evaluation of whether the society
> as a whole would benefit from training women in certain fields.
> Maybe it's because women graduate in very important fields and
> then become housewives and do not serve the community . . . then
> the effort spent on educating them is wasted.[27]

The idea that education is wasted on women is a prevalent one and
not only voiced by the men in charge, but also by some of the women
who are supposed to defend women's interests. Thus, for example,
Soraya Maknoun, University Professor, head of the research group;
Women for Cultural Research and member of the High Council of
Women's Cultural and Social Affairs, recently declared:

> If a woman truly wishes to serve the country, shouldn't she realise
> that by going to university she is depriving someone else of a place?
> If a woman gains access to a place to study mining or agriculture, in
> the end she will get married and her husband is not going to go and
> work in the villages and so she won't practise. We would have

spent so many millions from our scarce resources and our national budget to educate this woman and then she goes and sits in a corner in her home. How could such a woman claim to serve the community? I promise you most of us seek this kind of formal knowledge out of pure capriciousness.[28]

From such a position it is but a short step to argue for a bantu education for women, and Soraya Maknoun does so without hesitation:

> Women should be educated according to their needs. They should learn to identify their rights and their duties and appreciate all that our religion has to say about raising a family . . . Such an education will have the added advantage of being relatively inexpensive and not pose a heavy financial burden on our government.[29]

The problem of access to university education is considerably worse at the post-graduate level for women. Male graduates can gain places either at home or when necessary obtain government scholarships for post-graduate studies abroad. But as it is assumed that the sole function of women is to get married and reproduce, single women are not permitted to apply for government grants to study abroad. Thus even in appropriate fields such as arts they simply do not have the possibility of further studies. As Mrs Sepehri, Deputy Head of the Faculty of Art of El Zahra University, explains:

> The legal requirement of marriage to qualify for foreign grants prevents many of our women from going abroad . . . Of course it is best for women to be accompanied by their husbands, but what about those women who for a whole variety of reasons don't get married but do wish to continue with their education. What are they to do?[30]

The double standards, however, prevail, despite much complaint. The media continues to reflect the complaints of women, but without much effect. Thus a woman teacher tells a woman's magazine reporter:

> I went abroad for further education myself, before the revolution. I never did anything wrong. But there were plenty of Iranian boys behaving in the most corrupt manner.

Now that they don't allow women to study abroad, what facilities are they willing to provide at home?[31]

The answer is virtually none. This despite constant protests and criticisms from many women; the most remarkable of whom, Zahra Rahnavard, wrote a series of lengthy critiques of the government's educational policies in both daily and weekly journals. Rahnavard argued that the continuous undermining of women in education has not only been detrimental to women, but also it has eroded their support for Islam and their understanding of its importance:

The only religious education we offer women is to wear the veil . . . we have failed to impose the veil because of the absence of a proper analytical perspective and religious strategy. Our girls no longer understand that the veil is a liberating force.[32]

Addressing the question of funds and resources, Rahnavard states:

Our planners say 'We don't have the means to invest equally in men and women and must spend our limited resources on those who provide a higher return for society. Since women's domestic obligations, in terms of childbirth and raising a family, means that they do less work, we cannot allocate too great a portion of our scarce resources to them.'
We respond that this is the wrong approach since Islam demands education for all and does not discriminate in learning . . . scientific training is of the essence and there should be no barriers on this path. It is true that an educated woman may choose to stay at home for a time to raise her children but she may choose to work outside her home at another time.[33]

Rahnavard concludes by pointing out that the dependent images of women disempower a potentially important group in society:

In our society the muslim women is perceived as a consumer. That is, she represents consumption in every one of its dimensions. Not only in economic terms, but also in intellectual and emotional ones, in terms of choices and decisions and determination. Our women are not seen as people with independent and creative minds capable of making logical decisions . . . A creative, free independent and determined woman who makes her own choices is denigrated for being unfeminine and unwomanly.[34]

But of course Rahnavard's comments fall on deaf ears. Though the wife of the previous Prime Minister and one of the leading feminist ideologues of the revolution, Rahnavard's success in improving the conditions of women has been more illusory than real. She herself complains.of no one heeding her criticism and points out that although many of her books have been translated, published and reprinted many times abroad, they have been out of print for years in Iran.[35]

EMPLOYMENT

Much of the reluctance to educate women is hinged on the assumption that they would not use their education in the labour market and that in the long run they would not be employed. There are, however, a number of serious problems in this analysis, not least of which is the Islamic Republic's policy of gender segregation. Since there is an insistence that all public services should be segregated, there is an immediate doubling of the labour force in certain sectors such as health and education. That is an increase in the very sectors that adjustment policies are cutting back elsewhere.

Since the emphasis on segregation has been in the name of Islam, much of the discussion about the place for women in the labour market has been conducted in the context of Islamic discourse. In practice many typically feminine jobs such as typing and secretarial work revert to men, so that women who are health or education specialists are marginalised and encouraged to move out. As a civil servant with a post-graduate degree and eighteen years service explains: 'This emphasis on sexuality renders women inactive in our society . . . In all sectors other than health and medicine our way is barred by the perception that society has of our gender.'[36]

But in the domain of theory the problem is not so clear-cut. Abolqasem Sarhadizadeh, the Minister of Labour and Social Affairs and the only Minister to have a woman secretary, has argued that such an approach is contrary to the spirit of Islam:

We have lost the wonderful rapport that the Prophet of Islam had established with women at the height of Islam . . . it is is a great pity that we have lost our wonderful cultural heritage and the superb and fruitful gender relations established by Islam . . . so that now I am the only Minister with a female secretary and this seems to be cause for much comment[37] . . . why should such questions arise? . . . why do women not insist on getting more exacting jobs?[38]

Similarly Zahra Rahnavard argues:

In our country there is a complex understanding about women . . . which produces a culture of inequality . . . this culture is a far cry from the true Mohamadian Islam. So that although women have shown their political support fully and at all social levels, in the past ten years they have not been allowed to play their part properly in the economic and social construction of our country.[39]

Some of the activities that result in belittling women and lowering their status are conducted in the name of Islam. But these only have a religious cover and not a religious content. If we follow the true Mohamadan religion of Islam, then women would have no problems.[40]

Perhaps the best answer to the Minister's question and an example for Zahra Rahnavard's criticism was provided by Hushang Zamani, head of the National Office of Inspectorate of National Administrative and Employment Organisations (*Daftareh Barressihayeh Tashkilateh Sazemaneh Edari va Estekhdami Keshvar*):

Before the revolution women in many government organisations were given jobs that in no way accorded with the social principles indicated by Islam. For example women were appointed as secretaries to Heads of Departments. After the revolution the Public Sector Personnel Department decided to eliminate the post of secretary from the administrative hierarchy and replace it with office manager which is a male post.[41]

The domestication of women has found support among some women who ironically are both politically and economically active themselves. So, for example, once more we find Soraya Maknoun, herself a university professor and head of the research group on women's employment, declaring:

I am absolutely against the view that women can only succeed by gaining equal access like men to all jobs in all fields . . .
If a woman wants to work and her husband is against it, influen-

tial magazines such as *Zaneh Rouz* . . . should step in and give her appropriate advice and tell her that it does not matter where a woman is. The important thing is for her to be of service. You must explain to her that a husband depends on his wife's help to succeed and God will pay women a high reward for such service . . . In fact our society does not have a woman's problem: the critics have just imbibed western propaganda and imposed their western perspectives on our lives.[42]

A criticism that can hardly be levelled at Zahra Rahnavard, a muslim intellectual who has centred her analysis on the Islamic perspective.[43]

HEALTH AND EDUCATION SECTORS

The official segregation of the labour market, implemented more rigorously in the public than in the private sector, has on the whole proved detrimental to women. The only exceptions are in the fields of health and education. For example, the government has decided that only women should read midwifery and women are encouraged to become doctors. Thus the National leader Ayatollah Khameneyi declared: 'We must have as many female doctors as male ones so that female patients go to female practitioners, not only for feminine ailments, but for all their medical problems.'[44] This is a view that is echoed by the students: 'To fulfil the heartfelt desire of imam [Khomeini] we should seek to have male nurses for male patients and female nurses for female patients.'[45]

The President Rafsanjani thoroughly approves of the segregated labour market and proudly proclaims that:

women are free to engage in those activities that are permitted . . .
Our wives are basically the kind of people who in the past did not enter the social arena . . . but our daughters are not like this. They go to university and get jobs and work. Right now the imam's [Khomeini] daughter works in the cultural and educational sector. My daughters do so too as well as the wife of the Prime Minister [Zahra Rahnavard].[46]

There is, however, a short step from this to the conclusion that the only work permissible and suitable for women is in these two fields. Thus Sabah Zangeneh, the Cultural Deputy of the Ministry of

Ershad (Islamic Guidance), explains: 'In recent years they have come to the conclusion that women could only be active as teachers or at best as nurses or doctors.'[47] This is obvious in the announcement by Hushang Zamani, Head of the Office of Public Sector Personnel and Administration: 'The civil service laws have been revised to facilitate the departure of those ladies who no longer wish to work in the public sector.'[48] In addition he stated the need to reorganise those women who chose to stay:

If we don't pay attention to women's natural and physical and psychological characteristics in allocating jobs to them, we fail to gain positive returns from the managerial point of view.
. . . In management, men should undertake the more difficult and demanding jobs and the ones that are complex and complicated and better suited to their nature and give women jobs suited to their temperament.[49]

This view is reflected in the planning policies. Hosein Ali Mousavi, head of the Statistical Office and Human Resources of the National Personnel and Employment Bureau, explains:

To create a balance between domestic and social and employment duties of women, we are preparing the way for moving women to jobs that are suited to their physical needs . . . accordingly posts in the fields of agriculture, engineering and technology will be reserved for men and the areas of health and education will be open to women.[50]

This policy has already led to a marked decrease in the numbers of female civil servants in the Ministries of Agriculture, Mining, Heavy Industries, Road and Communications. But this has been compensated by a marked increase in female employees of the Ministries of Health and Education, so that overall the proportion of women civil servants rose from 1 in every 11 to 1 in 7 in 1976 and 1 in 5 public employees in 1986 (see Table 9.1).

The situation was eventually formalised by note 60 of the 1985 budget which prohibited the employment of women in any public sector other than health and education.[51] It is worth noting that whereas in 1978 the education sector employed 70 per cent of the public sector female workers, by 1986 it employed 86 per cent.[52] On the other hand, health and in particular nursing is becoming increas-

Table 9.1* Public sector employees 1966–86 showing number of women employees with more than 10 years employment

	1966	1976		1986
Total public sector employees	662 666	1 673 092	6 years+	2 454 427
Women in public sector employment 10 yrs+	56 833	245 918		407 634
Percentage of the total	8.5	14		16

Source: Statistical Centre of Iran, *National Census of Population and Housing*, November, 1966, p. 41, November 1976, p. 55, and Mehre 1365 (October 1986) p. 240.

ingly a male domain, with male nurses arguing that they are better suited to the job:

> Our warrior brothers are distressed for religious and personal reasons when they are tended by our sister nurses . . .
> Our warriors have to be undressed and their wounds have to be treated . . . at such times they don't want any women to be present.
> . . . evidence shows that our brother nurses are, from a practical point of view, more effective than our sisters . . . because of their strength and their ability to work night shifts etc.[53]

As a result there has been some attempt at 'preventing our sisters from participating in the hospital level health care and replacing them by male nurses'.[54] The Revolutionary guard hospitals are already attempting to segregate their hospitals:

> In the Revolutionary guard hospitals we use male nurses in the men's wards and female nurses for the women's. We even try and keep up the segregation in the operating rooms and use women technicians. When operating on men the entire team are male.[55]

WOMEN AND WORK

The net result of ten years of discriminatory policies in the labour market has been a marked fall in the rate of female participation. As

Mahmoud Hedayat, the head of Manpower planning of the Ministry of Plan and Organisation, has pointed out: 'The activity rate for women over the age of ten is 7 per cent and for men is 69 per cent. That is a ratio of 1/9. What this means is that a man is nine times more likely to find a job than a woman.'[56] This statement is clearly substantiated by the census figures (Table 9.2), which show a marked fall in the percentage of women workers in the labour force, from about 13 to 14 per cent in the two decades preceding the revolution to 9 per cent in 1986. What is more, the fall occurred when the Iran–Iraq war was at full swing and women from all over the Arab-speaking world were moving into the Iraqi labour market to replace the men.[57] But the war coincided with extensive underdevelopment of the industrial sector in Iran,[58] and the only expanding sector, that of the war industries, refused to employ women as a matter of principle.[59]

Thus the increase in the public sector employment of women has been more than offset by the dramatic fall in their employment in the private sector (Table 9.3). The policy of segregating the labour market resulted in pressure on women to leave the factory floor and on employers not to take on new female recruits. Not surprisingly there was a more than 75 per cent fall in the numbers of women employed by the private sector (Table 9.3). A survey of the central province's factories in 1987 indicated that none had taken on any women recruits in the previous five years.[60]

Table 9.2* Women as proportion of the total labour force

	Total labour force	Employed women	Women as proportion of total
1966	6 858 396	909 983	13%
1976	8 799 420	1 212 020	14%
1986	11 035 962	987 102	9 %

Source: Statistical Centre of Iran, *National Census of Population and Housing*, November 1966, p. 41. November 1976, p. 55, and Mehre 1365 (October 1986) p. 240.

The census also indicates a marked fall in the numbers of unpaid family workers. This may be in part a question of categorisation;

Table 9.3* Female employment trend

	1966	1976	1986
Female population	12 097 258	16 352 397	24 164 049 (–124 237 mobile pop.)
Employed	909 983	1 212 202	987 103
Civil service	56 833	245 918	407 634
Private sector	429 628	322 146	99 838
Self-employed	197 712	130 693	181 186
Managers	5 723	5 358	13 719
Unpaid workers	110 222	495 723	212 850
Unemployed	89 845	236 986	332 602
Not known	9 358	12 182	70 876
Male population	12 981 665	17 356 347	25 280 961 (–126 861 mobile pop.)
Employed	5 984 412	7 587 400	10 048 859
Unemployed	635 844	759 650	1 486 138

Source: Statistical Centre of Iran, *National Census of Population and Housing*, November 1966, p. 41. November 1976, p. 55, and Mehre 1365 (October 1986) p. 240.

some women may now see themselves as self-employed rather than unpaid family labourers, and the former category does show an increase. It may, however, be that the census questionnaire and data processors have returned to the gender-blind methods which systematically ignore female participation.[61] Given the war, the carnage of men and recruitment from parts of the rural areas, it is difficult to accept a *prima facie* fall of 50 per cent in unpaid female family workers in the economy.

Despite the many difficulties about assessing the rate of female employment,[62] it is obvious that there has been a sharp drop in the participation of women both in absolute and relative terms. Some, such as Marzieh Sadiqy, advisor to the plan organisation's infrastructural deputy chief and administrative head of the national transport and communication scheme, claim that female employment in Iran fell by 18.5 per cent in the period 1976–86 and that there was a six-fold increase in the numbers of women seeking work during the same period (Table 9.4).

Table 9.4*   Unemployment

	Female population	Unemployed female	Male population	Unemployed male
1966	12 097 258	89 845	12 981 665	635 844
1976	16 352 397	236 986	17 356 347	759 650
1986	24 164 049	332 602	25 280 961	1 486 138
	(– 124 237		(– 126 861	
	mobile population)		mobile population)	

WOMEN EXPERTS

Over the past thirty years the Iranian population has doubled, and so has the number of unemployed men, but over the same period female unemployment has nearly quadrupled (Table 9.4). Since public sector employment has increased, obviously the brunt of unemployment has fallen on the less educated, poorer working-class women, who should have been the obvious beneficiaries of the revolution.

The acute shortage of trained labour and continuous pressure by women, as well as women's magazines and some parliamentary representatives, have led to some interesting patterns both in terms of perception and in practice. Although in areas such as the judiciary professional women remain firmly excluded, they have found a place in some other fields. Even in the context of law it is becoming less acceptable to publicly deny the right of access to women. Here women are barred because they are said not to have the expertise; and they don't have the expertise because for some years they were not allowed to read law at all and even now they have a limited quota for entrance. As a result Ayatollah Muhammad Yazdi, the head of the Judiciary, could easily justify the exclusion of women even at the level of consultation for drawing up family laws:

There are very few women working in the judiciary and most of them are doing secretarial and clerical jobs; they hardly ever reach the higher level. So you cannot expect us to hand over to such women the problems of family laws at the national level.[63]

The venerable Ayatollah even went so far as to argue that 'There is no law barring the way to female employment . . . there is no discrimination against women neither in law nor in practice. In practice women do get jobs.'[64] This is a curious statement since women are only ever allowed to act as advisors, and that in very specific cases 'Suitably qualified women with the required level of legal training and education could be employed as advisors to Family courts and Courts dealing with Personal Law and Custody of Minors.'[65] When confronted with this anomaly, the Head of Iranian judiciary reverted to the usual excuses: 'Women don't have the patience to listen carefully to both sides of the argument . . . I have seen judges at work, believe me it's arduous work and not suited to women'.[66]

The view that there are no legal impediments to the employment of women is widespread: so much so that the Employment committee of the High Council of Women's Social and Cultural Affairs came to the conclusion that:

Existing laws and regulations are not so detrimental to the rights of working women or to their employment in the first place, as to need any revision. It is not the laws that are deficient but their implementation which is weak.

. . . It is male employers who refuse to employ women. Of course there are problems with women workers. There are times that because of giving birth and having to nurse their babies they cannot be at work. So men, when they need workers, prefer to employ men.

A woman graduate cannot expect to get the same kinds of jobs as are offered to male graduates; not even in the fields that she is permitted to work in.[67]

The argument is always that it is not the laws, but men's preferences and women's reproductive activities that prevent them from achieving high status in the labour market; arguments that are all too familiar for feminists the world over.

There are, however, some men in Iran who at least publicly state that women ought to participate in all domains. For example, Dr Ahmadi, member of the high council of the Cultural Revolution, objects to the tendency of men to employ men:

Some people make choices according to their own personal views. But their actions as individuals may prove detrimental to women as a whole in our society by alienating them and discouraging them from coming into the public domain.

If we bar women from entering into two or four areas then such limitation will be gradually extended to other spheres and we will be losing some of the best talents in the country.[68]

Similarly Ayatollah Kashani, the Speaker of the conservative Council of Experts (*Shorayeh Foqaha*) claims: 'women in our country are seen as noble and independent beings who, like men, can participate in all the political economic educational and social domains'.[69] And the Minister of Labour and Social Affairs, Abolqassem Sarhadizadeh, states:

> In my opinion the invisibility of women is the greatest barrier to progress. When you go to a government office, it is quite obvious that women's work and productive capacity has been ignored. Their path to management is barred. They are obliged to accept women headmistresses in schools, but that is the ultimate level. That is to say that women do have the ability to do much better and rise much higher, but they are not allowed to do so.[70]

Despite the unwillingness of men to employ women there is in Iran a critical shortage of expertise. Thus despite an estimated overall fall of 18 per cent, the fall in the participation rate of women in the labour market as a whole, and a 60 per cent fall in industrial employment of women in the period 1976–86, there was a 10 to 12 per cent increase in the numbers of women working in management and as expert advisors.[71] As shown by a series of interviews conducted by the weekly women magazine *Zaneh Rouz* as part of its campaign on female employment, most of the high-ranking women working in the public sector were educated in the pre-revolutionary era of equal access. Many graduated in fields that are now closed to women altogether, such as airline pilots or agriculture, or in fields that have restrictive entry requirements, such as electronics and planning. All of the women interviewed were married and had children and all combined their domestic duties with demanding full-time jobs, but none had been promoted to top positions, nor expected to be. As Marzieh Sadiqi, administrative head of the national transport and communication project, explains: 'In government organisations, when women reach a certain level they do not get promoted any more . . . To avoid this dead-end I have had to set up my own private company where I am the general manager.'[72] Similarly Nasrin Emad Khorasani, the only documentation expert in the Ministry of Agriculture, stated:

In government offices may . . . dislike working with women or even consulting them, even when they are the only expert in the field . . .

If I get invited to go to an academic conference, it is always a male colleague, who knows nothing about the subject, who is sent . . .

If work is done collaboratively with male colleagues, they are the ones who get the extra pay and promotions. In our section it is not possible for a woman to reach high management levels.[73]

Women in positions of responsibility are further constrained by the disdain of their colleagues and the general public. For example, a personal friend of the author who was a highly trained accountant returned from the US to join the war effort in Iran. She was recruited by the Red Cross, the only woman they employed out of a large pool of applicants. In a matter of months she uncovered a number of false returns from a supplier, who was charging well over the odds. When called up to explain his creative accounting, the man was genuinely shocked: 'I must have really come down in the world to be cross-examined by a woman', he announced. This accountant was one of ten recruits, the other nine were men and promoted to head various departments, but the woman found herself on the bottom rank throughout her post-revolutionary career.

There are, however, a few high-ranking women still working in the civil service. Surprisingly, many of them are in the Ministry of Agriculture which has been seen as ideologically unsuitable for female employment. At least three of its high-ranking experts are female; in addition to Nasrin Emad Khosravani, the Ministry's Deputy Chief of Public Relations is a woman, Dr Parvin Maroufi. The winner of the Ministry's agricultural prize in 1989 was also a woman – a bacteriologist, Nasrin Moazami, who works at one of the teachers' training schools. All three women, when interviewed, indicated that the prejudices against them would clearly prevent them from getting any further in the public sector.

Many were also aware that the trail they had blazed was to go cold after them, since not only were women not allowed to train in the subjects concerned, but even where they could qualify in the field, the employers would refuse to employ them. So, for example, Fatemeh Nikou, the Director of Plan and Engineering of the Electronic Telephone Centre, commented:

Despite the general public's view and the government's prejudices, electronics is a suitable field for women. I was the only woman in my class [she had began working for the telephone and communications company before the revolution in 1974], but this never posed a problem. Now women may be able to study electronics . . . but the real problem is after graduation, because employers are very reluctant to employ them and the problem is getting worse all the time.[74]

As a result women who are have done exceptionally well often try to hide the fact that they are not men. Thus Shahla Dehbozorgi, the only Iranian women airplane pilot and the head of practical training at a gliding school in Tehran, said:

It's best not to discuss being a woman, since once they find out, first they criticise you and then put you aside saying that women are not any good and can't work properly. But no one ever comes to see how women work, no one comes to praise them for their efficiency and their ability to run units successfully and train and encourage their colleagues.[75]

Even her employer was rather weary of the publicity: 'She is an excellent manager and has initiated many successful programmes. But I fear that writing about her in the press may well result in a lot of problems in her career.'[76]

Thus although there are women who have carved a niche for themselves in the public sector, they have done so despite the men and without help from the regime. As Marzieh Sadiqi of the Plan Organisation explains:

Of the 105 training grants allocated to the civil service last year, only 3 were offered to women. This when women form 30 per cent of the public sector employees and despite the fact that over the past decade the numbers of women experts working for the government has increased and could have potentially increased even more.[77]

Sadiqi, who qualified as a road safety programming expert, a subject which is now closed to women, deplores the dramatic 18 per cent fall in female employment, the elimination of women from certain sectors and the 60 per cent fall in female industrial employment. But she notes with some pride that the percentages of women working as consultants and in management have increased by 10 and 12 per cent respectively.[78] But this reflects a move towards the private sector of which Sadiqi herself is now a part:

> In government organisations, women are only allowed to reach a certain level beyond which they will not get promoted. As a civil servant I worked from 6 a.m. to 9 p.m. . . . . But in the end to avoid the dead-end I had to set up my own private firm where I could become general manager.[79]

Thus even the one woman who for years has represented the respectable face of the Islamic republic at the international women's meetings has had to admit defeat when it comes to getting rewards from her government.

CONCLUSION

Many Iranian women supported the revolution in the firm belief that it would offer them a higher status, more respect, a complementary role to men and liberate them from the chains of imperialism. But stripped of its rhetoric the revolution has done little other than envisage women as chained perpetually in the couple of decades of their lives in which they fulfil their maternal obligations. With the recent fears of a population explosion in Iran, even this commendable avenue is beginning to be closed to women. Nevertheless the government insists that women should continue to retain their familial attributes which delineate them in terms of their relationship with a 'protector', presumably a male one. Thus Dr Sadeq Aynehvand, Head of the Humanities Group of the Ministry of Higher Education, announced recently:

Women's status is rooted in:
 1 – motherhood . . .
 2 – being a wife
 3 – their female essence and
 4 – being a daughter.[80]

The problem is that all of these stages could be very temporary in Iran, given the ease with which men divorce their wives, the father's right to retain his children after divorce and the early age of marriage. Thus it is perfectly possible for a woman in her early twenties to have completed all three stages of being a daughter, wife and mother and be left with nothing other than her 'female essence', which would probably not procure a high price in the formal labour market in The Islamic Republic.

Given the high rate of male unemployment, the current paucity of resources and the need for the government to prove its religiosity by keeping women in purdah, there is little room for hope for the poorest women in Iran.

Notes and References

* I am most grateful to Dr Farhad Mehran for allowing me access to some of the data used in this Chapter. However, any mistakes or misrepresentation are entirely mine.

1. For further discussion, see Elson, Moser and others in this volume.
2. For further discussion, see Val Moghadam, 'Women, Work and Ideology in the Islamic Republic of Iran', *International Journal of Middle East Studies* (May 1988) pp. 221–43; and *Nimeyeh Digar*, no. 10 (Winter) 1368 pp. 16–51; and Haleh Afshar, 'Women in the Work and Poverty Trap in Iran', in H. Afshar and B. Agarwal (eds), *Women, Poverty and Ideology* (Macmillan, 1989) pp. 17–42.
3. For further discussion, see H. Afshar, 'The Iranian Theocracy', in Afshar (ed.), *Iran, a Revolution in Turmoil*, pp. 220–44.
4. For further discussion, see H. Afshar, 'Women, Marriage and the State in Iran', in H. Afshar (ed.), *Women State and Ideology* (Macmillan, 1987) pp. 70–86; and 'Behind the Veil: The Public and Private Faces of Khomeini's Policies on Iranian Women', in B. Agarwal (ed.), *Structures of Patriarchy* (Kali for Women and Zed Books, 1988) pp. 228–47; and 'Women and Reproduction in Iran', in N. Yuval-Davis and F. Anthias (eds), *Women–Nation–State* (Macmillan Press, 1989) pp. 110–25. Also A. Tabari and Yeganeh, *In the Shadow of Islam* (Zed Press); Guity Neshat, 'Women in the Ideology of the Islamic Republic', in G. Neshat (ed.), *Women and Revolution in Iran* (Boulder, 1983), among many more.
5. *Zaneh Rouz*, 10 February 1990.
6. *Zaneh Rouz*, 22 January 1988.
7. *Zaneh Rouz*, 30 January 1988.
8. *Zaneh Rouz*, 20 January 1990.

9. *Zaneh Rouz*, 30 January 1988.
10. For further discussion on sex ratio, see, for example, Barbara Harris and Elizabeth Watson, 'The Sex Ratio in Southern Asia', in Janet H. Momsen and Janet Townsend, *Geography of Gender* (Hutchinson, 1987) pp. 85–115, among many others. For further discussion of the Iranian case, see, for example, Val Moghadam, 'The Reproduction of Gender Inequality in Islamic Societies: A Case Study of Iran in the 1980s', *World Development* (1990).
11. Qolamreza Soleimani, secondary school teacher, interviewed by *Zaneh Rouz*, 9 May 1989.
12. *Zaneh Rouz*, 6 February 1988, 26 August 1989, among many more.
13. For further discussion, see Haleh Afshar, 'Epilogue', in H. Afshar (ed.), *Iran, A Revolution in Turmoil* (Macmillan, 1989) pp. 244–53; and 'Khomeini's Teachings and Their Implications for Iranian Women', in N. Yeganeh *In the Shadow of Islam* (Zed, 1982); as well as Val Moghadam, 'The Reproduction of Gender Inequality', *World Development*; and Sahar Qahraman, '*Siyasateh hokoumateh Eslami piramouneh dasressi zanan beh amouzesheh ali va asarateh an bar moqiyateh ejtemayi va eqtessadi zanan*' (The Islamic Republic's policies on women's access to higher education and its impact on the socio-economic position of women), *Nimeyeh Digar*, no. 7 (Summer) 1367 (1989).
14. Qahraman, 'Siyasateh . . .', *Nimeyeh Digar* (Summer 1989).
15. Ibid.
16. Ibid. p. 25.
17. Ameneh Masoumian, previously head of the college, interviewed by *Zaneh Rouz*, 27 January 1990.
18. *Zaneh Rouz*, 12 December 1988.
19. *Zaneh Rouz*, 27 January 1990.
20. *Zaneh Rouz*, 12 December 1990.
21. For example, Marzieh Mohamadianfar, head of the employment committee of the High Council of Women's Cultural and Social Affairs, told *Zaneh Rouz*'s reporter quite categorically that: 'some things like artistic works are specifically for women; men for example could never do tapestry.' 27 January 1990.
22. *Zaneh Rouz*, 20 January 1990.
23. *Zaneh Rouz*, 5 August 1989.
24. Marzieh Mohamadianfar, member of the employment committee of the High Council of Women's Social and Cultural Affairs, *Zaneh Rouz*, 27 January 1990.
25. Marzieh Mohamadianfar, head of the employment committee of the High Council of Women's Cultural and Social Affairs, *Zaneh Rouz*, 27 January 1990.
26. *Zaneh Rouz* occasionally runs articles about such women, for example 6 February 1988, 10 December 1988, etc.
27. *Zaneh Rouz*, 23 January 1988.
28. *Zaneh Rouz*, 27 January 1990.
29. *Zaneh Rouz*, 27 January 1990.
30. *Zaneh Rouz*; 20 January 1990.
31. *Zaneh Rouz*, 20 January 1990.

228   *Ideology at Work in Iran*

32. *Zaneh Rouz*, 10 February 1990.
33. *Zaneh Rouz*, 10 February 1990.
34. *Zaneh Rouz*, 10 February 1990.
35. *Zaneh Rouz*, 10 February 1990.
36. *Zaneh Rouz*, 3 November 1989.
37. For further discussion on the perception of the role of women in the labour market as a whole and as secretaries in particular, see Haleh Afshar, 'Women, State and Ideology in Iran', *Third World Quarterly*, vol. 7, no. 2 (April 1985) pp. 256–78.
38. *Zaneh Rouz*, 3 November 1989.
39. *Zaneh Rouz*, 26 August 1989.
40. *Zaneh Rouz*, 10 February 1990.
41. *Zaneh Rouz*, 14 January 1989.
42. Zaneh Rouz, 27 January 1990.
43. See, for example, Zahra Rahnavard, *Toloueh Zaneh Mosalaman* (Dawn of the muslim woman) (Mahboubeh Publication, n.d.) amongst many.
44. *Zaneh Rouz*, 27 January 1990.
45. Heidar Ali Abedi, teaching assistant at the Department of Nursing of the Medical Faculty of Isfahan and post-graduate student at Tehran Medical Faculty, *Zaneh Rouz*, 26 December 1987.
46. *Zaneh Rouz*, 22 January 1988.
47. *Zaneh Rouz*, 27 January 1990.
48. *Zaneh Rouz*, 14 January 1989.
49. *Zaneh Rouz*, 14 January 1989.
50. *Zaneh Rouz*, 5 November 1988.
51. *Zaneh Rouz*, 14 January 1990.
52. Hushang Zamani of the Plan Organisation, reported in *Zaneh Rouz*, 14 January 1989.
53. Heidar Ali Abedi, nursing student, quoted by *Zaneh Rouz*, 26 December 1987.
54. Heidar Ali Abedi, nursing student, quoted by *Zaneh Rouz*, 26 December 1987.
55. Muhammad Khoshnevis, head of the nursing group of Imam Hosein University, talking to *Zaneh Rouz* reporter, 26 December 1987.
56. *Zaneh Rouz*, 3 November 1988.
57. For further discussion, see, for example, Nadia Hejab, *Womanpower* (Cambridge University Press, 1988).
58. For further discussion, see Haleh Afshar, Iran, *Revolution in Turmoil* (Macmillan, 1989).
59. For further discussion, see Haleh Afshar, 'Women in the Work and Poverty Trap in Iran', in Haleh Afshar and Bina Agarwal (eds), *Women, Poverty and Ideology in Asia* (Macmillan, 1989) pp. 18–42.
60. Ibid.
61. For further discussion, see Arlene Dalalfar, *'Jayeh khaliyeh zanan dar mohassebateh amari'*, in *Nimeyeh Digar*, no. 5 (Winter) 1365; and Valentine Moghadam, *'Zan, kar va ideology dar Jomhouriyeh Eslami'*, in *Nimeyeh Digar*, vol. 10 (Winter) 1368 footnote 33, pp. 47–8.
62. See, for example, Arlene Dalalfar, *'Jayeh khaliyeh zanan dar mohasebateh amari'* (women's empty place in statistical accounts), *Nimeyeh*

Digar, no. 5 1365 (Winter 1986) pp. 16–23. Similarly, Marzieh Mohamadianfar, member of the employment committee of the High Council of Women's Social and Cultural Affairs, complained to *Zaneh Rouz* reporters that 'Unfortunately we don't have a single detailed disaggregated estimate giving exact details of the situation of female employment', 27 January 1990.

63. *Zaneh Rouz*, 20 January 1990.
64. *Zaneh Rouz*, 20 January 1990.
65. Article 5 of the 5 Additional Articles to the Code for Selection of Judges.
66. *Zaneh Rouz*, 20 January 1990.
67. Marzieh Mohamadianfard interviewed by *Zaneh Rouz*, 27 January 1990.
68. *Zaneh Rouz*, 24 February 1990.
69. *Zaneh Rouz*, 27 January 1990.
70. *Zaneh Rouz*, 3 November 1989.
71. *Zaneh Rouz*, 16 September 1989.
72. *Zaneh Rouz*, 20 January 1990.
73. *Zaneh Rouz*, 20 January 1990.
74. *Zaneh Rouz*, 13 January 1990.
75. *Zaneh Rouz*, 20 January 1990.
76. *Zaneh Rouz*, 20 January 1990.
77. *Zaneh Rouz*, 3 June 1989.
78. *Zaneh Rouz*, 16 September 1989.
79. *Zaneh Rouz*, 20 January 1990.
80. *Zaneh Rouz*, 3 January 1990.

Part III
Policies

10 Politicising Gender and Structural Adjustment
Georgina Ashworth

INTRODUCING THE STRATEGY

If the purpose of research is to reveal, the purpose of advocacy is to see the revelation into wider consciousness and then into policy and remedial actions. This chapter is concerned not with an analysis of the impact of structural adjustment on women, but of the process of making that impact known, and postulating damage limitation and even preventative measures, as well as proposing alternatives to current forms of adjustment. It is a somewhat personal history, since it is the nature of political advocacy – about unusual and innovative issues – to travel light, so to speak, forming coalitions and caucuses as the opportunity arises.

In the early 1980s, faced with the blatant ignorance of politicians, civil servants and academic developmentalists, as well as well-meaning NGO staff, this author became *de obligatio* a lobbyist and advocate on 'women in development' in general. Having formed the CHANGE publication series, it was the effort needed to sell each copy and to persuade readers to change their understanding and thereby their policies and practices which revealed the scale of this ignorance – and positive reluctance. The CHANGE country profiles on the 'status' of women automatically linked the individual, the micro, to the pressures of international relations, or the macro, and CHANGE's other publications, the Thinkbooks, were based on a series of live, participatory meetings and were intended to persuade with brevity and accessible language as well as policy options – to obviate dilatory thought.[1] The reluctance of the male target group to read materials about women, made another line of activity necessary. This was a deliberate but unfunded 'campaign' to raise the consciousness of senior decision-makers in development about the gender dimensions of their work by using a range of tactics, evolved and refined through trial and error.

Consequently it can be said that many of the pools of consciousness that exist today in the Overseas Development Administration,

233

amongst parliamentarians, and especially amongst NGOs are the outcome of that campaign, even though the source may have been forgotten. The newer consultative mechanisms between women's groups and government are an outcome of this personal advocacy, and the subjects they address, including violence and structural adjustment, have often been the proposal of this author. In 1986 the tactics and objectives of advocacy were extended to Europe, both through the European Community and its development institutions and networks, and in 1987 to the twenty-two countries in the wider Council of Europe. In 1987 and 1988 they were introduced into the North–South 'dialogue'.

Advocacy and lobbying do not form part of school or higher education curricula, so at present they have to be self-taught. Meanwhile the notion of democracy in predominant use in the United Kingdom and Western Europe is confined to parliamentary institutions, rather than understood as active participation in every form of human relationship or the continuous and organic extension of this participation to the excluded, predominantly women and of these the poorer and more greatly disadvantaged. The obstacles before the introduction of gender analysis to political decision-makers are numerous and well established physically and metaphysically in tradition. Advocacy is a literally thankless task and, as there are no financial rewards, the motivation has to be conviction; obdurate persistence and the capacity to make much out of little are also essential qualities. Nevertheless it is essential to have many more activist feminist advocates, particularly from the South, in rapid communication with each other to accelerate their effectiveness, and especially aiming at the more remote areas of economic policy formation such as the GATT and the IMF. As it is now, an important tactic, as well as a symbol of solidarity, is to use research and materials developed in the South, such as DAWN's *Development, Crises and Alternative Visions (1985)*,[2] and *The Invisible Adjustment: Poor Women and the Economic Crisis*[3] (1987), as support for self-devised arguments on gender with bureaucrats and politicians.

The fact that structural adjustment became a major part of this political advocacy is a reflection of history, rather than foresight. That 'development' policy and projects of all kinds had negative effects on women's control of income, their time and bodies, while women's contribution to the economy through paid and unpaid work was largely ignored, were general themes advocated during the first years of the 1980s, with specific regional applications – such as women being the farmers of Africa, or prostitution being the main source of foreign exchange in Thailand, the selfless 'madonna' domestication of women being the other side of military rule and economic reconstruction in Chile.[4] With research on the evident effects of militarisation on women, and in the formation of national indebtedness and causation both of active under-development and enforced adjustment, further linkages were made.[5]

Evidence (based on the CHANGE Reports) was also given to enquiries on Bangladesh and famine in Africa by the Select Committee on Foreign Affairs.[6] In 1985 CHANGE both organised (with others) a national conference on Women, Aid and Development and published information packs on 'Farmers, Food and Famine' and 'Women and Debt' which opened up wider discussion.[7] As international debt, structural adjustment agreements and inequitable terms of trade came to dominate relations between governments of North and South, they naturally came to the fore in the advocacy of the gender dimensions of economic relations: the essential cultural limitations to women's rights or entitlements in their society predetermines their weak negotiating power, and enables the more powerful to dispose of their time, income and bodies through both micro and macro-economic policy. In 1986 the author was appointed as a consultant to a coalition of 500 OECD-based development NGOs to co-ordinate their activities relating to debt, trade and structural adjustment, and – somewhat with the challenging anticipation that it would be impossible – to introduce the gender dimension into these.

GETTING THROUGH: 1985

In 1985 the final conference of the Decade for Women took place in Nairobi, and this author believed it was crucial to use this as a point and source of leverage with different government departments. The lethargy of the British government towards the Plans and Programmes of Action (as well as the International Convention on the Elimination of Discrimination Against Women) on a national basis, as well as in external development, provided more than adequate ammunition.[8] Before the world conference six meetings were organised in Parliament by this author and one other, as was a campaign of parliamentary discussions on the non-implementation of the Decade conducted with MPs from all parties over a period of six weeks, with particularly negative replies emerging on development. Reference has already been made to the Conference on Women, Aid and Development held early in 1985 which, amongst other objectives, was intended to draw in and educate the Overseas Development Administration – in which it did not really succeed, except that some guilty reactions were brought forth by a press release indicating ODA's ignorance of gender issues and attitude towards women demonstrated by their disregard for the conference.[9]

During and after the Nairobi World Conference the pressure was maintained by a number of individual and collective actions, ensuring daily consultations between the official delegation and British NGO representatives. Later the Home Secretary (Douglas Hurd) was persuaded by this author to initiate the Inter-Ministerial Working Group on 'Women's Issues', and a national conference was organised for the National Council for Voluntary Organisations (Women's Organisations Interest group) on implementation of the *Forward-Looking Strategies*, adopted in Nairobi, within Britain.[10] Both continue working to this day, although only the latter, now the National Alliance of Women's Organisations, publicly acknowledge these origins.

Early in 1986 a meeting of the All-Party Parliamentary Group on Development was organised at the prompting of this author, and well attended by senior male developmentalists from the Commonwealth and Overseas Development Administration, at which one MP declared 'women in development is the issue whose time has come'. The meeting was entitled 'Development Issues after the Decade for Women' and introduced the gender dimension to macro-economic issues using the *Forward-Looking Strategies*. The relevance of using the *Forward-Looking Strategies* is three-fold. As a universally accepted document it is applicable in all UN member states and cannot be dismissed as a personal nor a Northern feminist obsession, Second, the *Strategies* are essentially interdisciplinary, covering every subject and making the links between personal behaviour and global structures. Third, they are based in the context of human rights, justice and equity, which are also difficult to refuse to acknowledge, although they are often overlooked as pertaining to women. They also contain detailed *Strategies* for bilateral and multilateral development co-operation, as well as substantial sections on international trade and debt.

The encouragement of breaking through government resistance to feminist pressure and of recognising the slow but visible changes in the NGOs – despite visible setbacks as well – provided the stimulus to continue in other arenas, and to broaden both the intellectual base of arguments used and the targets for them.

THE EUROPEAN INITIATIVES

In 1986 this author happened to be present as an observer at the General Assembly of European Development NGOs in Brussels, an annual event organised by the EC-NGO Liaison Committee and attended by panels of delegates elected by their national 'platforms', networks or associations of such NGOs. As a very public forum, with the opportunity of visiting the funding sources of the European Community, the Liaison Committee and this occasion are attractive to senior male NGO administrators; meanwhile the structure and conduct of the national 'platforms' contain many disincentives to policy innovators or the active participation of women. So it was no surprise to find not a single agenda item on 'women in development', even though in the preceding year the Final Conference for the Decade for Women had addressed itself to NGOs as well as to governments. By quickly and informally calling a small caucus of women present, this author persuaded a delegate to introduce the *1985 Forward-Looking Strategies* into the 1986 workplan of the development education sub-committee, and was invited later in the year to expand on this with a presentation to a special meeting of its members. It was the inter-linkage of gender and economic issues which were the lines of argument advanced to the bemused members of the development education committee, who had never so much as considered whether their materials reflected the reality of both sexes in development, or if their objectives included a real egalitarianism between women and men.[11]

In 1987, better prepared, a fuller caucus was called with the help of a Dutch representative, and equipped with the *Strategies*, lines of argument, and some practical options to project, participants went out into the wider meeting and its workshops, and began an educational process which continues to this day. A resolution was drawn up and promoted by unlikely delegations such as Italy and the UK with the Netherlands, but tactically it was weak because it contained no firm framework or reporting system for a constituency both ignorant and inclined to neglect novelty or challenge to their *modus operandi*. So a firmer resolution had to be put forward the following year when

this author also introduced the idea of making 'women in development' the main subject of the 1989 General Assembly. The main
areas of debate in this successful session in 1989 were to be women
and debt and structural adjustment, with Peggy Antrobus (Women
and Development Unit, Barbados) making the chief presentation.[12]

Interwoven as these issues and activities are, using her position as
voluntary joint co-ordinator of the network (then in formation)
Women in Development Europe (WIDE), the author also introduced structural adjustment into its annual assemblies. In 1988 and
1989 it formed the main subject of the conference element of these
assemblies, generating awareness and agreed lines of action among
WIDE's members in almost all Northern and Southern European
countries. At the first of these, Zenedeworke Tadesse from CODES-
RIA and AWORD contributed an African perspective. In the second, again Peggy Antrobus with Neuma Aguiar from Brazil,
co-ordinator of the DAWN Network, gave the major presentations,
and collaborative advocacy and publishing activities between European and Southern women were initiated.[13] These perspectives are
therefore available for inclusion in research to be commissioned and
managed by this author under contract with the EC-ACP Cultural
Foundation in several African countries under the Lome Agreement.

European NGOs remain intellectually and structurally resistant to
the gender implications of their work. This resistance is evident in
many forms which appear commonly across the continent with minor
cultural variations. At a Day Conference held in 1987 by the NGO
taking the lead in France on Debt and Adjustment there were
twenty-six speakers, all white and male, making statements as representatives of various interests (academia, the Churches, the
Freemasons, farmers, *et al.*). No opportunity to question or space to
caucus was presented, and the concept that women's interests might
be of relevance was clearly absent. The Netherlands-based European
Debt Network operates the opposite to this bulwark strategy; it
diffuses its dialogue, accepting minor 'educational' points in conver-
sations, but never building them into its comprehensive documents or
into its contacts with the burgeoning debt protestors in the South
(who in turn avoid outreach to, for example, the DAWN Network).
Its meetings, drawn from all over Europe, are conspiratorially male,
as if the issues are too important to include women; yet the participants would claim to be neutral. The British members, who are taken
from Oxfam, War on Want, and the World Development Movement,
operate in a similar fashion. The German NGOs are distributed

throughout the country, but many are immensely wealthy and rarely inclined to challenge either their government or themselves; the anarchic radicalism and hard left mostly support a poorer federally-spread group, Buko, which produces the critiques of the banks and Government, as well as actions against them, but is as adamantly sexist as the 'operational' NGOs. The few feminists who worked in Buko, or in the new inter-agency network, found their spirit being murdered, and their effectiveness curtailed, and left by the end of 1988. The UN Non-Governmental Liaison Service in Geneva provides a masculine support network rather than a genuinely even-handed 'liaison service' which reaches out to ensure a wholeness to its representation and documentation.[14]

INTRODUCING GENDER INTO THE NORTH–SOUTH 'DIALOGUE'

To take up the space made for one of three full-status NGO representatives on the otherwise governmental European Organising Committee of the twenty-two country 'European North–South Campaign on Interdependence and Solidarity', was a unique opportunity to express opposition to structural adjustment in principle, particularly as pressed by the West German and British governments, and to introduce the gender dimension to all aspect of this campaign's work. Further, as the only woman on the organising Bureau of this Committee, this author had the access and right to persuade and influence the members, which included the political secretariat of the Council of Europe, into some – in many cases extremely reluctant – understanding of the issues involved. The Campaign was conducted on a national basis in the long run, but the themes of Debt, Trade, Agriculture, Environment, Culture and Aid, were marked by international Round Table sessions held in different European countries. Preparations also included many joint meetings with other organisations, such as the OECD Research Centre in Paris, and various agencies of the United Nations. At the invitation of the women's caucus, convened from amongst the Swiss, German, Dutch and Danish delegations, this author prepared a probably unique briefing paper on the gender perspectives of all these themes for use on a national basis and in the Round Tables, and some suggestions were made as to feminist 'experts' from both South and North who could attend and defend these perspectives.[15] While none of the arguments could be enforced in an essentially voluntary campaign, and government representatives are notoriously reluctant to accept innovation, many of them crept into the Round Tables' proceedings and into the reports prepared by male German and Dutch members of the Council of Europe.

Subsequently (mid-1988) there was a special session (uniquely badly organised by the Council of Europe) on 'Women's Voice in the North–South Campaign' where the original women's caucus, with some additions from the Philippines and Africa, drew up strategies and tactics for the final conference of the North–South Campaign in Madrid, with particular reference to the impact of structural adjustment on women and the disposal of their time. Tactically, again this conference presented an unparalled opportunity to reach and educate the senior representatives from the IMF, World Bank and European institutions at one go. As frequently occurs to even the best lobbied clauses, however, the final rapporteur omitted the specific arguments, and 'Women's Voice' became a whispered appendix to the main document. While overall the Campaign was not of huge significance, and did not change the direction of European relations with the South, as was intended, the tactical penetration of the gender perspectives will, it is hoped, have some durability and be carried on into the formation of the prospective North–South Institute in Lisbon.

In the autumn of 1987 the Non-Governmental Liaison Service, based in Geneva, organised with Oxfam-UK and UNICEF a conference on Debt, Adjustment and the Needs of the Poor.[16] Held in Oxford, this event was again attended by representatives of the financial institutions as well as the UN and NGO networks from the South. A token effort to invite some women had been made, happening upon the feminist Noeleen Heyzer from the Asia Region network of DAWN, and the Asia Pacific Development Centre, but Oxfam's own gender unit was prevented from linking up with them to form a caucus or create any 'distraction' from the 'mainstream' discussions. Belatedly Heyzer and this author organised a small discussion, since the poorest and most disadvantaged in any country are always of the female sex, and current programmes of structural adjustment are making more women even poorer: facts which were being steadfastly ignored by the NGOs and institutions alike, even though the conference was intended to be discussing the UNICEF book *Structural Adjustment with a Human Face*.[17] While Oxfam had recently published a pamphlet on the effects of adjustment in Zambia, and had 'discovered' woman-headed households to be in a worsening position, their analysis left out any reference to inequitable gender relationships and the overall exclusion of women, on grounds of customary sex discrimination, from development institutions such as agricultural credit, despite constitutional equality.[18] Likewise, concerning the 'vulnerable groups' of UNICEF's analysis, the opportunity was missed to record what process and maldistribution of power and resources make that vulnerability in the first place. While recognising the critical contribution of women in food production and in the provision of household health care, these are contradicted by the strategic recommendations which demonstrate their class and sex bias clearly in their utilisation of women's sex-roles, and disposal of their time: 'While such an approach may increase time-costs for women it will place extremely modest monetary costs on the households; and will lead to substantial savings in the public sector.'

UNICEF's inverted care for women, as the instrumental bearers of children, rather than recognising their intrinsic humanity, is an improvement of the original separation of the category child from any adult, but it still requires examination. Health, education, gainful employment become necessities to ensure the well-being of the next generation, rather than of the child-bearer, or of women as a social category.

Again, the efforts of this small critical caucus were distorted in the final document, which cautiously referred to 'women and children' in safe and conventional terms, even thought the conference was intended to be a radical breakthrough in recognising the relationship between poverty and powerlessness. However, this author was subsequently invited to participate in the Asian DAWN[19] meeting to present a 'Northern feminist perspective on structural adjustment and the development crisis' (from which she was prevented by teaching obligations: a women's studies summer school on trade and development) and to the Gender and Equity seminar held in advance of the Society for International Development Tri-Annual Conference (New Delhi 1988). Both events pressed forward consciousness of inequity and economic restructuring, on which further strategies and interaction in both Southern and Northern women's groups.

Being invited to create a framework for NGO activities and to manage the NGO newspaper at the July 1987 UNCTAD VII Conference gave another opportunity to educate an almost entirely male audience of civil servants, and some politicians, from North and South, on different gender dimensions to the issues of debt, trade and development. Prior to the conference, this author circulated a number of women's groups and NGOs in the South, urging them to lobby at home, or to attend the conference as NGO representatives, if possible, or to contribute articles to the newspaper. The object was for them to project their own perspectives into what is essentially the only South–North negotiating forum; it was an object a little ahead of the funding available for such exercises. A feminist Canadian government representative who happened to be in Geneva for a meeting of UN ECOSOC shortly before the conference drew up a resolution on implementation of the *Forward-Looking Strategies* for the official conference, which also enabled some tactical link-ups to be made, although the resolution was later lost. CHANGE also designed and published a poster series for the conference, entitled 'Women: Backbone of the International Economy',[20] showing how the female sex 'contributes' in unpaid and lowly-paid time, and in personal sacrifice and gender-assigned roles, not only to national production but also to international trade; and how adjustment and other macroeconomic policies affect this contribution. The 'pupils' for this educational tool were intended to be the delegations.

As manager of the newspaper, it was the selection of the editor and journalists, again from North and South, rather than direct writing contribution that made the difference, although the speed of events and reporting requirements over four weeks made polished gender arguments rare.[21] Tactical caucusing of the women, and male sympathisers, with rapid training enabled some debate on gender and structural adjustment to take place during the uneven NGO mid-way assessment conference. Finally, having requested a space on the agenda to make an intervention which was written during the proceedings to reflect their directions, as well as to incorporate the concerns of the organisation represented, this author made a contribution which included the following:

Mr President, our concept of development is indigenous, democratic, sustainable and local, in which women as well as men have rights and dignity and economic self-determination. We reject enforced adjustment which increase social and gender inequality or forces one generation to be sacrificed to the putative well-being of another . . . all technical agreements for Commodities, Services, Manufacturing – and any further instruments – should include research to study their social implications. Mr President, the greatest inequity and inequality in the distribution of resources in the world today is between men and women . . . National debt servicing and structural adjustment widen this inequality because they assume the free disposition of women's time in lieu of financial resources.[22]

Later the UN Institute for Training and Research for the Advancement of Women (INSTRAW), in the Dominican Republic, was to pick up this text and make use of it to illustrate the objectives of 'mainstreaming women in development' in international economic negotiations. This author was able to further this process as a consultant to INSTRAW, and to develop their understanding of 'gender', as distinct from 'women in development', as well as present arguments for their research and 'mainstreaming' agendas for the 1990s.[23] Although the UN Division for the Advancement of Women in Vienna at first resisted the subject of structural adjustment, and the officer promoting research on SAPs was obliged to publish elsewhere,[24] they eventually convened an expert group meeting (to which this author was invited, having advanced various documents using Consultative Status with UN ECOSOC) in the autumn of 1989, discussed again early in 1990 at the UN Commission on the Status of Women.[25] Although this report was presented and received with some passion, acceptance of the negative impact of SAPs on women within the rest of the UN system is still very limited. Considerable internal awareness-building and lobbying is still required, making use of external research materials (such as this book) rather than internal studies only.

The much-needed social analysis of trade agreements has begun amongst non-governmental organisations, such as the Industrial Restructuring Education Network of Europe (IRENE), based in the Netherlands, whose initiatives on Trade in Services are sadly unique. Responding to the concerns of this author after participating in a high-level seminar on this subject before the opening of the Uruguay Round of the General Agreement of Trade and Tariffs, IRENE both held a general workshop and has now started a specific programme of analysis of the gender implications of trade in services.[26] The variety of services makes this peculiarly difficult, but the questions of the potential displacement of women from income earning either in the formal or informal sectors will be important, or the removal of control over their own labour into low-paid 'organised' services, as will be the issues of consumption of services, a dimension much neglected by economists. While effective services for distribution and communication are necessary elements for development, the external control of such services is likely to lead to increased financial flows from South to North, and indeed, if present patterns of gender-stereo-typed employment are extended into this field, from poorer woman to richer man.

With Spain's democratic transformation from 1975, it has begun to take a much more significant part in international affairs, which is also reflected in the rapid growth of non-governmental organisations. These are hungry for contact with other European NGOs, while having strong relations with Latin America – some based on guilt, some religion, some the democratising process, and some the common Hispanic traditions alone. Their rapid manufacture tends to be in traditional political and hierarchical forms, with men dominant and women in secretarial or documentary roles. However, some enterprising individual women are attempting to integrate gender into the very beginnings of operations, and to do this have organised tours by feminist 'experts', courses, summer schools and publications. The audiences, nevertheless, tend to be female: the unconverted not attending. The Basque North–South Institute invited this author, among others, on an enterprising decentralised rotating conference, ensuring outreach through the region, intended to mobilise a far greater consciousness of the gender dimensions and political consequences, of macro-economics.

As Japan, too, has decided to recycle its surplus in the form of very tied aid, as well as to open up to non-Japanese skills in a range of social areas, so there are now more contacts in international and local conferences. The reshaping of North–South relations with the presence of Japan, makes the principle that gender interests are in at the beginning imperative. Consequently, opportunities have been taken by this author both through students theses on this new phenomenon and through direct advocacy at international seminars, to direct proposals for Japanese aid to woman-beneficial programmes – and away from 'traditional' adjustment. A lecture tour of Japan in 1988 on issues for 'Women's Networks until 2000' gave some impetus to these somewhat isolated initiatives.

THE COMMONWEALTH EXPERT GROUP

In the autumn of 1989, the Commonwealth Secretariat released the first authoritative publication on structural adjustment and women,

Engendering Adjustment for the 1990s.[27] An Introduction by the Secretary-General, Sir Shridath Ramphal, stated clearly that women's lives had been set back twenty years, and that the report provided an 'incisive and moving analysis of the special difficulties women are now facing in different parts of the world'. An Expert Group, chaired by the then UNDP Permanent Representative in Uganda (now at the International Labour Office), of Ghanaian origin, Mary Chinery-Hesse, had been formed in 1987. Composed of Indian and Malaysian economists, Bina Agarwal and Jamilah Ariffin, Tendai Bare of the Zimbabwe Ministry of Community Development and Women's Affairs, and Dharam Ghai of UNRISD, Marjorie Lamont-Henriques of the Planning Institute of Jamaica, and Hilda Lini from Vanuatu, Iola Mathews from the Australian Council of Trade Unions, and Carolyn McAskie, Canadian High Commissioner for Sri Lanka, the Group also included Richard Jolly and Frances Stewart who had co-edited the UNICEF *Human Face* (with Andrea Cornia). Containing (secondary, rather than original, for reasons of cost) case studies from a range of countries, *Engendering Adjustment* emphatically recognised women's many roles, and chose four of these for the purposes of their analysis: producers, home managers, mothers, and community organisers.

This in itself was innovative, since the meaningless expression 'the role of women in development' has become standard language of most intergovernmental documentation, obstructing rather than contributing to understanding of the complexity of rights, time, and rewards denied for numerous responsibilities. The conjunction of two domestic and two public roles is helpful in raising awareness of the economic contribution made by women through activities which are unpaid and paid, unrecognised and partially observed. Such raised awareness should, in the longer run, attract policy and development strategies, and moves away from the consistent objection of economists that projects for women to overcome their social disadvantages are always a cost to the exchequer.

The recommendations were themselves grouped under the four roles, and are targeted towards various organisations and agencies; they include a section on 'securing implementation', in which a 'key element' is 'the empowerment and organisation of women themselves', affirmative action, institutionalising women's concerns, and general education on 'women's issues', each of which is elaborated. However, they do not include an alternative adjustment programme, which would have completed the challenge which *Engendering Adjustment* otherwise presents. This places the onus for this innovation on the voluntary advocates and lobbyists again.

RECENT NATIONAL INITIATIVES

From 1987 the suggestion was made to the nascent ODA/women's consultative mechanism that one of its immediate future sessions should be on women and structural adjustment; until the publication of the Commonwealth's *Engendering Adjustment* justified this proposal, it was rejected as unnecessary and abstruse by the head of the economics division of the ODA. It is a feature of political advocacy towards bureaucracies that acceptance often only takes place when a 'higher authority' repeats the same message; ironically the 'higher authority' may have been a target of persuasion from the same source, unaccepted at home!

Earlier, in March 1989, projected at the meeting of the IMF Development Committee/Finance Ministers, this author drew up a letter to the Chancellor of the Exchequer, then Nigel Lawson, with Helen O'Connell, then women's officer of War on Want. The major objective was two-fold: to reach the most senior financial decision-maker in the country in an appropriate and timely context; and to win the support of male directors of development NGOs to the cause of women, by presenting the letter to them for joint signature.[28] Both were undertaken as educational processes, rather than in the expectation of instant policy change. The letter outlined the main forms of impact of structural adjustment on poor women and their time, both direct and indirect, and included the contradictions of cuts in health services and Northern governments concern on population increases. It also included recommendations to the Chancellor for action. To this author it was essential to retain the strategic emphasis on women's right to enjoy and exercise their human rights and to make economic and personal decisions for themselves, instead of have them made in the IMF boardroom in Washington, or in the village council. To the religious-based NGOs this presented some problem when understood as including reproductive rights, but wording was reached which did not lose the emphasis on women's humanity or rights, without immediately offending the believers in God's control of women's fertility:

Public expenditure cuts in housing, transport, childcare, health and education have well-documented immediate effects and serious long-term implications for future development. The burden of coping with these cuts in social programmes is transferred to women's time and personal resources . . . rarely mentioned effects of public expenditure cuts are higher rates of women's morbidity and mortality. The cuts greatly diminish women's basic rights at a time when they are least able to cope.[29]

The letter quoted the World Bank, and the Commonwealth Heads of Government summit 1987 and Finance Ministers meeting 1988, anticipating *Engendering Adjustment*, to legitimate the issues as well as to remind government of its responsibilities to Intergovernmental Organisations and international instruments to which it is party. Perhaps it should have quoted UNDP who have been charged with providing the mopping-up World Bank 'compensatory measures' for all of US$8m. The following were requested within the letter:

- an analysis of the impact of the proposed measures (in adjustment programmes), both positive and negative on women;
- proposals on how women may be consulted and involved in policy reforms;
- an explanation of how women are intended to benefit from the policy reforms;
- targets for improvements in key specific indicators, such as women's income, nutritional levels, literacy, morbidity and mortality;
- a clear indication as to how the actual impact on women will be monitored and how the results of the monitoring programme will be used to reformulate the overall adjustment programme.

The letter was released to the press, and some limited use was made of it by non-mainstream international news networks. Tactically the letter can now be used in several ways, not least in referring back to the directors of NGOs, who tend to evade a real understanding of gender in their theoretical or practical day-to-day work, in support of money for women's initiatives, projects, or publications. The recommendations for action – which were educative in the context rather than anticipating a comprehensive response – can also be followed up, and the policy wheel does not need to be reinvented. It also formed the basis of a non-governmental position paper for the

ODA/Women's Consultative meeting, alongside the Commonwealth's *Engendering Adjustment* early in 1990.

Tactically the Women's Consultative Group for ODA agreed that a response to the Group's position paper should be required of ODA after their own presentation, followed by a concentration – for reasons of time – on the Executive Summary of *Engendering Adjustment*. In this our emphasis was to be approval of the Commonwealth Expert Group's recognition of all women's roles, and the use of positive language (domestic management; social organisers), with the clearly expressed linkage between credit, infrastructure, land and legal rights, etc. (in lieu of the usual recommendation that education alone is women's panacea).

The ODA spokesman defined adjustment as 'economies adjusting to the resources they have' without any hint of irony concerning either the imposition of these measures onto the populace while also referring to democratisation, nor of the fundamental ignorance of what the resources are when sex-disaggregated statistics are not used and the household is the focus of convenient attention – which leads to the multiplicity of demands now being placed on women. He attributed to adjustment an inevitability as substantial as Smith's 'invisible hand', and attached 'order' to minimise the as-inevitable 'pain', without any clarity on who would be bearing the pain. The primary objective was growth, 'even if it may not trickle down', with trade liberalisation, currency devaluation, and every form of deregulation possible. Again there was no consciousness of the overall need of women for regulation to guarantee equal pay, safe conditions of employment, *et al.*, in the deeply gendered market. 'All the evidence shows that successful economies are those which allow private energies to flourish', came as dismal hearing to the group, since our perception was of the exploitation of women's 'private energy' by the entrepreneur in the interests of commercial and national competitiveness in a skewed market, paraded as one where the forces are free.

Further intrinsic contradictions emerged over the 'proper roles of government' of the restructuring country which had been 'muddled up' and should be characterised by a non-interfering 'light touch', although meanwhile the 'donor collective should get more control'. At the same time the language of 'bottom-up' development as distinct from 'top-down' was also used, but without convincing the consultative group since it was clearly attached to this invasive policy, because of the fundamental ignorance of the realities of who is at the 'bottom', and because no methodology was proposed (nor was it our experience that participatory democracy is fully encouraged in the United Kingdom). Likewise there was a strange rebuttal that the terms of trade in any way cause the current financial flows from South to North, and a denial that tariff or non-tariff barriers exist at all in the US, Japanese and European Community against processed commodities from Africa. While South–South trade was inadvertently recommended, the absence of substantial technical support for commodity processing and diversification demonstrates a conscious policy of ensuring continued 'recipient' docility towards donors, rather than encouraging economic independence or self-sufficiency. The Economic Commission for Africa's own plans for Adjustment were dismissed as of no real consequence, demonstrating that some countries' sovereignty is very much more equal than others.

An ODA spokeswoman on Ghana's PAMSCAD made it clear that in all matters the ODA took its 'cue' from the World Bank, concentrating two-thirds of expenditure on Programme Aid to support the liberalisation of the exchange rate (whereby the money does not actually reach Ghana), with an expressed 'liking' for conditionality. The remaining third is divided between rehabilitation of diesel power stations and water, with support for a World Bank project in cocoa and 'sustainable' management of tropical forests, and technical co-operation, particularly in the supply of primary teacher education, syllabus development, etc. There was some willingness to listen to criticism of the noticeable absence of gender analysis (e.g. in access, consumption and use of electric power, ownership of land or trees, etc.), although another spokeswoman essayed to pin this on the World Bank's household survey in Ghana. 'The integration of women' was, in this context, solely the potential training of female engineers, while the masculinity of language (manpower, man-hours, over-manned) betrayed ignorance of the basic bias of economic theory which obliterates women in all their many roles. The question, even after ODA's several series of gender training, was always one of 'women's – um – issues'.

Faced with these mental barriers, the Consultative Group's repeated insistence that ODA should ensure that all SAPs and PAMS-CADs, and other policy measures, should at the very least be planned to 'enhance the quality of life and self-determination of women', across all sectors and in all their roles, seemed a very small triumph indeed. However, a second meeting on the subject was arranged, as well as a discussion meeting with the new Minister for

Overseas Development, Lynda Chalker. Subsequently, this author made arrangements for a meeting with, and parliamentary questions for, the Shadow Secretary of State for Development Co-operation; the World Development Movement will pursue the issues of structural adjustment in its forthcoming two-year campaigns; and the accumulated perspectives of CHANGE will be transmitted to the Conference on the Least Developed Countries late in 1990. The quest continues.

Notes and References

1. *Of Conjuring and Caring: Women in Development* (CHANGE, 1982); *Shaming the World: The Needs of Women Refugees* (CHANGE, 1985); *Of Violence and Violation: Women and Human Rights* (CHANGE, 1985).
2. First published in 1985; a second edition was published in 1987 and 1988 respectively by Monthly Review Press and Earthscan.
3. Caribbean and Latin America Office of UNICEF, Santiago, 1987.
4. 'Providence and Prostitution: Image and Reality for Women in Buddhist Thailand', Khin Thitsa, for CHANGE, 1981; 'Military Ideology and the Dissolution of Democracy', Anon, for CHANGE, 1983.
5. Georgina Ashworth: 'Women, War and Under-Development', paper for WILPF Conference on Women and Military, Brussels, February 1983, and FAO Human Rights Committee, May 1983, published in *Pax et Libertas*, 1984; 'Women, Militarisation and Under-Development: Case Studies from Kenya, Sri Lanka and Chile', for Women and Militarisation Seminar, Siunto, Finland 1987 (unpublished).
6. Grace Akello, 'Self Twice Removed: Ugandan Woman', CHANGE, 1983; Tsehai Berhane Selassie, 'In Search of Ethiopian Women', CHANGE, 1984; Naila Kabeer, 'Minus Lives: Women of Bangladesh', CHANGE, 1983.
7. 'The Cost of Debt: Women and the Debt Crisis', Information pack, 1985; 'Farmers, Food and Famine', Information pack, 1985.
8. See Georgina Ashworth and Lucy Bonnerjea, *The Invisible Decade: UK Women and the UN Decade* (Gower, 1985); also Georgina Ashworth, 'The International Women's Movement and the UN Women's Conference', in *Pressure Groups in the Global System*, ed. Peter Willetts (New York: Frances Pinter Publishers and St Martin's Press, 1981).
9. See 'Hard Cash: Man-Made Development and its Consequences: A Feminist Perspective on Aid', CHANGE and War on Want, 1986, for an account of the conference.
10. See UN, *The Nairobi Forward-Looking Strategies, 1985*, Report of the UK Conference on the Forward-Looking Strategies (NCVO, 1986).
11. 'An Introduction to the Forward-Looking Strategies', Georgina Ash-

worth, unpublished paper for Development Education Subcommittee, December 1986.

12. See proceedings of the EC-NGO General Assemblies 1986, 1987, 1988, and 1989, EC-NGO Liaison Committee, Brussels; also Peggy Antrobus and Georgina Ashworth, *More Women Needed in Lome*, Lome Briefings, EC NGO Liaison Committee, 1989; Peggy Antrobus, 'Gender Implications of the Debt Crisis in the Commonwealth Caribbean: The Case of Jamaica', for Conference of Caribbean Economists, July 1987; Peggy Antrobus, 'The Situation of Women in the Caribbean: An Overview: Including the Impact of Structural Adjustment Policies on Women', for UNDP/UNFPA/INSTRAW, December 1988.

13. See proceedings of the Annual Assemblies of WIDE, Leuvenn 1987, Oxford 1988, Copenhagen 1989; Peggy Antrobus, as above. Neuma Aguiar, 'The Impact of the Latin American Crisis on Women', draft for DAWN Latin America Group on Food Energy and the Debt Crisis in relation to women, undated 1987?; also Neuma Aguiar, 'The Economic Crisis and Women', for WIDE, Denmark, 1989.

14. Georgina Ashworth, 'An Elf Among the Gnomes: A Feminist in North–South Relations', *Millenium*, vol. 17, no. 5 (1988).

15. Georgina Ashworth, 'Women and the North–South Campaign', unpublished paper for European North–South Campaign, Strasbourg, 1988.

16. UN NGLS/Oxfam, 'Debt, Adjustment and the Needs of the Poor: Final Statement', September 1987 and Full Report 1988.

17. Andrea Cornia, Richard Jolly and Frances Stewart (eds), *Adjustment with a Human Face* (OUP for UNICEF, 1988).

18. J. Clark, and C. Allison, *Zambia: Debt as Poverty* (Oxfam, 1989).

19. Noeleen Heyser, 'The Impact of Food–Energy–Foreign Debt Management on Women: Concepts and Issues', for Southeast Asia DAWN Network, 1987.

20. 'Women Backbone of the International Economy', poster series for CHANGE, 1987.

21. 'Trade-Off: *The NGO Newspaper for UNCTAD VII*', Geneva, 1987, (appeared in twelve issues, in English and French).

22. Intervention for the International Coalition for Development Action at the United Nations Conference on Trade and Development, Geneva, 27 July 1987.

23. Georgina Ashworth (ed.), *Bridging the Gap: Issues for Women's Studies and Development studies for the 1990s*, for Krishna Patel, INSTRAW, 1989. See also Marjorie Williams, 'The Global Economic Crisis, Structural Adjustment and the Fate of Women', a concept paper for the Women's Alternative Economic Summit, July 1988; 'Statement and Recommendations' from Women and the Debt Crisis Working Group, The Hague, March 1988.

24. Margardia da Gama Santos, 'The Impact of Adjustment Programmes on Women in Developing Countries', *Public Enterprises*, Llubjana (May 1985).

25. United Nations, Report: 'UN Interregional Seminar on Women and the Economic Crisis: Impact, Policies and Prospects', CSDHA, Vienna, October 1988.

26. IRENE, Trade in Services: NGO Perspectives, Tilburg, 1989; and network enquiry 1990.
27. 'Engendering Adjustment for the 1990s', Report of a Commonwealth Expert Group on Women and Structural Adjustment, Commonwealth Secretariat, London, September 1989. See also Commonwealth Secretariat, 'Structural Adjustment and Women's Agriculture', Report of a Colloquium on Agricultural Policy in Commonwealth Africa, May 1986; 'Questionnaire to Selected International Organisations' for Commonwealth Working Group, undated; Diane Elson, 'The Impact of Structural Adjustment on Women: Concepts and Issues', for Commonwealth Secretariat, May 1987.
28. 13 March 1989: signed by Julian Filochowski, Cafod; Michael Taylor, Christian Aid; Frank Judd, Oxfam; Kate Young, Womankind; Charlotte Mbali, World Development Movement; Mandy McDonald, National Women's Network; Francis Khoo, War on Want; Jane Grant, WOIG/ NAWO; Georgina Ashworth, CHANGE.
29. Ibid.

11 Final Declaration . . . Beyond the Debt Crisis: Structural Transformation
Maxine Molyneux

The following statement was produced by the participants in an all-woman seminar on global economic issues which formed part of the ongoing work of the Women's Alternative Economic Summit. It was timed to coincide with the United Nations special session of the General Assembly on international economic co-operation which took place from 23 to 28 April 1990. The seminar, which lasted three days, brought 50 women together from 22 countries with an additional 12 representatives of international organisations. Most of the women were from the developing countries, but among our European group was a Hungarian sociologist, a warmly welcomed presence and one which reflected the new contours of a changing world. Participants came from all regions of the world and from a variety of different contexts; there were women grass-roots activists, government ministers, project designers, campaigners and academics, representing a broad spectrum of experience and opinion. The agenda for discussion at the seminar focused on the issues raised for women by stabilisation and adjustment policies; topics ranged from macro to micro level issues, including food security, privatisation, the informal sector and waged employment, household structure, political responses, and increasing violence against women. The purpose of the declaration was to assist in campaigning work, to draw attention to the gendered effects of economic policies and world recession. All workers and activists with an involvement in these issues are welcome to use it if they wish. To build on the momentum of the conference a group of us have now set up a new international network entitled Gender-Focused Alternative to Structural Adjustment Programmes: the network will be planning our meetings and research priorities over the coming months, and hope to add our weight to the growing pressure for change.

FINAL DECLARATION
BEYOND THE DEBT CRISIS: STRUCTURAL TRANSFORMATION

1. Because women play a central role in economic and social life, we must look directly to women's experiences to reveal the real depth of the current global economic crisis. Women in their vast majority are concentrated in the most impoverished and oppressed sectors of our societies. Yet it is women who are being made to bear the brunt of what have been called 'structural adjustment' strategies for managing international debt.

   It is within this context that women are struggling for viable long-term alternatives: transformative approaches with a gender perspective. The burden of adjustment programmes must be lifted from the shoulders of the poor and shifted to those who profited most from the economic policies that led to the current crisis.

2. Under the present system, aid from the World Bank and the International Monetary Fund (IMF) is conditional on the adoption of 'adjustment' packages that are imposed regardless of the cultural and economic diversities of women around the world, as well as internal political conflicts. These rigid prescriptions have added to women's responsibilities for family survival and social reproduction, reduced the resources at our disposal, and restricted options for women's participation and leadership in public life.

3. The use of an unchecked and unregulated market model for economic restructuring has aggravated existing inequities in both 'developed' and 'developing' countries. Women have found our traditional usage of land undermined, our access to other resources circumscribed, and the return on our labor reduced. Under the pressure of prevailing market forces, poor women are compelled to submit our labor to exploitative relations in both the formal and informal sector of the economy.

   East and West, North and South, women are pitted in competition against one another for investment, jobs, and aid, although in fact we share many common experiences of oppression. Transnational corporations, with a power surpassing that of many national governments, are a central institution in promoting such competition.

   Governments remain unaccountable to women. Instead, the logic of the 'free market' has led many governments to turn to militarism and ideological oppression to control women's labor and our bodies. Our resistance to such oppression is inextricably linked to sexual politics, because government and market control has extended even to the realms of sexual relations and biological reproduction.

4. Women are demanding an equal voice in redefining development priorities for our societies. All too often, development agencies – many times working under the misleading label of 'women in development' – make exploitative appeals to women's needs to solicit funds for the perpetuation of unjust and unequal economic and social arrangements.

5. We are concerned about how the sweeping changes in Eastern Europe are being interpreted. While they expose the false promises of authoritarian governments, they do not discredit efforts to create cooperative alternatives to conventional, market-driven development strategies, nor do they justify the imposition of such strategies by economic intimidation or overt military intervention. Many Eastern Europeans see their responsibility in avoiding any rivalry for resources. Already women from Eastern Europe are seeking new forms of cooperation with Third World women's movements.

6. We as women recognise our differences as well as our commonalities, and the need to analyze our situation in terms of gender as it relates to class, caste, nationality, race, ethnicity, and religion. This in no way condones emerging currents of national chauvinism and religious fundamentalism. Different values, needs, and perceptions of different groups of women must be acknowledged and engaged within the process of struggling to make a better and more just world.

7. Women are by no means passive victims who are unaware of our own situation. Women have developed multiple, complex, and innovative responses to the global economic crisis, both individually and collectively. Researchers and activists have joined forces with grassroots women at the local, national, and international levels to organise for survival and change.

   Donors and governments are called upon to recognise and support efforts by women to act on our own behalf. Such actions express the true meaning of 'empowerment'.

8. We propose an alternative approach to give women equal participation in decision-making and control over resources: the alternative of economic democracy. Economic democracy means that all women must have access to all resources; that women must be active shapers in decisions at every level of society – within the family, in our communities, and in the political process, nationally and internationally. Poor women in particular must be included at the negotiating table in setting funding priorities and development policies.

   To make this vision a full-fledged reality for ourselves, we as women will need to organise collectively – in our communities as well as nationally and internationally. Key to the success of such collective efforts is joining forces in coalition with other sectors.

9. Development and strengthening of a critical popular economics education is one of the most important strategies for realising the visions outlined in this declaration. In addition, women's organisations worldwide need to increase their capacity for international cooperation – in research efforts, policy proposals, and action campaigns. There is a pressing need for more direct interchanges among grassroots women from different nations and regions, and for more research into the effects of 'structural adjustment' on women worldwide.

   Likewise, more dialogue is needed among women at the grassroots, researchers and scholars, and policy makers. We see a crucial role for nongovernmental organisations as facilitators of a two-way communications flow between grassroots women's organisations and national and international institutions.

New York
April 1990

Bibliography

The following select bibliography lists works of relevance to the theme of this book which have appeared in English since 1985. Where a complete book is cited, no reference is made to individual chapters. This list has been compiled by Gwyneth Morgan, Librarian at the Development and Project Planning Centre, Bradford University, in consultation with the editors.

AFSHAR, H. (ed.), *Women, Development and Survival in the Third World* (London: Longman, forthcoming).

AFSHAR, H. and AGARWAL, B. (eds), *Women, Poverty and Ideology in Asia* (London: Macmillan, 1989).

ANTROBUS, P., 'Consequences and Responses to Social and Economic Deterioration: The Experience of the English-Speaking Caribbean', paper prepared for the Workshop on Economic Crisis, Household Survival Strategies and Women's Work, Cornell University, 2–5 September 1988.

ANTROBUS, P., 'Gender Implications of the Debt Crisis in the Commonwealth Caribbean: The Case of Jamaica', paper for the Conference of Caribbean Economists, July 1987.

ANTROBUS, P., 'The Situation of Women in the Caribbean: An Overview: Including the Impact of Structural Adjustment Policies on Women', paper prepared for UNDP/UNFPA/INSTRAW, 1988.

ANTROBUS, P., 'Women and Development: An Alternative Analysis', *Development*, 1 (1989) pp. 26–8.

ASHWORTH, G. (ed.), *Bridging the Gap: Issues for Women's Studies and Development Studies for the 1990s* (Santo Domingo: INSTRAW, 1989).

BERGER, M., 'Women's Response to Recession in Latin America and the Caribbean: A Focus on Urban Labour Markets', paper presented to the Workshop on Economic Crisis, Household Survival Strategies and Women's Work, Cornell University, 2–5 September 1988.

BERRIAN, D., 'Tracing the Consequences of Macroeconomic Policy on Income, Poverty and Nutrition: Incorporating Women's Role in the Economy into Political Analysis', paper prepared for the Workshop on Economic Crisis, Household Survival Strategies and Women's Work, Cornell University, 2–5 September 1988.

BEULINK, A., 'Women and the Debt Crisis', *Development*, 1 (1989) pp. 88–94.

BIENFELD, M., *Structural Adjustment and its Impact on Women in Developing Countries* (Ottawa: CIDA, 1988) (CIDA/RC/Project 839/11109).

BOCAR BA, I., *Sustained Growth and Development with Equity in Sub-Saharan Africa: Mali* (Washington, DC: World Bank, forthcoming).

BUVINIC, M., LYCETTE, M. and McGREEVEY, W. (eds), *Women and Poverty in the Third World* (Baltimore, MD: Johns Hopkins University Press, 1987).

CAMPBELL, B. and LOXLEY, J. (eds), *Structural Adjustment in Africa* (London: Macmillan, 1985).

CHANGE, *The Cost of Debt: Women and the International Debt Crisis* (London: Change, 1985) (Change international reports: Women and Society: thinkpack) (Information pack).

COMMONWEALTH SECRETARIAT, *Engendering Adjustment for the 1990s: Report of a Commonwealth Expert Group on Women and Structural Adjustment* (London: Commonwealth Secretariat, 1989).

COMMONWEALTH SECRETARIAT, *Structural Adjustment and Women* (London: Commonwealth Secretariat, 1990) (video).

COOTE, B., *Debt and Poverty: A Case Study of Jamaica* (Oxford: Oxfam, undated).

CORNIA, G., JOLLY, R. and STEWART, F. (eds), *Adjustment with a Human Face: Protecting the Vulnerable and Promoting Growth* (Oxford: Clarendon, 1987).

DA GAMA SANTOS, M., 'The Impact of Adjustment Programmes on Women in Developing Countries', *Public Enterprise*, 5 (3) (1985) pp. 173–9.

DEERE, C. and DE LEON, M. (eds), *Rural Women and State Policy: Feminist Perspectives on Latin America* (Boulder: Westview, 1987).

DEMERY, L., and ADDISON, T., *The Alleviation of Poverty Under Structural Adjustment* (Washington, DC: World Bank, 1987).

ELSON, D., 'From Survival Strategies to Transformation Strategies: Women's Needs and Structural Adjustment', in Beneria, L. and Feldman, S. (eds), *Economic Crisis, Household Strategies and Women's Work* (forthcoming).

ELSON, D., 'How is Structural Adjustment Affecting Women?', *Development*, 1 (1989) pp. 67–74.

ELSON, D., *The Impact of Structural Adjustment on Women: Concepts and Issues* (Manchester: University of Manchester, IDC, 1988) (Manchester discussion papers in development studies, 8801).

ELSON, D., (ed.), *Male Bias in the Development Process* (Manchester: Manchester University Press, 1990).

FOOD AND AGRICULTURE ORGANISATION, *Impact of Development Strategies on the Rural Poor* (Rome: FAO, 1988).

GIDWANI, S., *Impact of Monetary and Financial Policies upon Women* (Santo Domingo: INSTRAW, 1985) (INSTRAW research studies, 1).

GONZALES DE LA ROCHA, M., 'Economic Crisis, Domestic Organisation and Women's Work in Guadalajara, Mexico', *Bulletin of Latin American Research*, 7 (2) (1988) pp. 207–23.

HAGGBLADE, S. and HAZELL, P., *Prospects for Equitable Growth in Rural Sub-Saharan Africa* (Washington, DC: World Bank, 1988) (PPR working papers, 8).

HELLEINER, G., 'Growth-Oriented Adjustment Lending: A Critical Assessment of IMF/World Bank Approaches', paper prepared for the South Commission, Geneva, 1988.

HEYZER, N., 'Economic Crisis, Household Strategies and Women's Work in South East Asia', paper prepared for the Workshop on Economic Crisis, Household Survival Strategies and Women's Work, Cornell University, 2–5 September 1988.

HOJMAN, D., 'Neo-Liberal Economic Policies and Infant and Child Mortality: Simulation Analysis of a Chilean Paradox', *World Development*, 17 (1) (1989) pp. 93–108.

HOJMAN, D., 'Prospects for Rural Employment and Wages under Neo-Liberal Policies: The Case of Chilean Agriculture', *Bulletin of Latin American Research*, 8 (1) (1989) pp. 111–21.

IBRAHIM, B., 'Policies Affecting Women's Employment in the Formal Sector: Strategies for Change', *World Development*, 17 (7) (1989) pp. 1097–107.

INTERNATIONAL LABOUR ORGANISATION, *Employment and Incomes in Zambia in the Context of Structural Adjustment* (Lusaka: ILO/ SATEP, 1987).

JAYAWEERA, S., ALAILIMA, P., RODRIGO, C. and JAYATISSA, R., *Structural Adjustment and Women: The Sri Lanka Experience* (Colombo: Centre for Women's Research, 1988).

JIGGINS, J., 'How Poor Women Earn Income in Sub-Saharan Africa and What Works Against Them', *World Development*, 17 (7) (1989) pp. 953–63.

JOEKES, S., 'Gender and Macroeconomic Policy', paper prepared for AWID Colloquium on Gender and Development Co-operation, Washington, 1988.

JOEKES, S., LYCETTE, M., McGOWAN, L. and SEARLE, K., *Women and Structural Adjustment* (Washington, DC: International Center for Research on Women, 1988).

JOEKES, S., *Women in the World Economy: An INSTRAW Study* (Oxford: Oxford University Press, 1987).

JOLLY, R., 'The Crisis for Children and Women: What Can Be Done?', *Journal of Development Planning*, 15 (1985) pp. 99–112.

JOLLY, R., 'Women's Needs and Adjustment Policies in Developing Countries', an address to the Women's Development Group of the OECD, Paris, 1987.

LELE, U., 'Women and Structural Transformation', *Economic Development and Cultural Change*, 34 (2) (1986) pp. 195–221.

LESLIE, J., LYCETTE, M. and BUVINIC, M., 'Weathering Economic Crisis: The Crucial Role of Women in Health', in Bell, D. and Reich, M. (eds), *Health, Nutrition and Economic Crisis: Approaches to Policy in the Third World* (Dover, MA: Auburn House, 1988).

LESLIE, J., 'Women's Work and Child Nutrition in the Third World', *World Development*, 16 (11) (1988) pp. 1341–62.

LONGHURST, R., 'Rural Productivity, Malnutrition and Structural Adjustment', in Clay, E. and Shaw, J. (eds), *Poverty, Development and Food* (Basingstoke: Macmillan, 1987).

LONGHURST, R., KAMARA, S. and MENSURAH, J., 'Structural Adjustment and Vulnerable Groups in Sierra Leone', *IDS Bulletin*, 19 (1) (1988) pp. 25–31.

MASSIAH, J., 'Weathering Economic Crisis: Women's Response to the Recession in Commonwealth Caribbean', paper presented at Weathering the Economic Crisis: Women's Response to the Recession in Latin America and the Caribbean, Racine, Wisconsin, June 1988.

MBILINYI, M., 'The Invention of Female Farming Systems in Africa: Structural Adjustment in Tanzania', paper prepared for the Workshop on Economic Crisis, Household Survival Strategies and Women's Work, Cornell University, 2–5 September 1988.

McFARLANE, C., 'Women and the Impact of the Economic Crisis', paper prepared for the Centre for Social Development and Humanitarian Affairs International Seminar on Women and the Economic Crisis, Vienna, 3–7, October, 1988.

McKEE, K., 'Microlevel Strategies for Supporting Livelihoods, Employment, and Income Generation of Poor Women in the Third World: The Challenge of Significance', *World Development*, 17 (7) (1989) pp. 993–1006.

MITTER, S., *Common Fate, Common Bond: Women in the Global Economy* (London: Pluto, 1986).

MOSER, C., 'The Impact of Recession and Structural Adjustment on Women: Ecuador', *Development*, 1 (1989) pp. 75–83.

MOSER, C., *The Impact of Recession and Structural Adjustment Policies at the Micro-Level: Low Income Women and Their Households in Guayquil, Ecuador* (New York, NY: UNICEF, 1989) (Invisible adjustment, 2).

MUNACHONGA, M., *Impact of Economic Adjustments on Women in Zambia* (Lusaka: University of Zambia, 1986).

OLUKOSHI, A. and OLUKOSHI, H., 'Structural Adjustment and Female Labour in the Nigerian Textile Industry', *Zast*, 4 (1989) pp. 25–34.

ONIMODE, B. (ed.), *The IMF, the World Bank and the African Debt* (London: Zed, 1989).

OVERSEAS DEVELOPMENT INSTITUTE, *Adjusting to Recession: Will the Poor Recover?* (London: ODI, 1986) (Briefing paper, November 1986).

PEET, R., *International Capitalism and Industrial Restructuring: A Critical Analysis* (London: Allen & Unwin, 1987).

PHILLIPS, A. and NDEKWU, E. (eds), *Structural Adjustment Programme in a Developing Economy: The Case of Nigeria* (Ibadan: NISER, 1987).

PITTIN, R., *Women, Work and Ideology in a Context of Economic Crisis: A Nigerian Case Study* (The Hague: Institute of Social Studies, 1989) (ISS working papers. Women's history and development: themes . . ., 11).

POLLACK, M., 'Women's Poverty in Latin America: A Three Country Study of Short and Long Term Trends', paper presented at Weathering the Economic Crisis: Women's Response to the Recession in Latin America and the Caribbean, Racine, Wisconsin, 1988.

ROSE, T., *Crisis and Recovery in Sub-Saharan Africa* (Paris: OECD, 1985).

RUBERY, J., 'Women and Recession: Some Problems of Comparative Analysis', paper presented at Weathering the Economic Crisis: Women's Response to the Recession in Latin America and the Caribbean, Racine, Wisconsin, 1988.

SCHULTZ, T., *Women and Development: Objectives, Frameworks and Policy Interventions* (Washington, DC: World Bank, 1989) (PPR working paper, 200).

SEN, G. and GROWN, C., *Development, Crisis and Alternative Visions: Third World Women's Perspectives* (London: Earthscan, 1988).

SERAGELDIN, I., *Poverty, Adjustment and Growth in Africa* (Washington, DC: World Bank, 1989).

SINGER, H. and PRENDERGAST, R. (eds), *Adjustment and Development* (London: Macmillan, forthcoming).

STOECKEL, J. and SIRISENA, N., 'Gender-Specific Socioeconomic Impacts of Development Programs in Sri Lanka', *Journal of Developing Areas*, 23 (1) (1988) pp. 31–42.

SWANTZ, M.-L., 'The Effect of Economic Change on Gender Roles: The Case of Tanzania', *Development*, 2/3 (1988) pp. 93–6.

UNESCO, *Women's Concerns and Planning: A Methodological Approach for Their Integration into Local, Regional and National Planning* (Paris: Unesco, 1986) (Socioeconomic studies, 13).

UNICEF, *Ghana: Adjustment Policies and Programmes to Protect Children and Other Vulnerable Groups* (Accra: UNICEF, 1986).

UNICEF, *The Invisible Adjustment: Poor Women and the Economic Crisis*, 2nd rev. edn. (New York, NY: UNICEF, 1989).

UNICEF, *The State of the World's Children, 1989* (Oxford: Oxford University Press, 1989).

UNITED NATIONS, Interregional Seminar on Women and the Economic Crisis, Vienna, 1988.

UNITED NATIONS DEVELOPMENT PROGRAMME, *Regional Programme for Africa: Fourth Cycle: Assessment of Social Dimensions of Structural Adjustment in Sub-Saharan Africa* (New York, NY: United Nations, 1987) (RAF/86/037/A/01/42).

UNITED NATIONS, ECONOMIC COMMISSION FOR AFRICA, *African Alternative Framework to Structural Adjustment Programmes for Socio-Economic Recovery and Transformation* (Addis Ababa: United Nations, 1989) (E/ECA/CM.15/6/Rev. 3).

WORLD BANK, *Sub-Saharan Africa: From Crisis to Sustainable Growth: A Long-Term Perspective Study* (Washington, DC: World Bank, 1989).

Index

263